Inside the Palace

INSIDE
THE
PALACE

The Rise and Fall of
Ferdinand & Imelda Marcos

BETH DAY ROMULO

G. P. PUTNAM'S SONS / NEW YORK

Published by G. P. Putnam's Sons,
200 Madison Avenue, New York, NY 10016.

Published simultaneously in Canada by
General Publishing Co. Limited, Toronto

The text of this book is set in Caslon.

Library of Congress Cataloging-in-Publication Data

Romulo, Beth Day, date.
Inside the palace.

Includes index.
1. Marcos, Ferdinand E. (Ferdinand Edralin),
1917–   .   2. Marcos, Imelda R. (Imelda Romualdez)
1924–   .   3. Philippines—Politics and
government—1946–1973.   4. Philippines—Politics
and government—1973–   .   5. Philippines—
Presidents—Biography.   6. Philippines—Presidents—
Wives—Biography.   I. Title.
DS686.6.A2R66   1987   959.9'046'0922 [B]   87-2407
ISBN 0-399-13253-8

Printed in the United States of America
1   2   3   4   5   6   7   8   9   10

Contents

Inside the Palace

Prologue

THE last time I saw Imelda Marcos was at my husband's funeral, on December 15, 1985. "The First Lady!" "The President!" I heard the urgent whisper ripple down the line of people who crowded the small mortuary chapel adjacent to the church. Imelda Marcos came first, a towering figure all in black: black dress, black stockings, black shoes. The President was behind her. People pushed back against the floral displays that crowded the little room, to clear her passage. A statuesque woman, Imelda has become even more regal with the passing years of uncontested power.

She came forward to where I was standing, embraced me, and said in a low sympathetic voice, "Poor Beth. You are all alone now. You must come and stay with me."

Friends who overheard her joked with me later: "You might have ended up on that plane for Honolulu!" For, a scant two months later, her empire had collapsed around her and she and her husband were exiles on the face of the earth.

I greeted the President and the three of us stepped for-

ward to the side of the casket, so that they could pay their
final respects to my husband, General Carlos P. Romulo.
He had served President Marcos as Foreign Minister for
fourteen years. Before that he had enjoyed a distinguished
multiple career as soldier (he was aide to General Mac-
Arthur in World War II), publisher, writer, educator, and
diplomat. He was a signatory of the United Nations Charter
and the first Asian to become President of the UN General
Assembly.

We had brought his body to the lovely old Spanish-style
Santuario de San Antonio, our parish church, for the three-
day wake before the funeral. Despite a request for dona-
tions to the Kidney Center in lieu of flowers, many of his
friends had sent both. Huge baskets of orchids, an-
thuriums, and roses filled the small chapel and spilled out
to line the walk to the driveway. Individual white cattleya
orchids with the names of the members of his immediate
family were pinned inside the soft lining of the open casket—a Philippine tradition.

On the morning of the funeral, we first observed a simple
private Mass at the Santuario de San Antonio, with Jaime
Cardinal Sin, the Archibishop of Manila, officiating. Then
we took the General's body to Manila's beautiful Cultural
Center overlooking Manila Bay. There a state funeral was
held, attended by President and Mrs. Marcos, the entire
cabinet and diplomatic corps, and the guests from abroad
who had flown in for the funeral. The President spoke for
the Philippines, and the foreign ministers of all the neighboring Asian countries read statements from their heads of
state, as did a former foreign minister from Japan. Undersecretary of State for Political Affairs, Michael Armacost,
who had been an ambassador to Manila, read a letter addressed to me from President Reagan. It was a stunning,
dignified event that extolled my husband's half century of
public service. When he had retired only two years before
his death, he had been the world's oldest foreign minister,

second only to the USSR's Andrei Gromyko in tenure of that office. General Romulo was a figure of international stature and considered a national treasure by his countrymen.

The night he came to my husband's wake, I sat with President Marcos in front of the bier. "I suppose you will be campaigning a lot now?" I asked. "No," he said, rubbing his leg. "My knee is bothering me. Old war wound." (He always made references to his guerrilla past.) He nodded toward Imelda. She had already left us and was working the crowd—towering over the others, eyes bright with excitement. She told me once she was like a fish: If you take it from the water, the eyes grow dim. If you take Imelda out of the crowd, she dims. By a conscious act of will she had become one of the world's foremost political animals.

President Marcos was looking toward the casket, deep in his own thoughts. Finally he said, in a soft voice, as much to himself as to me: "He should have been President."

It occurred to me the job had not been open for the past twenty years. But I refrained from saying so, since I knew he was thinking of the many "near misses" that had kept General Romulo from succeeding to the presidency of the Philippines. At the end of World War II, President Sergio Osmeña had asked him to run as his vice president. Romulo refused. Then Osmeña's popular political opponent, General Manuel Roxas, had also asked Romulo to run as his vice president. Again he refused. Roxas defeated Osmeña and died in office. Once, in 1953, my husband did run briefly but when he realized there was a popular CIA-backed ground swell for Ramon Magsaysay, he withdrew in his favor. Since then, there had been periodic rumors that if the Marcos government ever fell and an interim government were established in its place, Romulo would be the national choice to hold the country together until elections could be held. Unfortunately, he was already too ill and too old when that came.

Imelda insisted on taking me home from the Heroes' Cemetery in her car. I protested that I had my own car and my stepsons for escorts, but she was adamant. "Shouldn't you be with the President?" I asked. He looked small, ill and suddenly old to me that day. He had delivered a very nice tribute at the memorial service, and he was obviously moved by the occasion. At one point I caught him crying.

"No, he has people with him," she said. The President drove off alone with his security guards. And then her identical black limousine pulled up and we stepped in. We were alone in the spacious back seat. There was a glass partition between us and the driver and security officer. Another security car followed us.

"You're something else," she marveled. "You didn't even cry."

In the Philippines widows cry abundantly in public, and even men close to the deceased are expected to shed tears. One persistent army major had even kept trying to open the casket at the last moment so I could say a tearful farewell in front of all the other mourners, but I refused so sharply he finally gave up. Obviously at that moment I was out of sync culturally, although my husband would have approved of my stoicism. He didn't like public displays of emotion.

"I wasn't especially sad," I told the First Lady frankly. "It was such a beautiful service, with all his friends and colleagues there."

Mrs. Marcos handed me a flat box. Too shy to open it in front of her, I waited till I was home alone. Inside was a double strand of small black and white pearls, a large perfect black pearl ring set with diamonds on each side, and matching black pearl earrings, each also accented with a small diamond. The perfect set of jewelry to wear with black or white mourning attire.

She loved to give beautiful gifts. Lady Bountiful. His-and-her eight-thousand-dollar diamond watches for Christmas. After the funeral, she sent me three roses for thirty days. I asked the maid what the number three was for. She said it meant "I love you."

Love. Imelda liked the word. Manila was to be a city of love. Forget the terrible garbage dumps where the scavengers lived, the shantytowns hidden from public view behind the city's whitewashed high walls. She was the goddess of beauty and love. Defending her lavish clothes, her collection of jewels, she said: "The poor people want me to be their star." It appeared to be true. Traveling in her private air-conditioned "Love Bus" to Tacloban, her childhood home, or viewing her special projects—the Philippine Heart Center, the Children's Hospital—in Manila, she would open the window, reach out, and the slipper-clad, ragged throngs would swarm around the bus, fighting to touch her hand. Lined, sun-creased brown faces looking up adoringly, dazzled by the aura of her beauty.

As the long black limousine inched into my circular drive, the First Lady peered curiously at my house. She had often been our guest in the big old Romulo compound, but she had never seen this small house that we had taken since the General retired from government service.

"Would you like to come in?" I asked.

"Yes," she said decisively, getting out of the car. Since the maids were still at the cemetery, there was only the cook to open the door, holding back one of my exuberant cocker spaniels who was intent on jumping all over us.

She walked inside, looking around with interest. I showed her through the whole house. It wasn't much of a tour, since everything is on one floor: There was our big comfortable bedroom in the back with the Betamax and armchairs, the General's dressing room with its own barber chair and Exercycle, his book-lined formal study where he often received guests. I thought of the time, not long ago, when Michael Deaver had sat there to arrange President Reagan's visit to Manila—which was later canceled.

We sat in the airy, open sala facing the orchid garden and the pool. "You planned this whole house to please him," she commented, more to herself than to me. "What are you going to do now?"

"Well, there are a lot of things to clean up here," I began, thinking of the more than one thousand cables, letters, and condolence cards spilling over in my study, yet to be acknowledged.

"What about New York?" she asked suddenly. She loved New York and we had often been there together, the General and I ensconced on the 36th floor of the Waldorf Towers, in the same suite he had always used since 1935, she on the 37th in the lavish suite once occupied by General MacArthur. We came each fall for the opening of the United Nations General Assembly, when my husband took over as head of the Philippine delegation; Mrs. Marcos came for any number of reasons, but mostly, I wager, for fun: She loved the opera, the theater, the restaurants and nightclubs, most of all the pace and excitement of the city. She usually had a large entourage, and she stayed weeks or months depending on when the President summoned her back to Manila. "New York is my R and R!" she once exclaimed to me.

"Oh, I'll get there—maybe in the spring," I said. "I'll see my family, take care of business. And then I'll come back here."

"You're coming back!" She seemed surprised that I wouldn't leave when I could. For the past two years, ever since the needless and brutal assassination of the popular opposition leader, Benigno Aquino, Jr., the Philippines had been sliding downhill economically, politically, and in international prestige. Many had emigrated. Those who could afford to—including some of her own Blue Ladies* (the name given to the women who were members of Imelda's inner circle)—had bundled up their jewels and their cash and fled to Hong Kong, New York, Switzerland, and Morocco.

"I've been here nearly thirteen years, Mrs. Marcos," I reminded her. "I have family and friends here. It's home to me now."

She seemed pleased that I felt so at home in her country. We chatted a bit about old times, when I had first become part of her official family. "How he flaunted you," she laughed, recalling my early visits to Malacanang Palace with my husband.

It was the last time I saw her.

Within weeks the country was rocked by a burgeoning revolution, as Ferdinand Marcos tried to hold on to his waning power.

All her political skills and charm were to no avail. The people rose against him. I couldn't help but think of what she had said about the downfall of her friend, Chiang Ching, whom she had exuberantly predicted would outlast any change in the Chinese government: "She didn't position herself correctly."

Neither, alas, did Imelda.

---

*Socialite political supporters of the Marcoses, the Blue Ladies first appeared at the 1964 Nacionalista Party at which Ferdinand Marcos won the nomination. They wore white *ternos* (traditional native Filipino dresses with butterfly sleeves) with "Marcos blue" sashes. After his victory and inauguration, they became the intimates of Malacanang Palace, often helping Imelda to host visiting dignitaries.

The Diplomat and the Politician

WHEN I first met President Marcos in January of 1973, he had already been in power eight years—longer than any other Philippine president. By the time he was forced out of office, in 1986, he had ruled for twenty years—half of the total period that the Philippines had been independent. There were many young people—50 percent of the population of 56 million are under twenty—who never knew any other president.

Marcos emerged on the political scene as a product of World War II. When the Japanese invaded the Philippines, he served in the Philippine army. Escaping imprisonment when the islands were occupied, he fled to the hills of his native Ilocos Norte province and became a guerrilla. After the country was liberated by MacArthur's forces, Marcos entered politics. In 1949, at the age of thirty-two, he became the youngest member of Congress. He had worked his way to the position of Senate President by the time he made his first bid for the presidency of the country in 1964, and he challenged the incumbent, Diosdado Macapagal, who was seeking reelection.

The Philippines has never developed a political system with two strong, opposing parties of clearly defined ideological differences. Elections have always been a personality contest, with candidates switching parties as easily as they changed their shirts. Political elections have also tended to be characterized by considerable corruption and chicanery, with leading candidates trying to buy each other out. Since the mass base of the electorate is poor, votes go to the highest bidder.

There is also no strong loyalty to the government per se. For four hundred years the Philippines was under the rule of Spain, which was viewed as the oppressor. Later, the United States controlled the Philippines for forty years; again, there was no residue of goodwill for American governor-generals. What Filipinos have always looked for, however, is a *datu* ("chief"): a father figure, a single leader who will take care of his people. No one has understood this national yearning, and taken better advantage of it, than Ferdinand Marcos. He fashioned himself into the man his people wanted: strong, cool, slightly stern, given to flights of passionate nationalism. He also played continuously on the war-hero image, judiciously releasing stories of his phenomenal bravery and courage.

Promoting himself as "the most decorated guerrilla fighter" of the occupation years, Marcos cut a dashing and charismatic figure. He was already a prominent Senator when he met—and wooed—Imelda Romualdez. The daughter of the poor branch of a distinguished family (her uncle was in the Senate), Imelda was working in a bank and studying voice when the shrewd and ambitious Senator saw her and decided she would be the perfect partner for his grand design of achieving political power.

They were a formidable pair of campaigners—Ferdinand with his trim, athletic body, glittering dark eyes, and powerful oratory, exuding an aura of strength and charm; Imelda with her masses of shining black hair, round Spanish eyes, feminine manner, and pleasing soprano voice. Pushed into political activity by her husband (who was eleven years her senior), the young Imelda proved to be a real trouper and a good vote getter, covering the many islands of the Philippine archipelago by plane, car, *banca* (Philippine canoe), and ferry, singing to the crowds and selling her husband.

The most glamorous political duo the Philippines had ever produced, they aroused the sort of romantic anticipation and excitement in crowds that the young John and Jacqueline Kennedy inspired in the United States.

Once he had invented his role, Marcos played it to the hilt. A clever lawyer, who was always outguessing his opponent's next move, he was also a well-read man who drew frequently on references from history and literature in his speeches. He also conveyed the impression that he had a strong sense of his personal destiny. Sitting across a desk from him, many found it difficult not to believe everything he said, including the subtle allusions to his personal courage. Self-contained, steely, eminently self-confident, Marcos was a crafty power player who had made himself into the image that best satisfied the needs of his people. Years later Senator Paul Laxalt compared Marcos to Richard Nixon in their shared love of political intrigue and their chameleonlike ability to seem to be whatever their roles demanded.

On my first visit to Manila, General Romulo warned me: "This is not a classless society." And indeed it was not. Spanish rule had brought with it a feudal society that has not basically changed over the centuries. A few entrenched families—perhaps 10 percent of the population—control the wealth and the power. Because such a small group of people control the wealth and power in the country, Philippine society, despite a population as large as France, seems like a small town. Everyone knows, or is related to, everyone else. Gossip *(chismis)* is a favorite pastime: inventive,

colorful, often funny. Even when loose talk came to be
labeled a crime punishable by imprisonment under martial
law, the gossip continued unabated—albeit reduced to
whispers. Much of it centered around Imelda's extravagance and her "favorites." She could not tolerate criticism
or "bad news," so her favorites tended to be sycophants
who used her for their own ends.

At the time I moved to Manila, and for a few years
thereafter, the Marcoses appeared to be popular despite
the imposition of martial law the previous fall. An invitation
to the palace was sought after. A few families were bitter
and distraught over losing their businesses to Marcos cronies, or having a member of their family jailed, as was
Benigno Aquino, Jr., but in general Manila was a politically
passive society. Some of the wealthy matrons occasionally
sniped at Imelda Marcos because of her love of luxury, but
the President himself seemed immune from attack.

There is a minuscule middle class and a huge number of
poor people. During the American period the Philippines
was supposedly tutored in the democratic system. A presidential government was established, with a bicameral legislature and a judiciary. But it was so shallowly rooted that
when Ferdinand Marcos changed the system, to insure his
own retention of power, there was little resistance.

He abolished the Congress, which many considered a
roadblock rather than a means to legislation. The constitution was rewritten so that the government could be
changed from a bicameral to a parliamentary system. Laws
could be passed quickly in this way, though in fact Marcos
ran the country by presidential decree. Having done away
with Congress and made the judiciary subservient to his
office, he was able to operate without any accountability or
checks and balances.

Yet he remained enormously popular, the beloved *datu*.

The President preached "democracy," but what he truly
believed in was one-man rule, a concept not unusual in

Asia. And once he declared martial law, which gave him free access to all the built-in systems of checks and balances, he began methodically and systematically to destroy them, one by one. He abolished the office of the vice presidency. He muzzled the press and made dissent a punishable crime. He struck down the writ of habeas corpus so that victims had no legal recourse at their disposal.

He got by with all this without too much protest from his people. He slipped it in, one teaspoon at a time, like so much bad-tasting medicine, in the name of national progress and "restructuring society." He rationalized everything he did in terms of this necessary restructuring, and, for the most part, Filipinos accepted that. Everyone agreed that the old feudal order had to go, and perhaps Ferdinand Marcos was the leader who could break with the past. He called his Master Plan, which was supposed to unleash the inherent vitality and wealth of the Philippines, the "New Society." His personal political party became the "New Society Party" and its most glamorous star and leader was his wife, Imelda.

Both Ferdinand Marcos and Carlos Romulo rose in fame from the ashes of World War II. But their paths did not cross at that time.

Carlos Romulo (he was twenty years older than Marcos) was the son of a provincial governor and one of the bright young Filipinos who were helped to study abroad by the American governor-general. His sponsor, when he went to Columbia University in New York to get a master's degree in 1918, was President William Howard Taft. Returning to the Philippines with his degree in American literature, Romulo became a professor of English at the University of the Philippines and worked as a newspaper reporter and editor.

Considered apolitical, Romulo served every president of

the Philippines, usually in posts abroad, and was not active in any political party.

He became friends with both General and Mrs. Douglas MacArthur when they came to Manila in 1935. MacArthur served as military advisor to the Commonwealth government until the Japanese attacked Pearl Harbor in 1941, at which time he was recalled to active duty with the United States Army and given command of the military forces in the Philippines. At that point, he selected Romulo, by then a newspaper publisher and a reserve officer, to be his aide and press officer, giving him the rank of Major.

When the Japanese attacked Manila, the MacArthurs, President Manuel Quezon, Romulo, and others escaped to the island of Corregidor at the mouth of Manila Bay and eventually worked their way to Australia before the Philippines fell. (Romulo later wrote of his experiences in a best-selling book, *Last Man Off Bataan.*)

In Australia MacArthur waited out his chance to retake the Philippines, and tried to keep the war in the Pacific fresh in the minds of Americans back home. With no materiel or men coming his way from the United States which, with its allies, was concentrating on the war in Europe, he sought ways to keep up the morale of the people and guerrilla fighters in the occupied Philippines. He arranged airdrops of cigarettes, candy, and oranges to the islands, all stamped "I Shall Return. MacArthur." Whenever Romy heard his former boss attacked for the "egotism" of that terse message, he bristled.

"General MacArthur wanted to stamp them 'America Won't Let You Down.' But I persuaded him to use 'I Shall Return.' Because the Filipinos knew MacArthur, and if he said he would return, they would believe him."

Jean MacArthur, the general's wife, and Carlos Romulo were about the same age—some twenty years younger than the general. They had been through a lot together during the war years and they remained fast friends thereafter. The very hour that we arrived in the Waldorf Towers, each fall, on our annual trip to New York, Romulo would order flowers sent to Jean. Pretty soon the telephone would ring: "Romy, you're back!" (His American friends always called him Romy.) It was always a joyful reunion. The day after General Romulo died, Jean MacArthur called me in Manila. "I feel like there's a big chunk gone from my life," she said sadly.

Teacher, writer, and eventually world diplomat, Romulo was the first (and so far only) Asian to win the Pulitzer Prize in Journalism, which he received for a series of articles predicting the outbreak of World War II. It was General MacArthur who called him in to his office, in Australia, to tell him he had won. Romulo was so startled at the unexpected news that he said, without thinking, "Are you pulling my leg?" And MacArthur replied, with mock severity, "Am I in the habit of pulling your leg, Carlos?"

In certain ways, Carlos Romulo was better known abroad than he was in the Philippines. Early on, he set his sights on the international scene, and many of his accomplishments were played out in that arena. A fervent advocate of world peace, he was one of the original signers of the United Nations Charter in San Francisco in 1945. The Philippines' permanent representative to the United Nations for many years, he became the first Asian to be elected President of the General Assembly (1949–50). He would also have been elected Secretary-General were it not for the repeated veto of Soviet Russia. The Russians felt, and frankly told him, that they believed he was too "pro-American."

Soon after the Philippines became independent in 1946, Romulo was named his country's ambassador to the United States, while concurrently serving as the representative to the United Nations. He retired in 1961 during the Kennedy administration and returned home to become President of the University of the Philippines.

It was while serving in the latter capacity that President Marcos asked him to join his cabinet as Secretary of Education. Well aware of the General's international prestige, Marcos later offered him the post of Minister of Foreign Affairs.

General Romulo and President Marcos appeared to have an excellent working relationship and mutual respect for one another's talents. Courtesy always characterized their interchanges: Even though he occasionally teased Marcos (he could not resist teasing anyone), Romulo was never familiar with him, and he always addressed him as "Mr. President." The President, in turn, always addressed Romulo as "General," the title of his choice. Romulo considered President Marcos the "most studious" of all the presidents he had worked for, and the best prepared on issues. He also admired his coolness under fire.

A man of impeccable integrity himself, General Romulo seemed scarcely aware of the misdoings and evil around him. Totally without cynicism, he was content to answer to his own conscience and let others do likewise. After the charges of corruption engulfed Marcos's administration, the most I ever heard General Romulo say against the President was that he should step down. Which Marcos, of course, had no intention of doing.

President Marcos's declaration of martial law on September 21, 1972, caught General Romulo completely by surprise. He had been given no clue of what was to happen when he left Manila to attend the opening of the General Assembly in New York that fall.

Privately distressed, he wrote the President a long confidential letter warning him, in effect, that this would make it harder for him to defend the Philippines abroad. He hoped the situation was only "temporary," for "the longer martial law stays in effect, the longer will the impression persist that those cherished liberties for which our fore-fathers fought . ... have been killed permanently. . . . Rule by martial law, if unduly prolonged, will be governed by the familiar dynamics of dictatorship. Succession in such governments is achieved by violent coups, leading inexora-bly to the total defeat of the democratic processes."

Marcos didn't listen. He had already taken a poll of his military and found that 85 percent were in favor of martial law. According to the election laws, a president could serve one term and be reelected (which he had been), but he could not run for a consecutive term—although there was no rule against his running again at a later time.

As early as 1969 Imelda's name was being floated, through the instructions of the President, and the efforts of her brother, Benjamin "Kokoy" Romualdez, the family gofer and bagman, to stand for the 1973 election. It did not occur to anyone that Marcos was well on his way to setting up a family dynasty, in which his wife could hold the seat for him, thus permitting him to run again.

As it turned out, the 1973 election was never held. By the time Marcos declared martial law in 1972, he must already have decided it was better to hold the post himself than let his wife have a shot at it.

With no challenger on the horizon, both were soon con-tentedly entrenched at Malacanang Palace. Perhaps, like the Duvaliers of Haiti, they assumed that Marcos would be "President for life."

A Foreign Affair

G ENERAL Romulo's romance with an American journalist had been one political hitch that the Marcoses
could simply not have anticipated. When one of his spies
first reported to the President that his eminent and aging
Foreign Minister was courting an American woman, Marcos
was caught off guard. *"Not* the General!" he exploded. Any
other member of the cabinet and he could have understood
it—they were men in their forties and fifties. General
Romulo was seventy-four. It was ironic, I suppose, that it
was the oldest member of his cabinet, holding the premier
post next to his own since Marcos had abolished the vice
presidency, who was caught up in an international romance.

But the Marcoses and I were stuck with each other. The
General would not give me up and they would not give him
up.

A classic Capricorn who always got his own way, the
General liked to tell his friends exactly when he decided to
marry me: "When I saw her walk in the revolving door of
La Côte Basque, the night of my dinner for George Bush."

It was the fall of 1972—the first time I had seen him in twelve years. "You have matured and mellowed," he told me. "What was I like before?" I asked, curious about his impression of me then. "You were attractive then, too," he replied, "but—different. You hadn't matured yet."

I first met General Carlos P. Romulo in 1957 when I was assigned by the *Reader's Digest* to write an article about the death of his eldest son, Carlos Junior, in a plane crash. Called "A Bridge of Helping Hands," it was a straightforward, emotional tale that won the high readership award for that month. The reason it was so appealing was that Romy was first and foremost a journalist. Throughout many distinguished careers—as publisher, in the military, and finally as an international diplomat—he always thought like a reporter: He had an alert, receptive attitude that instinctively sensed the news value of any information, combined with a genuine affection for and curiosity about people.

When I got the assignment I called him in Washington, where he was serving as his country's ambassador to the United States. Since he was also head of the Philippine delegation to the United Nations and commuted regularly between New York and Washington, he asked me to meet him for a breakfast conference in New York. There he gave me the story precisely as he knew I needed it—in a fast, concentrated hour. It practically wrote itself. When I got back to the Digest headquarters in Pleasantville, I told my editors it was the easiest interview I had ever had.

Unlike most subjects whom a reporter never sees again, General Romulo followed up our initial interview with gestures of friendship. Interested that I too wrote books, he offered to exchange volumes of his for mine, which we did. On one of his trips to New York he brought his wife and widowed daughter-in-law, and invited me to lunch with them.

In 1960 Romulo retired as ambassador and returned to the Philippines to become president of the national university. This was when I lost track of him, except for an occasional Christmas card, not realizing that he came to New York each fall to attend the United Nations. In early 1972 I read that he had survived a near-fatal auto accident in Manila, yet he was reported to be back at the United Nations that fall. My *Reader's Digest* editors said, "There is probably another story. Go see him."

When I called him for an appointment, Romulo invited me to attend a dinner he was hosting in honor of George and Barbara Bush at La Côte Basque. At that time Bush was the US representative to the United Nations. I enjoyed the Bushes; they were easy, friendly people and obviously good friends of the General.

I was surprised to see that the General's widowed daughter-in-law, Mariles, was acting as his hostess and I asked her son, Mike, where his grandmother was. It was only then that I learned that Virginia Romulo had died four years before. The General, I was soon to discover, was a much sought-after widower.

A dapper, fastidious man, the General, despite his small stature (he was five feet four), managed to dominate a room when he entered it through a combination of self-assurance and great charm. He seemed much younger than his seventy-four years. He was such a strong and winning personality that as I became close to him and spent time with him, I quite forgot about the differences in our age.

General Romulo considered good grooming and being a good host important adjuncts to diplomatic life and gave them serious attention. "A person who is well dressed is at ease and sure of himself," he maintained. His clothes— even pajamas and robes—were all custom tailored. He would spend twenty minutes selecting the perfect tie and pocket handkerchief. Shoes must be shined before each wearing. Sometimes he went in for rather daring colors— orchid shirts and the like—but the ensemble was always pleasing.

He was most famous perhaps as a speaker. He had built a

career on oratory and won a prominent place for himself in world affairs, despite the fact that, as he was first to admit, he was merely "a small man from a small country."

Wherever Romy appeared, he drew crowds. Once, at a flag-raising ceremony when he was pinch-hitting for President Marcos, the crowd surged around him, asking for autographs, wanting to shake his hand. Defense Secretary Enrile, who was standing by, said, "General, they like you."

Romy turned to him and said softly, "No, Johnny. They love me." Turning to me, he added, a bit wistfully, "That is what I wish someone would write about me one day. Instead of all the stories about the honors and awards." (He had eighty-four honorary degrees, nearly a hundred special medals and citations, including the Philippine Medal of Honor and the US Medal of Freedom.)

Although I had known him since 1957, and written about him several times, I had yet to hear Romulo speak. That fall of 1972, when we first started courting, he invited me to a Philippine-American Chamber of Commerce luncheon at which he was to be the guest speaker.

Every seat was sold out. Apparently the General was a great favorite. His audience responded with enormous enthusiasm, giving him a standing ovation when he was introduced and when he concluded his speech.

Afterward in the limo, as he was dropping me off at my apartment, he asked me what I thought of his speech.

"You're a great performer," I said.

His face fell with disappointment.

"I mean it," I explained. "There are many orators. But you know how to work an audience. I'd put you up against Bob Hope anyday." Actually he reminded me more of Jack Benny—he was so sure of himself he could use long pauses to build up a punch line. His speeches usually were serious in content, but he used anecdotes and jokes to keep the audience interested. Then, when they were laughing, he slipped them some important thought. They loved him.

However, he also had a dark side—he could be very demanding. He didn't countenance fools gladly and would flare up at inefficiency, tardiness, or plain garden-variety stupidity. He also appeared to have a ravenous appetite that attacked like a knife at certain hours and he would get very testy if meals were late. Whoever was close caught the flack—whether it was an aide, his host, or his wife. A close friend warned me early on, "You will find they don't call him the General for nothing!"

We continued to get acquainted after the Chamber of Commerce luncheon. Over subsequent meetings it came out that I had lost my husband in 1967; Romy's wife had died the following year. He invited me to come to Manila and meet President and Mrs. Marcos, and suggested I do a story on why Marcos had declared martial law. No one from the Western media had as yet interviewed the Philippine president on this subject.

I flew to Manila in January 1973, and my interview with President Marcos was a cover story for *Saturday Review/ World*. By then I also had an assignment from the *Ladies' Home Journal* to see Imelda Marcos and get a first-person account of her recent brush with a would-be assassin. She had been handing out plaques at an outdoor awards ceremony on December 7, 1972, when one of the "awardees" suddenly lunged at her with a bolo—the long curved knife used by Filipino farmers to cut cane. This horrifying scene had been captured on live television.

I arrived in Manila, armed with my two legitimate assignments, as a guest of the government. Later I was told that some women guests from abroad were propositioned by Mrs. Marcos's brother Kokoy, or the President himself, or one of the lesser officials. No one bothered me. But I did notice that General Romulo seemed relieved that the government had provided me a suite at the Intercontinental Hotel rather than in one of the guest quarters at Malacanang Palace.

The General himself met me at the palace for my first

meeting with the First Lady, on January 15. The first few minutes were spent with his introducing me to both the President and his wife. Then the men retired to the President's study.

Imelda Marcos received me in the Music Room, which was also used during state dinners by both the President and Mrs. Marcos to receive their VIP guests. Just off the long public reception hall, the Music Room was small and antique-laden, studded with family photographs, a few paintings. A Louis Quinze settee with matching chairs faced the door. No one entered this room without knocking. And it was considered a great privilege during a large dinner to be invited inside while the other guests milled around in the public reception hall.

Tall for a Filipino, with heavy black hair swept to the side in a chignon, Imelda Marcos had a classic beauty that, even allowing for periodic fluctuations in weight, is striking. That day she was dressed in a Pucci silk print dress and a long double strand of pearls that she used as a sling for her injured arm. (She later attended the Nixon inaugural using a more elaborate pearl sling.) I don't know whether she had ever been taught the tactics of survival (she denied it), but when attacked, she had crossed her arms over her body, protecting her heart, throat, and back, thus saving her life. Her attacker was eventually killed by her security guards, but not before she had been badly slashed. Her arms still bore deep scars when I saw her, and she was anticipating corrective surgery.

Since then, understandably enough, she has been haunted by the prospect of assassination. She wears a scarf or kerchief at her throat, since an old soothsayer in her native province of Leyte told her it would ward off a beheading. And her incredible wardrobe collection stems in part from the fact that she was also warned never to throw away any personal article of clothing lest it be used for voodoo rites to unleash evil spirits against her. When she redid the palace a few years after the assassination attempt, all the windows were covered over and bullet-proofed. Bullet-proof steel plates completely lined the ceilings.

The First Lady's manner, at that time, was somewhat shy and diffident. She answered my questions simply, without affectation, speaking softly, talking of her husband, her children, her Catholic faith ("I am not afraid to die, because if I die I meet my God, you see?"). Although I had heard that she was a formidable vote-getter who had much to do with her husband's success in the 1965 presidential elections (he acknowledged she delivered the one million vote margin he needed to be elected), she still seemed something of a neophyte, who gave the impression "my husband is older, smarter, and he is the boss"—an attitude that was to alter radically as time went by. Her idea of a political speech was a few lines about "I know my husband is a good man. Please vote for him," followed by an appealing native song crooned in the local dialect.

Later, when our interview was over, Romy told me she asked him, "Did I do all right?" The nonstop strident monologues and political arrogance of her later years was not yet apparent.

During my three-week stay in Manila, I interviewed President Marcos as well, made one quick tour of the islands, and spent every lunch and evening with General Romulo. One afternoon he took me to the beautiful old San Agustin Church, within the ancient Walled City (Intramuros), and asked me to stay in the Philippines and marry him. He explained that while an ambassador must ask permission to marry a foreigner, he was "the boss" in his ministry. However, he would need the approval of the President.

"And if the President doesn't approve?" I asked him.

"Then I'll resign." He answered firmly.

The news came as a shock to the President—not to say a frightful nuisance. Marcos was so disturbed by it that he closed himself in his office and took no calls while he composed a long, handwritten letter to the General, pointing out how ill-timed the proposed union was (he even compared the General's situation to that of the Duke of Windsor). The note was delivered to the Romulo house by the secretive General Fabian Ver. Romy told me that Ver was devoted to the President and that "if you are going to have a bodyguard, he's the one to have." He described an incident when the President's car was being attacked by student demonstrators and Ver literally threw his own body across the car, spreadeagled, to take the stones and shots himself. No wonder Marcos clung so tenaciously to Ver.

The President reminded his minister of foreign affairs that the US military bases in the Philippines were up for renegotiation. The General was head of the Philippine panel and it would not be appropriate at this critical juncture for him suddenly to take an American wife. "Any concessions you make to the other side," the President warned, "our people will blame you and say it is because of her influence."

Eventually we worked out a compromise. Since I was the "free agent," I suggested that I return to New York, get a contract to write a book on the Philippines, and then come back. I would live in a hotel and pursue my profession, but be close to the General and serve as his constant companion, hostess, and eventually—when history permitted—as his wife.

And so my visit to Manila ended. When he saw me off at the airport, Romy wanted to know what my life would be like back in New York. "What do you do when you get up in the morning?" he asked.

"I fix my breakfast," I told him.

"I'll send you a Filipino maid."

I laughed. "I've been fixing my own breakfast all my life!"

Before I left, he called for a plebiscite among his grand-children to determine whether I should come back and live with them.

All voted yes, except for ten-year-old Rowena.

"Why?" he asked her.

"Because you are going to marry her anyway, so there is no reason to vote," she answered with unarguable logic.

Seven-year-old Anton wrote his grandfather a note saying that there were "three things wrong with Beth Day: "1) She's too young to be my grandmother; 2) She's taller than Popsy; and 3) She don't even know me yet."

While I was in New York, preparing to return to the Philippines, the General made several trips in Asia, including Saudi Arabia, and called me each day from wherever he was.

He was upset by his hotel accommodations in Saudi Arabia. He told me that he had called the President from Riyadh, where he was on a mission to get more oil for the Philippines, and informed him that the telephone was bugged.

Startled, Marcos replied, "Security is tapping our line? How do you know?"

"Two cockroaches just jumped out of the telephone."

From a neighboring Asian country he called me, gleefully, to report that the host government had offered him a girl. Not just any girl, but an American, since the word was out he liked Americans.

I was furious. This was, I learned later, a rather common practice in the diplomatic world. "Girls" were provided VIP guests on the rather cynical rationale that if they were thus entertained they would be less likely to wander around a foreign city alone. The practice is also sometimes used by hostile governments to entrap diplomats.

Romy assured me that he had told the protocol officer to take the girl away. "To begin with, she was a blonde"—he considered all blondes albinos—"and she was drenched in

Joy!" He was inordinately fond of good scents, but didn't like overpowering ones.

Wherever he went, he apparently made it clear to his hosts that he missed me. At a dinner in Hong Kong, his host set a place to the General's right that remained empty throughout the meal. When it came time for the toasts, the host offered one to "the lady whom you wish were here tonight."

In Pattaya, Thailand, a beach resort where official conferences are sometimes held, he ordered a special telephone line installed just so he could make his daily call to me in New York.

I wrote him regularly. Once when he was complaining to me on the phone that he was lonely, I remarked with uncharacteristic coyness, "My letters kiss you for me."

There was a moment's silence. Then he said drily, "Well, they aren't *that* good!"

I always tried to tell him precisely where I would be at what hour, but he didn't always figure the time change correctly. I had told him I was spending Easter Sunday out of town with my brother's family, but when I walked into my apartment that night the phone was ringing. It was Romy, in an absolute snit. "Where have you been all day?" It seems he made a call, with the President and First Lady beside him, so that the three could thank me for the stories that had by now appeared in the *Saturday Review/World* and *Ladies' Home Journal*. When there was no answer at the apartment, the President had turned to Romy and said, "See? She's two-timing you!"

At a meeting of the Security Council in Manila a few days later, the General failed to hear a question directed at him. "His mind is in New York," teased the President.

"No, sir," Romy corrected him. "My heart is in New York. But my mind is here."

Word of the General's romance got around. At a dinner party at the palace, the guest of honor, an American banker, said to the President, "Well, I understand your Secretary of Foreign Affairs is going to be a bridegroom!"

"Yes, he is very much in love," Imelda Marcos chimed in, "and he is having her come back here to be near him."

"I sent him to escort a guest," grumbled President Marcos, "and he took his job too literally!"

When I returned to Manila in March, Romy told me that my biggest competition for his time would be the President and his barber, Peter. Peter had been coming faithfully every morning to shave and massage him since his return to the Philippines in 1961. It was a part of the morning ritual he enjoyed and he would not let anything interrupt it. Peter was also the barometer of local opinion. He told the General that when his customers heard I was back in Manila, they asked, "Why couldn't the General find a Filipina?" Peter apparently had risen to my defense explaining that although the General could certainly find a Filipina who was prettier, he was an intellectual man and he wanted "a woman he could talk to."

Romy told me this, adding with a twinkle, "If they only knew!" He later told me that he had originally chosen me as a companion and hostess, since entertaining was a large part of his diplomatic tasks. That the relationship also proved to be a romantic one was a delightful plus.

Since we could not yet be officially married, I took a suite in the Manila Hilton, only a few blocks from the General's office. I had a little kitchenette and I often made simple lunches for him there. If we went downstairs to his reserved table at the Rôtisserie, our meal would invariably be interrupted six or seven times by people who had failed to catch him at the office.

Soon after my return to Manila, the General arranged for a private weekend and we flew to a new beach resort, Punta Baluarte, in Batangas, only a half hour by helicopter from Manila. When we returned early Monday, he discovered the President had been calling him persistently at his house. He drove directly to the palace and found Marcos quite angry that he had been unable to reach him by phone.

"Don't go there again," he told Romy. "What if a war was declared and I couldn't talk to you! You can't go where I'm unable to reach you by phone."

That was the end of our spontaneous vacations. After that, if we left Manila for a weekend, we had a protocol officer in tow and were in constant communication with the palace.

Since I didn't have a clear social position or any rank beyond that of resident journalist, I often felt uneasy in the amorphous role of "girlfriend of the General." But the Marcoses treated me very well. They understood that my position was a result of the President's request to delay our marriage, so I was included in their gatherings as though I was a Cabinet wife. At state dinners, Romy sat at the presidential table, while I was assigned to Table Number One, which was directly below and included members of the Cabinet and foreign guests.

I tended to stay on the sidelines unless I was called for. Very often, Imelda Marcos would beckon me to approach the small presidential group that included the President, herself, the General, and perhaps a guest of honor. I was never certain that I should. And sometimes I felt the animosity of other palace regulars who had more rank than I did. But if she insisted, of course I joined her.

As Henry Kissinger once modestly commented, "Power is an aphrodisiac," and there always were a lot of pretty ladies around to flatter and cajole the President. Mrs. Marcos kept a sharp eye on them. On several occasions when there were some aggressive beauties around as we were ready to leave on a flight, she revised the passenger list so that I was the one assigned to ride with the President. I guess she figured I was no threat.

Imelda and I were always at something of a stalemate. In general, she treated me with consideration, but we were not at ease with one another. She lived on praise and I have a poor tongue for praise. Each time we met there would be that strained moment—waiting. And all I could think of to say was something lame about her lovely dress. That was not what she wanted to hear from me. She wanted my good opinion of her intellect, her grasp of political affairs, her speeches.

We would never have chosen one another for friends. She and I were locked by historical accident in a relationship that left both of us a bit uncomfortable, wary, but on the face of it, friendly. It was actually much easier for me to talk to the President than to her.

To the President, his minister's romance was an embarrassment. Imelda, on the other hand, was openly curious and interested in the romance, as were most Manilans. At a small dinner in the Cultural Center shortly after my return, she toasted the General: "To your success—in whatever way you wish *most* to succeed!"

Once he came to my hotel suite directly from the palace and showed me a package the First Lady had given him: capsules of Royal Bee Jelly imported from Europe. "She said it was to help uphold the Philippines' honor," he laughed. He never took them.

Imelda and the Jet Set

I HAVE a recurrent fantasy. I see Imelda Romualdez—a tall, leggy, warm-eyed girl, on the beach at Tacloban. She is barefoot. Her dress is a hand-me-down. But she is a happy child. Her huge black eyes sparkle with vitality. She is holding her little brother's hand. She loves her brother dearly, and since her mother is both frail and depressed, it is Imelda who protects and cares for the little boy. She is always singing, her sweet soprano voice wafting out on the soft tropical breeze.

There are many stories of Imelda's spontaneous generosity, her kindnesses, her desire to please. Even after all the years of uncontested power that had made her arrogant, she was capable of genuine gestures of concern. Beneath the arrogance the warm-hearted, coltish girl would sometimes appear.

I often wonder, if she had married a more ordinary man—a banker, lawyer, or doctor—what sort of woman would she have become? Would she have remained ordinary herself? Or was she also driven, like her husband, by a relentless, gnawing urge for power?

I don't think so. She learned it. She became accustomed to it. And by this period of her life, she had forgotten any other way to live.

But I don't believe she wanted it at the beginning.

When I interviewed her for the first time in 1973, she told me that the rigors of being a senator's wife very nearly had done her in when she was a young matron with small children. The constant crowds of people in her house, the lack of privacy, the political demands were too much for her. She suffered a nervous breakdown. Sent by her husband to doctors in New York, she was treated and then told the brutal truth: Either learn to live the public life of a politician's wife, or leave your husband. You won't change him.

She learned to handle it, with a vengeance. Like most converts, she became more of a politician than her mentor. She not only embraced the public, political life, she learned to draw her strength from it. Crowds became her best friends, her source of energy. "Touching the flesh" revitalized her. Ferdinand Marcos had the relentless ambition. But it was Imelda Marcos who became the more effective politician.

Desite my lack of a title, I was adopted into the official family at Malacanang Palace and became a de facto Cabinet wife, performing the normal routines and duties of the other wives. There was airport duty: meeting and saying farewell to all the visiting VIP guests. There were the formal dinners at Malacanang, sometimes two or three a week. There were the trips on the presidential yacht, and domestic interisland flights on the President's or the First Lady's planes, to their respective hometowns.

In June of 1973 the Marcoses gave a dinner in honor of Van Cliburn, who had won the Tchaikovsky piano competition in Moscow. Mrs. Marcos decided to make me a "special guest" to share the honors for the evening and promoted me to the presidential table, to the right of her husband.

I don't know how long Cliburn had known the Marcoses, but he appeared to be a familiar and welcome guest. Over the next few years, I saw him at the palace fairly regularly, along with Cristina Ford. At that time the Ford Company had heavy investments in the Philippines. (The Ford plant in Bataan was closed in 1984.) Imelda Marcos clearly enjoyed Van's company, and to a great extent their common bond seemed to be music. He guided her in setting up a program for talented Filipino children, whom she sent abroad to study.*

In those days the remodeling of the palace had not yet begun and it was still a charming, old-fashioned, rambling white colonial house open on two sides to the Pasig River. Used by the Spanish governors, it later became the residence of the American governor-generals, and finally— after the establishment of the Philippine Commonwealth in 1935—the official residence of the Philippine presidents. Mrs. Douglas MacArthur recalled that in her years in Manila (1935–1941) guests walked between great blocks of ice set on either side of the palace's entrance path to cool off after an evening of dancing. (By 1973 the public rooms of the palace were all air-conditioned. But no one had been able to do much about the mosquitoes that hid under the tablecloths, then attacked during dinner. I once asked why the dining room wasn't sprayed before the guests came in and was told that President Marcos was allergic to sprays of all kinds and none were used in the palace.) Dinners were held in another old building on the palace grounds, Maharlika Hall. Guests were received by President and Mrs. Marcos at Malacanang and then walked around to Maharlika, a distance of about one city block.

---

*The most famous perhaps is the brilliant young pianist Cecile Licad, who became a protégé of Rudolf Serkin.

On that evening when I shared the spotlight with Van Cliburn, Romy and I walked with him and President and Mrs. Marcos through a flower-lined entrance, then through a trellised archway woven with fresh sampaguita (jasmine) up the stairs to the second floor of Maharlika Hall. This circuitous route was actually a security device. As we appeared, the band struck up "Mabuhay" ("Long Life"), the traditional spirited Philippine song of welcome, and we walked down a red carpet between the lines of waiting guests, to the presidential table, on an elevated dais on the left side of the room. The table was covered with embroidered tablecloths decorated with sampaguita and white orchids. And every few feet there were heavy silver candelabra surrounded at the base with fresh flowers. The orchestra played throughout dinner. Then there was a program of native songs and dances. (Later a modern fashion show was added to this format to entertain palace guests.)

That evening was really my debut in Manila society. When the presidential party walked down the red carpet, there was much nodding and greeting and the General slipped out of the official party every few feet to greet some dear friend. A man I had not seen before grasped my arm as I passed by. When I paused, he whispered in my ear: "You have the best Filipino of them all!"

Whenever we went to the palace, we never knew how long a wait it would be until we went in to dinner, or whether any refreshments would be served. Sometimes there were waiters with trays of juices and hard drinks. Other times I didn't see any. The larger the crowd, the fewer waiters and drinks there seemed to be. I never discovered whether it was a deliberate policy to discourage drinking or just an oversight in arrangements. I was told part of the problem was that, though enough wine was bought, the waiters poured as little as possible then sold off the unopened bottles—a little black market on the side. Several of the ambassadors and their wives told me they fortified themselves at home before they came to the palace. I was afraid to do that in case drinks were available and I didn't want to have more than I could handle.

Once I saw a waiter with glasses of champagne—a rare treat—and shamelessly tackled him, to the delighted laughter of Minister Ongpin and some other Cabinet members who caught me at it. The reason I had to literally pull at the waiter's arm is that if liquor was available, it would be offered to the men first and only on demand to the ladies. Most Filipino waiters assume that women drink nothing but orange juice.

Neither of the Marcoses care about liquor. President Marcos takes no alcohol at all and even for a toast would merely touch his lips to the edge of the glass. Imelda would play around with a glass of white wine, or sip champagne. She always ordered Dom Pérignon for her European guests when she took them out in Manila or New York.

Romy was sympathetic to my taste for wine. While he too enjoyed wine, his consumption was small. The goblets at the presidential table were large; the glasses at the round tables below were about the size I would use for sherry. My husband would watch me and when he saw my glass was empty, he signaled a waiter from the presidential table who would appear at my side with Romy's goblet, half full. My tablemates were generally a bit startled, but my momentary embarrassment did not diminish my pleasure.

As I became more and more a familiar figure at Malacanang, I grew a bit bolder and sometimes scolded the waiters for their lack of service, urging them to do better. Once, at a luncheon at the Manila Hotel for Japanese Prime Minister Takeo Fukuda, the newly accredited British Ambassador Bill Bentley, finding his place next to mine, said, "Oh I'm delighted to be seated next to you." I preened prettily. Then he added, in a jolly loud voice, "I hear you're very stern about the wine!"

General Romulo used to complain that Mrs. Marcos put

all her attention on spectacle and that no one minded the kitchen. A gourmet himself, he didn't like the food served at Malacanang and often ate at home before he went. The quality of food was uneven, with the catering being given out to different restaurants or hotels according to whichever was currently Mrs. Marcos's favorite. When I'd see the trucks of Via Mare, a quality local restaurant, parked outside I felt reassured. A fastidious European chef once told me he was horrified when he came to the palace kitchen to check it out before bringing in his food. "There was an old Chinese cook asleep in a chair, and a cat asleep on the table."

Occasionally parties were held outside. I remember attending one for American investors: The palace lawn had been turned into a village fairground, with bamboo stalls, vendors, and even lechon—piglets roasted over live coals. Favors in the form of small capiz shell lanterns and pieces of native jewelry in shell and wood were strung in the trees and guests were encouraged to jump up and get one—to whoops of encouragement from the musicians and dancers. There was also a fiesta "queen"—one of the top Filipina models riding around in a flower-decked pony cart with her bevy of attendants walking alongside in long embroidered native dresses.

At Malacanang Palace, the tables were always set with traditional European-style silver service. In private homes, however, Filipinos used a large dessert-sized spoon along with their fork, instead of a knife. It works much better than a knife when handling rice, which is served at every meal. Often a bed of rice is topped with meat, egg, fish, or a stew and the whole mixture is scooped up with the spoon. In the Chinese and Japanese embassies guests were offered a choice of conventional silver or chopsticks.

I didn't have much experience with chopsticks before I came to Manila, and I found my efforts similar to the time, as a child, I was learning to post to a trot while riding. If I got the rhythm right, I was okay. But if I got off to a wrong start somehow, I never could catch up.

We were guests at the Japanese embassy one night at a dinner the ambassador gave in honor of President and Mrs. Marcos. (Lavish dinners were held regularly in the embassies, in honor of the Foreign Minister, President and Mrs. Marcos, or visiting dignitaries.) I was deep in conversation with a delightful Japanese on my left who had spent a good deal of time at the UN and spoke excellent English, when the first course was presented. I started off with a splendid grip, amazed at my own dexterity with chopsticks.

A second course was served. And then a third. Since I was doing so well with my chopsticks I was afraid to put them down and I kept nipping away at everything set before me, talking all the while. I maneuvered my way through every morsel of white, pink, and red raw fish. Then tempura, and after that a plate of Kobe beef and vegetables. I manfully worked my way through the lot, even managing to use my chopsticks as a saw to separate pieces of steak. By the time the final soup course arrived and I at last put down my chopsticks, I suddenly felt sick. I had gone through about seven different courses.

Too late, I looked up from my lacquer tray and realized that other—wiser—folk had taken only small portions of each dish while I had eaten everything!

I massaged my taut, cramped fingers, rose with as much dignity as I could muster, and waddled out of the room, hating myself.

When I moved to Manila, Ferdinand Marcos was still a sexually attractive man. At close range, say across a small dinner table, he projected a sort of glittering animal magnetism. One evening, sitting at a round table at an informal palace dinner, I became fascinated watching him eyeing one of his wife's guests sitting beside me, a rather voluptuous Italian. I could literally see his nostrils flare, like in an old Valentino movie. Marcos did not marry until he was thirty-seven and by that time he already had a mistress and four children whom his old schoolteacher-mother protected and Imelda pointedly ignored. He was also said to have had affairs with several wives of American service personnel, which accounted for their husbands' hasty transfer to other countries. One of his closest cronies with whom he was involved in secret business enterprises had an extraordinarily pretty wife; her husband did not allow her to attend palace parties after he saw the President eye her. Later, when the President was clearly ill, she resurfaced at palace functions.

On June 27, 1973, a palace dinner was held in honor of Mrs. Henry Ford and the Apollo 17 astronauts and their wives who were then touring Asia. When the dance music began, the President danced the opening number with his guest of honor and then excused himself and disappeared from the dining room. I murmured to one of the Blue Ladies at my table, "I guess she's not his type."

"They say she leads instead of follows," the lady whispered.

The tawny, sexy Cristina Ford was not one of the President's favorites. She was clearly his wife's friend, not his. It was through the two women's friendship that the Ford Motor Company built a stamping plant in Bataan. And so Cristina was duly accorded all the attention and honors given foreign investors whenever she was in Manila.

Actually, I could easily understand why Imelda was so fond of Cristina and enjoyed her company so much. In her position of power, Mrs. Marcos was surrounded by sycophants and people wanting favors, and by those whose wealth was already based on her largesse. But these were hardly friends. Cristina did not need Imelda; she already had her own place in the sun. She was irreverent and full of fun. She was not in awe of the First Lady or anyone else.

When she was in Manila, which was fairly frequently,

Cristina sought out General Romulo as a dinner partner, then proceeded to flirt outrageously. Her charm and audacity amused them both. A woman like that needs a partner for whom she can perform publicly and not have to lock her bedroom door later.

Physically, she was a knockout in those days, with her natural tiger look, flowing hair, impeccable body, bronzed, healthy coloring. She always dressed with conscious simplicity, to show off her excellent figure.

The first time I saw Cristina Ford was at a dinner at Malacanang Palace to celebrate Philippine-American Friendship Day. A fleet of Mrs. Marcos's jet-set friends attended: the Duchess of Alba, the Villaverdes (Franco's daughter and her husband), the Countess of France. Cristina wore a dark burnt-orange matte jersey with a tank top and no bra. She wore a small feather boa of the same color slung over a shoulder, but no jewels and announced insolently to General Romulo, "Henry's money could buy out the lot of them!"

She complained about all the jewels the ladies were wearing, including Imelda and her own Italian friends: "They all wear too much jewelry and they spend too much time in the beauty parlor. Why should I endanger my life by covering myself with diamonds someone would kill me for?" She told Romy she had protested to Princess Pignatelli and the other members of her own party that they were wearing too many jewels. And Pignatelli said, "But everyone knows who you are, Cristina. No one knows us!"

She told the General that, to be a social success, a woman has to be something of a witch. He promptly dubbed her "La Bruja Hermosa"—"the beautiful witch."

She held his hand throughout most of the dinner. The Marques de Villaverde, seated on her other side, wanted to get in on some of the fun. But Cristina froze him out. "He thinks he's a great Don Juan," she told Romy. "But he has halitosis."

She asked Romy if he still had his "American girl," and when they left the presidential table he called me over to greet her. We chatted a moment but I didn't feel she was all that interested in talking to another woman.

Romy told me later that at one point during dinner she was holding forth about "natural" hair versus the stiffly formal styles of most of the ladies. "Mine is loose, natural, soft," she said. "Here, feel it," and she offered a strand of her long swaying golden hair. Romy dutifully felt it.

The Countess of France, observing the little tableau, asked Romy, "How was it?"

"A bit coarse!" he announced with a mischievous twinkle.

"Oh you!" Cristina huffed, pretending to box him.

At another point, he told me, he commented on her skintight dress and she told him, "I have nothing underneath."

"Not even a panty?" he asked with interest.

"You ask too much," she sniffed. She had meant no bra.

When the distinguished-looking American ambassador, William Sullivan, rose to offer a toast to the Philippines, Romy said, "Isn't he handsome?"

Cristina took a sharp look and answered, "It's only that white hair that makes him look handsome."

When the President offered his toast, she whispered to Romy, "Can you understand what he is saying?"

"Yes," the General told her.

Cristina shrugged her pretty bare shoulder. "Well, I can't."

On the way home that night, I was teasing the General about his evening with La Bruja Hermosa.

"A bitch. But sweet, eh?" he said.

The one sign of age the General betrayed was that he folded early and didn't like to stay out too late. He had special permission from the President and First Lady to slip away from state dinners as soon as the toasts were made and not stay for all the entertainment. I had to keep an eye on him from the entree on because he often signaled me before coffee was served, and I would leave my table and meet him in the corridor. The later he stayed the more tired and crochety he got. Once we were trapped in a small private party at which we were seated at the round presidential table and couldn't escape. Midnight arrived and there were song requests:

"What would you like to hear, General?" the First Lady asked him.

"Either 'Home Sweet Home' or 'Good Night, Ladies,'" he replied grumpily.

On evenings when we weren't at the palace, we dined at my hotel or one of the nearby restaurants. One warm evening in August of 1973, we had an early dinner at a small French restaurant near the hotel, then decided to walk in the Luneta Park, near Manila Bay. The next morning the General called me from his office, laughing: "The police chief just called me and read an item from last night's police blotter. Quote: 'Our Foreign Secretary was seen strolling in the Luneta with a white woman!'"

I attended my first Philippine wedding in July of that year. It was the wedding of a son of the Chief of Staff, General Espino, and it was held in the garden of his official residence at Camp Aguinaldo. An altar was set up with a red carpet leading to it and chairs for the guests on both sides. There was also a magnificent buffet set for at least five hundred people who attended the reception afterward.

It was, to my thinking, an exceedingly long Mass and ceremony, with candle sponsors and veil sponsors performing their parts of the ritual (at one point a veil is placed around the bridal couple and pinned with a satin cord, which later must be removed). There were ring bearers and coin bearers as well as flower girls, ushers, and bridesmaids. And, at the end, two white doves were released from a wedding bell. I held my breath praying they would still be alive after being stuffed in that closed area so long in the heat. Fortunately they were, although the General told me that at one wedding he attended, a luckless dove fell out dead at the bride's feet. I was to learn that a long, elaborate ceremony was standard for weddings in Manila. And if it involved one of the leading families, who considered it a social coup to have Imelda Marcos present, she often served as a sponsor.

At the wedding I attended the President and Mrs. Marcos were principal sponsors, and Mrs. Marcos was resplendent in an elaborately embroidered *terno* of red silk, with rubies at her throat, ears, and hands. The General and I were seated near the front, and we noted that the entire General Staff was also present. "What a moment for a coup d'état!" Romy said, mischievously.

Imelda Marcos's ideas of how she liked to appear did not always jibe with the wishes of her hosts. In Rome once to visit the Pope, she wanted to wear a white *terno*. Vatican protocol informed her that she must wear black, with long sleeves. Only the Catholic Queens—the Queen of Spain and the Queen of Belgium—were allowed to wear white when they are received by the Pope. Even Princess Grace of Monaco had to wear black with long sleeves, since she was a princess and not a queen.

Miffed, Imelda put aside her white *terno* and donned a demure long-sleeved black gown as protocol decreed. However, she did not forget the ruling. When the Pope visited Manila in 1981, every woman waiting at the airport to greet him was bare-armed and wearing a bare-throated white *terno* with butterfly sleeves. I and the others had gotten orders from the First Lady that we must have white *ternos* made for the Pope's arrival, with matching white parasols. We wore them in all innocence, not realizing it was a tasteless joke being played on the Pope and flaunting his protocol. One Cabinet wife who arrived in a pastel dress was hastily covered over with an extra-large white *barong*, a native men's shirt, so that she too became one of the white "butterflies," ready to greet the Pope when he stepped off the plane.

Since the President hardly left the palace, he increasingly sent his wife on official visits to other countries as a de facto vice president. In April of 1974, Imelda flew to Indonesia to set up a summit conference between President Suharto and her husband. That same year she visited Communist China, inaugurating trade relations between the two countries, and arranged for a shipment of Chinese crude oil to the oil-starved Philippines. A trip to Mexico that same fall also involved oil for the Philippines. In 1972, she initiated the first of many trips to Russia, which were on the face of it "cultural missions" but also had to do with the eventual establishment of diplomatic relations between the two countries.

The General used to tease President Marcos: "Where are you going to send the First Lady this time?" He claimed the President had a map and stuck a pin in the spot farthest from Manila, and then sent Mrs. Marcos there on an official mission.

Imelda never went anywhere without a flock of security. The President, on the contrary, when she was abroad, was often seen slipping away from the palace with only the ever faithful General Ver in attendance. Once, when Romy and I were leaving a palace dinner, the President nearly knocked me over in his race down the steps and into a car he drove himself. I decided the girl must be very pretty indeed.

Security was a headache for whoever entertained any of the Marcos family. Six, eight, ten, twelve—one was obliged to feed them all. And they could be pretty arrogant. The former owner of Philippine Airlines, Benny Toda, told of the time Imelda's security people demanded six bottles of Dom Pérignon from his house when Imelda attended a party.

In New York a friend of Romy's, Mrs. Richard Berlin,

whose husband was then Hearst chairman, complained that when she gave a small sit-down dinner for Imelda in her Park Avenue apartment the serving quarters were cluttered with hungry security men. "Never again!" she vowed.

Marcos's yacht, *Ang Pangulo* (The President), was used to entertain visiting dignitaries. We would board in the morning, then float around Manila Bay, perhaps stopping at the Marcos beach house in Bataan for swimming or we would put in at Corregidor, then take army helicopters to the historic monument and tour the tunnel where Romy, General MacArthur, and President Quezon among others withstood Japanese bombardment in the early days of World War II.

But for all the money they spent on its maintenance, the yacht was in questionable condition. Some of the bulkheads, for instance, were painted shut to look pretty. I always wondered what would happen if the old tub caught fire at sea.

On board the yacht there was a full-scale buffet and bar going at all times, and always a group of professional musicians and singers, often joined by talented members of the Cabinet. Since neither Romy nor I could sing (he was one of the few Filipinos I ever met who couldn't), he was called on to emcee the entertainment. Serious talks were held behind the closed doors of the main cabin, with only the President, a few hand-picked members of the cabinet, and the visiting guest present. The rest of us lolled on deck or went down below to the cabins assigned us to freshen up.

During the music hour, no matter how many professionals or eager amateurs were aboard, Imelda eventually would sing. She has a sweet soprano voice and she had had training in the traditional Filipino love songs, which she sings in a charming way. It is when she strays from what she knows how to do and attempts pop songs that she sometimes runs into trouble. It requires a different technique, one she really has not mastered.

If the President was in a good mood, he sometimes

joined her, singing romantic duets and Ilocano songs—the sort of performance that worked well for them in the provinces when they were campaigning.

The presidential plane was an old sixteen-passenger Fokker–28, which for some reason Marcos preferred despite occasional mechanical problems. True to his frugal personal style, the interior was spartan and guests were not offered so much as a glass of water. In the First Lady's plane, by contrast, the accoutrements were plush. There were always small baskets of fresh orchids and candies on the little tray tables and food, drink, champagne were offered. These were the private planes they used for short-range domestic flights. When she went abroad, Mrs. Marcos customarily appropriated two of the national airline's carriers, one to fly on and one for back-up; invariably PAL ran short of planes for the line's regular customers when she did so. Whenever her plane was coming in or leaving, the entire airport operation was frozen. Sometimes there were delays of two or three hours when "Ma'am" decided to dawdle over lunch. The story went that when Benny Toda once sent the palace a bill for Mrs. Marcos's use of its planes the airline was promptly nationalized. The Marcoses insisted they paid Benny but he insisted he never got the money; today he is trying to get it back from the new government.

On the President's birthday each September we either flew to Sarrat for an all-day fiesta or attended a luncheon at Malacanang Palace that lasted at least four hours. All of his Cabinet and all of the generals and their wives were required to perform in his honor. Even I, despite my legitimate claim to having a complete monotone, was pushed into the line of Cabinet wives, to serenade him.

On Imelda's birthday, in July, we flew down to her beachside palace at Olot (in Leyte province, near where she was born) for a long, lavish weekend of beautiful girls, models, dancers, musicians, flowers, and fashion shows. Of the several sitting rooms, there was one—off limits to most of the guests except Imelda's Blue Ladies—where caviar and champagne were served round the clock. Those were Imelda's playthings, not her husband's. Simple, austere in his taste, the President dined sparingly, usually on broiled fish and boiled vegetables.

Whenever she had VIP guests to entertain, Imelda liked to scoop up a party of people—a whole flock of "broken-down aristocrats," as Cristina Ford called them—and head down to Tacloban, an hour's flight from Manila. There we were loaded onto air-conditioned buses, helicopters, or private limousines, depending on the size of the party, and taken to Olot, a few miles from Tacloban.

I don't know when she started building up Olot, or what was there when she started, but by the time I became a member of her official family she had turned it into the equivalent of a luxurious beach resort. There were three heliports, two Olympic-size swimming pools, an auditorium, a chapel, and an 18-hole golf course. Besides the big main house, with its dining room overlooking the sea, there was a string of connected guest suites, individual beach houses, and guest cabanas. There was also a huge flood-lit outdoor *pelota* court with bleachers for the onlookers. While Imelda sipped champagne and danced with her guests, her husband smiled indulgently from the sidelines, or rounded up some of his aides for a game of *pelota*, the Spanish version of racquetball.

Imelda liked to load her guests into the open electric cars for a tour of her beach. One point she always stopped at was the elaborate marble monument she had had erected to her father. Apparently dissatisfied with the way he had been buried in Manila, she had had his body exhumed and brought home for the recognition she felt he deserved.

Joining us at Olot in 1973 was the Russian poet Yevgeny Yevtushenko. A big, strong-looking, blond-haired man, he was constantly prowling about shooting pictures and taking notes. I wondered if he were doing a book on the Philippines, but when I asked him about it, he claimed, "Only Graham Greene could do justice to this place."

The General and I swam with him one afternoon. Most of the aristocrats wouldn't go into the sea, which is warm but a little rough. It is the same beach, only a few miles farther up the road, where MacArthur made his first landing when he came to liberate the Philippines. Today lifesize bronze figures in the water commemorate the historic spot where MacArthur (and General Romulo) landed.

Yevtushenko was a fine, powerful swimmer. He swam far out into the sea, alone, while we stayed nearer the safety of the shoreline.

That evening, when we were milling about in the open patio, having cocktails, he asked me if I had any children. When I said "No," he told me that I should adopt one, because "you have mother's eyes." He showed me the photo of a blonde boy of about six or seven, whom he said he had adopted and who gave great joy to his life.

He was clearly appalled at all the affluence and ostentation he saw at the palace, and here at Olot, which was in such startling contrast to the poverty of much of the country. Perhaps he likened it to the days of the Czars.

That night I told Romy about my talk with the Russian poet. He nodded in agreement. "There is too much ostentation here. If I were President I would continue to live in my own house and only use Malacanang Palace for official functions. I would sell off the yacht and the private planes and travel on commercial airlines. It would be much more appropriate for the president of a small, poor country."

But Imelda never saw it that way.

Mrs. Marcos loved theatrical effects and was actually quite good at creating them. Arrivals at Manila International Airport were staged as spectacles, with hundreds of costumed schoolchildren bussed in to line the tarmac, playing native bamboo instruments and swaying to the music as VIP visitors stepped off their plane.

I was told by some of palace insiders that it was after her visit to the Shah of Iran's extravagant celebration* at Persepolis, in 1972, that Imelda took a cue from the Shah and began introducing "spectacles" to the Philippines.

Before arriving in Persepolis the First Lady passed through Paris and bought daytime dresses at Dior, Balenciaga, Schiaparelli, and Jacques Fath to add to the evening wear she had brought from the Philippines: six *ternos*, made by the three leading Philippine designers: Pitoy Moreno, Ramon Valera, and Christian Espiritu. Her personal party for that trip included her doctor and her hairdresser, Cristina Ford, and two of her Blue Ladies. The trip seems to have whetted her appetite for grandeur as well as provided her with a social introduction to some of the world's wealthiest people, contacts she strove to maintain.

At Persepolis each guest was assigned a protocol officer. For the Shah's first reception, Imelda put on a diamond tiara, but was told discreetly by her protocol officer that only members of royalty wear crowns.

She promptly yanked it off, then reversed it around and pushed it into the back of her heavy black hair.

She held her head high in the wind, as if to show the world that the Philippines could be as grand, as lavish, as decadent as any society on earth.

---

*The festivities commemorated the 2,500th year of the founding of the Persian Empire.

Make Mine Manila

LIFE in Manila, for the favored few, is so pleasant, so seductive, that I still live there, finding myself unable to wrench myself free from a lifestyle to which I have become addicted. My orchids, my garden, my pool, my dogs, my household help, and the warm cocoon of extended family life give me a security I can find nowhere else in the world.

Manila, of course, is really two worlds—the world of wealth and the world of poverty. And wealth is relative: I could never duplicate half of the services I have in Manila if I returned to live in New York.

When I first arrived to take up permanent residence there, in 1973, the lifestyle was even more elegant and old-world than it is today. Ladies "dressed" after six, and long gowns were de rigueur.

It was a whole new world to me, a never-never land for the elite of society. The lifestyle was beyond the imagination of a working New Yorker: chauffeur-driven cars; houses filled with servants; romantic evenings with grand dinners in vast orchid-filled gardens lighted by capiz shell lanterns glowing in the giant, sprawling acacia trees; beautiful women moving languidly in their flowing gowns, their jewels glittering in the moonlight.

When General Romulo held diplomatic dinners in his garden (it could seat 300 at dinner and accommodate 1000 for receptions), there were always strolling musicians. Sitting at the head table, watching the bejeweled women in their trailing gowns, listening to the music, sipping the champagne, I felt I had slipped back into the nineteenth century.

Manila is a tropical city of annual typhoons and monsoon rains and occasional earthquakes, all of which limit social life to some extent. The great dinners on the lawns and in the gardens are usually scheduled for the dry months of the year—December, January, February, March, April. The General used the Intercontinental Hotel to cater his garden dinners, because, in addition to their efficiency, the hotel was only about three blocks away, across the highway, and if we were ever rained out, we could move the party to one of their banquet rooms.

Earthquakes, of course, were unpredictable. The natives were used to them; I found them pretty scary, especially when I was living in my hotel, a tall building constructed to sway—which it did most mightily. The roomboys would tell me to stand in the doorsill, the strongest area, until a quake was over. One night when the General had asked me to stay at his house since he wasn't feeling well and didn't want to be alone, I awoke at 5:30 in the morning to a grinding sound of moving walls and the tinkle of swaying chandeliers. I jumped out of my bed—mainly because it was under an altar with heavy religious statues that I did not want falling on me—and decided to go outside. High waves were slapping against the concrete walls of the swimming pool then spilled out onto the grass.

On another night I was in Malacanang Palace. It was past nine in the evening. The dinner was late because we had all—including President and Mrs. Marcos—just come from a wedding in the Manila Cathedral. Again I heard that funny grinding sort of sound and looked up to see the chandeliers swaying. The Chief Justice, seated to my right, said, quietly, "Earthquake." We simply sat there, clutching the edge of the table and waited for it to pass. The dancers kept on dancing. The waiters kept on serving the food. Next morning when I looked in the paper it was reported to have registered five on the Richter scale.

The worst thing about the typhoons was the unearthly mad howl of the wind, like all the hounds of hell unleashed at once. There is nothing anyone can do, no way to sleep, read, or concentrate until the furor dies down. Then there's flooding in the garden, and sometimes the house, and the inevitable mopping. The trees that have toppled over have to be pulled up and roped until they root again. It never ceased to amaze me how the fragile orchids weathered the worst winds and storm. They looked as though they had gone through nothing more serious than a face-washing.

"Orchids are our strongest flower," Imelda Marcos once told me. "They live on air."

Life is very pleasant for the monied of Manila because of cheap labor. I pay my driver fifty dollars a month. His kid brother, who tends the yard, gets half that. If they left me there would be lines of applicants waiting for their jobs. They come from the provinces, where there is no employment. If they live in, as my help do, they have the added advantage of not being squatters, hiding in illegal shanty housing where most of the provincials live while looking for work.

The favored few live in well-guarded villages: Forbes Park, Dasmarinas, Magallanes, across the highway from the high-rise postwar financial district, Makati. Professional security guards are on duty around the clock as well as roving village guards. At Defense Minister Enrile's house, across a vacant lot from us, several security vans were always parked in front. The Romulo compound consisted of a main house with several adjoining apartments and a garden that extended through to the next block. The main house was a two-story Spanish-style structure with wrought-iron grillwork and open terraces. More modern houses are for the most part sprawling, one-story houses of native stone, low, cool, and surrounded by perfectly kept lawns. Some have grillwork fences, others are open to the street.

Full-scale help is abundant in the wealthy villages—maids, cooks, gardeners, drivers, laundrywomen. In the Romulo compound there was a staff of twenty-one to serve the nine members of the family in residence. (It is customary in the Philippines for various generations to live together, and married children often continue living with their parents.) All have ID cards so they can pass in and out of the gates freely in order to meet their friends and family outside. Household help has a hierarchy of its own. At the General's house, the caretaker had been there longer than anyone else and his word seemed to be law with the younger maids, yard boys, cooks, etc. Calixto Pascua, the General's driver, who was actually an employee of the Foreign Ministry, had one of the most responsible jobs, as personal driver and, in effect, security guard (the General did not have an official security officer). The maids always bowed deferentially to Pascua, calling him *Manong*—Big Brother.

For every privileged child there is a *yaya*—the equivalent of a Chinese amah—usually a young provincial girl who takes care of the baby from birth and often becomes emotionally deeply attached to the child. Philippine children of well-to-do families can be seen going to their classes, even at the age of ten and twelve, with their *yayas* carrying their books.

Servants consider their employers "masters," and the relationship is far more personal than that of American or European help and their employers. Once the "master" has taken a maid or houseboy into his family, he is in effect responsible for that person's health and happiness. The master is supposed to understand that if a relative of the servant dies or is ill the servant in all impunity will disappear back to the provinces for weeks or even months. If funeral expenses can't be met, a loan is provided.

After I moved in to the General's house, and the servants saw that I could take care of some of my husband's minor ailments, they brought me their burns, cuts, headaches, and other small complaints, with a mystic faith that I could doctor them all. During my tenure as householder I coped with crises that ranged from gunshot wounds to heart attacks and broken hearts—problems no Western employer would be expected to deal with.

The relationship between servant and master or mistress is not all roses, however. When I was a new arrival in Manila, I recall being shocked when a soprano, who was to sing at a breakfast meeting, confided she was not in voice so early because "I haven't even shouted at my maids today." In due time, I understood what she meant. The little maids who flood into Manila from their parents' farms in the provinces are apt to be pleasant and honest, but also untrained, inefficient, unmotivated—and clumsy. All pans get bent. All sharp knives get blunted. Television sets, mixers, and electric coffee pots get plugged into the wrong outlet and burn out. Crystal is smashed. Food that should never have been frozen finds its way into the freezer (cheese, caviar, pâté). Food that should be frozen is left out to rot.

A friend told me she had one maid that she automatically greeted each morning with "What have you broken today?" I asked what happened to the trained help. "They have all emigrated," she replied ruefully. As soon as a maid or cook becomes really good, a visiting foreigner will arrange for them to go abroad. The trick of maintaining a smoothly running household in Manila is to train your help yourself and then pray they won't leave you.

One of the perks of Cabinet life was having a car with a siren, a flashing red light when you wanted to use it, and a car phone. The first car phone that the General had when I came to Manila was something of a frustration since one had to go through the telephone company's "mobile operator." She seemed to be either asleep or out for a beer most of the time—I guess she didn't get enough business to stay at her post. Later he got a new improved model that was tied in directly to an operator at his ministry. The code name for the car-phone operator was "Ringo." ("Ringo, come in.") I was "Sunshine." ("We have Sunshine on the line, sir.")

The General was delighted with this new toy. It made him better-humored, also. Whenever we got stuck in one of the interminable traffic jams that are a given of Manila life, I usually had a magazine to read or a crossword puzzle to work. But he fumed. Now, with an efficient car phone, he could call up his secretary and dictate letters. He could make calls to ambassadors. Arrange appointments.

Since my own Toyota served as backup when his official Mercedes was in the shop, he had a second car phone installed in my car. One afternoon I was caught in the midst of a horrendous traffic jam on Taft Avenue, a main artery of downtown Manila, when I happened to glance out of my window and saw Romy's sleek black Mercedes two lanes away, also stalled. I promptly called his car, and we weathered the rest of the snarl happily by flirting and chatting over our car phones.

Each fall, when we went to New York for the opening of the United Nations General Assembly, there was a car and driver provided the General by the Philippine consulate. When he was in session or had meetings at the hotel, the car was at my disposal. I usually used it only for such mundane things as going to my old apartment to pick up my mail, or to pick up some food for our breakfast and occasionally lunch if we were not going out. I sometimes saw

Filipinos I knew from Manila using hired limos to go to the five-and-dime in New York. On the face of it, it seems ridiculous. But after a year of living in the Philippines, I knew what they were there for: all those marvelous gadgets for kitchens and bathrooms and closets that simply don't exist in Manila. There is nothing equivalent to the American dime store in the Philippines.

An adjustment that was difficult for me to make was that I was no longer anonymous in Manila. I didn't really mind making the effort to look as elegant as I could at night, for the formal dinners. But during the daytime, in my previous life in the States, I was accustomed to being a barefoot worker, who maybe got into a pair of slacks to run out and do errands. One morning at the Hilton I slipped down to the lobby to get stamps for my mail, without makeup or much of a hairdo. I was recognized and greeted by one businessman, one ambassador, and the hotel manager on the way. After that I stayed hidden unless properly attired.

The General showed me a report by a protocol officer assigned to escort me during a quick tour I had made of the provinces. "Miss Day," she noted, is "too friendly." "A beautiful woman," the General chided me, "should always be aloof."

I blew up. "Listen," I snapped, "I am middle-class, middle-aged, and midwestern. I'm friendly by nature and I don't intend to change. That's the person I am and if you don't like it, find someone else!"

He got used to it. Actually, General Romulo was himself, by nature, a friendly man. He could pull rank when protocol required, but he genuinely cared about people and treated those around him with kindly consideration. One of the reasons he got such a great press (which made him the envy of the rest of the Cabinet, and even the Marcoses) was that, as an ex-newspaperman he always had a friendly, personal relationship with the press, both at home and abroad. He was what we reporters would call "good copy," always willing to take the time to chat, and usually coming up with a quotable quote.

For the Westerner, one of the delights of Manila life (which would probably prove true in other major cities of the Orient as well) is what is known as "the colonel's lady" syndrome—the cheap cost and easy availability of personal services.

Whenever I found I had an unexpected free afternoon, I would wander down to the beauty salon in my hotel. I would get a sauna, a one-hour body massage, a color-rinse for my hair, a shampoo and set, a manicure, and a pedicure. It took up four full hours and involved the services of five different girls—yet the total bill came to P68, which at that time was a little over 10 US dollars, with another dollar for tips. When I was in New York I had to spend $26 just for a shampoo and set!

Traditionally, Philippine society is a matriarchy. Men may hold top political office, or serve as Chairman of the Board of major companies—but it is the women who handle the money. Romy told me that in the weddings of his youth, the groom handed over what money he had to his bride on his wedding day. After that, it was the wife who ran the show, at least momentarily. She did the household buying, paid the help, and doled out to her husband what she considered was an appropriate allowance for his cigarettes, booze, girls, or whatever else befitted his lifestyle. In hacienda country, where major crops such as sugar or rice are grown, it is often the woman who runs the operation. In the cities, housewives of professional men are apt to be engaged in a little business on the side—for export generally.

When I eventually took over the General's household, I was dismayed to find that I was responsible for the accounts, payroll, investments, etc. I have always been fairly frugal, and managed not to be in debt, but I've also always found it difficult to balance a checkbook. I suggested to my husband that rather than a personal maid what I really needed was an accountant: "I can dress myself, and wash my own stockings, but I do have a problem balancing books." It was his son Dick's wife, Tessie, the daughter-in-law who had been running Romy's household, who kindly showed me how to keep the daily records of expenditures and handle the payroll. I found the latter especially intriguing. No one was paid by checks, as I would pay my cleaning lady in New York. Everything was a cash transaction, which meant having cash in hand twice a month. In addition, it was always assumed that the help would need to borrow, so there were columns for "loan" and "salary due" after deducting the loan.

One of the things that disturbed me, as I got to know some of the couples and their marriages better, was how Philippine women tended to indulge—even infantilize—their men. In several marriages that I observed in which the family's money clearly came from the wife, the husband would use her money to play around with other women. I found this odious. And it wasn't a case of some ugly old hag "buying a young husband." These were couples of comparable ages, and the women were as attractive as their husbands. I did not know whether it was because of the national predominance of Catholicism (women put up with one husband for life no matter how he behaved), or whether it was part of their matriarchal society that considered men "boys" to be cosseted and indulged and never expected to be responsible. Perhaps the reason was a little of both.

Like most Asian women, Filipinas have a passion for gemstones and invest in them whenever possible. It is said that the first major investment after a house for one's family is a diamond. This is considered a good business move, a kind of all-purpose insurance. During the Japanese occupation in World War II, many Filipinas obtained rice for their families by trading in, one piece at a time, the stones they wore in belts around their waists and under their dresses.

It is practically a duty to assemble a great collection of jewelry, which is then passed along to one's daughters, or the wives of one's sons. Since most Filipino families, rich or poor, have a minimum of six children, it has to be a pretty big collection to go around. Once I warned a wealthy Philippine assemblywoman not to wear her ruby-and-diamond choker on the streets of New York. Then it occurred to me that she probably wasn't in any real danger, since the stones were so enormous no one would believe they were real!

When the General's first wife died, Romy told me that, although the family was not wealthy, she had managed to collect enough jewels over the years that he was able to call in an appraiser and have the lot divided into four parts and distributed to his daughters-in-law. "And there was plenty for everyone."

In the new circles I began to travel in, jewels, though kept in vaults and safe-deposit boxes, were meant to be worn daily, and taken out in wholesale for display at formal dinners at a the palace. I arrived in Manila with a few bits of gold, my mother's engagement ring, and two necklace, ring, and earring sets—one of jade, the other of coral. Everything else I owned was costume jewelry. As companion to the Foreign Minister, Romy told me, I needed to hold my own with the palace ladies, so he started buying me good stuff, a piece at a time, for my birthday or Christmas or Valentine's Day.

I had never thought much about jewelry, and the idea of wearing anything of considerable value made me uneasy. I decided I must have my ears pierced so I wouldn't risk losing earrings of real stones—I had lost plenty of costume-jewelry earrings over the years. Meanwhile the General had ordered my first "important" jewelry: beautiful long ruby and diamond evening earrings. Before my ears could support them, I had the dangling parts set on a gold chain and wore it as a necklace.

A few years later I was discussing with the General, in all seriousness, what I would do with a bib of silver and turquoise that a departing Indonesian ambassador's wife had given me. I was considering having the breastplate-sized piece dismantled and getting earrings, a ring, and a pin out of it. Romy said, amused, "You never used to think about jewelry—or fashion." It was true.

The Filipinas—shopgirls as well as society matrons—have a different approach to fashion than many Western women. Instead of proudly wearing their finest gowns and jewels over time, they are humiliated to be seen wearing the same thing twice. I recall that Mrs. William (Bootsie) Hearst, who always makes the Best Dressed List and is a stylish beauty, appeared at two consecutive dinners I attended in New York one season wearing the same dress—a beautiful apricot chiffon. She had no doubt paid thousands for it and it was her big dress of the season. In Manila, women pay their dressmakers about $35 for a dress, and order seventeen new little dresses at a time. Really wealthy women get seventeen lavish designer dresses at one fell swoop.

Another Philippine custom I found hard to get used to was the constant giving of gifts. If you have been away on a trip, for instance, you are supposed to bring back a gift for everyone. It's called *pasalubong*, "Welcome gift." Birthdays, anniversaries, going away, coming home—all require gifts, not just for one's immediate family, but for close friends as well. One day I was looking around my hotel room and saw that it was full of gifts—mostly from people who were close to the General or wanted to curry favor with him. There were several bowls of fresh flowers. Brandy, marrons glacés. A length of batik for a dress. An amethyst pin, a bolt of silk from Peking. Sometimes the General teased me, calling me a "walking gift." Luckily, the things most people gave me were wearable (the fabrics all found their way into dresses) or edible or drinkable. I didn't have to face the possibility of having to return them if Romy left office, like poor Pat Nixon and her diamond earrings.

Visitors to Malacanang Palace usually brought expensive gifts to Imelda. And the Marcoses always had elaborate gifts waiting for all their guests. Storerooms in the palace basement were full of gift items to be given away. Part of the ritual of a state dinner was the exchange of gifts. After the Saudi minister for foreign affairs came to Manila, I watched Imelda looking quite gorgeous in her gift from the Arabs: a red gown, trimmed with gold thread, with a train of the same material and gold ornaments in her hair.

Early poverty (always denied) had left its mark on Imelda Marcos. She never had enough of anything. Nor could she make up her mind. The 3,000 pairs of shoes: If she saw a pair she liked, she ordered a dozen at a time. That depressing "department store" in the basement of Malacanang Palace today is a bewildering mix of good and bad, worn and unused. Twenty years of impulse buying—and of the need not to be seen wearing the same dress twice.

There is one Filipino custom I found gratifying after living in America: Filipinos touch one another easily, without self-consciousness. In the Philippines, relatives and friends all kiss on greeting—usually both cheeks, although the grandest ladies touch very lightly to avoid smearing their makeup. No one in Manila seeing women kiss would conclude they are lesbians, or that men are unmanly when they embrace. Several times when I was standing near Imelda, sharing some scene or music, she would put a light hand on my arm or shoulder or waist. I found it charming and warm, although I would probably be too shy to do it myself.

Children are taught to kiss all "friendly" adults, that is, anyone their parents socialize with. During one of the first

parties in a private home I attended in Manila, I was left
alone briefly in the sala while my hosts greeted the next
arrivals, and five strange children suddenly appeared, lined
up, and began solemnly kissing me. Coming out of Mass
with the General one Sunday, I was introduced to a young-
ish couple, and their children promptly put their faces up to
be kissed. Not a word was spoken but the intention of the
gesture was very clear. The General teased me, "You've
probably never been kissed so much in your life!" and it
was true.

Nose-kissing, which was once traditional among the Ma-
lays, is still practiced by the old people, and by some of the
middle-aged who come from the provinces. This consists of
touching the side of the face with a quick, sharp sniff. The
first few times I experienced this, I thought the poor souls
were suffering from sinus trouble!

Margaret Mead once observed that Filipinos know how
to handle death: It is a communal affair. As is birth, illness,
hospitalization. Members of families are expected by the
hospital staff to stay with the patient. During the General's
various illnesses and surgeries, I slept at the hospital, going
home only to get fresh clothes. It may not be the most
antiseptic way to run a hospital, but Filipino doctors believe their patients are happier—and recover faster—if
family members are allowed to stay with them.

To survive in Philippine society it is necessary for the
newcomer, especially a Westerner, to learn "utang na
loob"—the principle of reciprocity of favors. It is a sort of
I-scratch-your-back-you-scratch-mine system using a cur-
rency other than money. At first I was shocked at how many
services were "given" if you were considered a relative, a
friend, or the relative of a friend. A doctor or a dentist
would treat you and refuse payment. In return, he would
feel no compunction about asking for help to get a visa or a
passport, or a letter of recommendation for a relative. I

have always found it much neater to pay for services and be done with it. But this is definitely not the Philippine way.

The custom affected my relationship with Imelda Marcos. She *expected* me to ask her for favors. And I did not. She would have been far more comfortable with me if I had—because then I would have been indebted to her. One of her Blue Ladies once said to me, "You're a fool. Look at Chesnoff [a *Newsweek* writer who quit the magazine to do a picture book on the Philippines for the Marcos government and then a biography of Imelda, which never appeared]. Look at Lollobrigida [the Italian actress had contracted to do a picture essay on the Philippines; Imelda later turned it down and refused to pay for it]. They get millions. You haven't got anything!"

I did write a book on the Philippines. My publisher did pay me—although the advance was modest. And the manuscript did actually see the light of day.

I was putting the finishing touches on the manuscript one fall day in 1973 in our suite at the Waldorf Towers when President Marcos called the General. After he had finished the business part of his message, he asked Romy, "And how is Miss Day?"

"Fine, Mr. President," the General answered. "She is finishing her book."

Wicked fellow that he is, Ferdinand Marcos quipped so loudly I could overhear him:

"I hope she is not finishing *you!*"

VIP Guests and Official Visits

By early 1974, the Philippines was apparently enjoying good relationships with other countries throughout the world and we had a rash of VIP guests in Manila, including Prime Minister Tanaka of Japan, Prime Minister Lee Kuan Yew of Singapore, Under Secretary Rush from the United States, and Prime Minister Gough Whitlam of Australia.

The one on whom Imelda Marcos lavished the most attention was Prince Juan Carlos of Spain and his delicately pretty wife, Princess Sofia. Their official visit to the Philippines in February of that year included a decoration for the Prince at the palace, a barrio fiesta held in the couple's honor on the palace grounds, a yacht trip to Corregidor, a concert at the Cultural Center (Imelda ordered all the boxes draped in mantillas), and a state dinner. And then, of course, there was a return dinner, given by the Prince in honor of President and Mrs. Marcos.

The General and I first saw Their Royal Highnesses at the fiesta. The guests were assigned seats to watch the entertainers. In the presidential row were President and Mrs. Marcos, Juan Carlos and Sofia, General Romulo and his opposite number, the Spanish Foreign Minister, and the Chief Justice. I was assigned a seat in the second row, among a bevy of former president's wives.

Everyone was dressed to the hilt. The men wore their medals and sashes and the women their best formal clothes and grand hairstyles. The Prince was very tall and distinguished looking and his Princess slender, with soft blonde hair. I wondered if he would ever be King?

The return dinner for the Marcoses was limited to forty guests. The Spanish Ambassador called Romy: "Do you object, sir, if I invite Miss Day?" Romy assured him he would object if he didn't.

It was the first time I ever sat in the small private dining room of Malacanang Palace (the previous dinners I had attended had all been in Maharlika Hall). It is a long room, off the main reception room, and only large enough for twenty to forty guests. It looked very elegant—the Spaniards had brought china and stemware from their own embassy and they served good Spanish wines, then French champagne for the toasts.

The guest list had been carefully chosen: a few members of the Cabinet—Secretary Enrile, Virata, and Executive Secretary Melchor with their wives; a few of the leading Spanish families of Manila, among them the Sorianos and the Santamarias. I was seated beside Chief of Staff Espino, which was just as well, as we were probably the only people at the table speaking English.

Juan Carlos did indeed become King of Spain. But later Imelda's relationship with the Spanish Crown deteriorated. When she went to Madrid and wanted to be received at the palace, she was snubbed. Enraged, she blocked the appointment of every Philippine ambassador suggested for assignment to Madrid, leaving the post vacant for several years to show her pique. General Romulo was able to fill that post only after Imelda's temper had cooled; he selected a Spanish-speaking golfing partner of her husband.

Since Ambassador Nieto liked the golf courses in Manila better than those in Madrid, he became known as the absentee ambassador. It often seemed to me that Mrs. Marcos's childish fits of anger did as much as anything to damage the Philippine image abroad.

In May of 1974, Dame Margot Fonteyn and her husband, the Panamanian diplomat Roberto Arias, arrived in Manila. At the Cultural Center, Dame Margot performed one traditional ballet and a Filipino one that had been created especially for her. As she took her curtain calls, there was a snowstorm of rose petals that covered her and the stage. Another Imelda special. Dame Margot and Van Cliburn were both later proclaimed National Artists of the Philippines for their work in helping to promote Philippine music and dance.

This was one area of Mrs. Marcos's prodigious activities that I applauded. There was so much young talent in the Philippines, it was appropriate to promote it and see that the most promising performers were able to study abroad. Today there are still a large number of Philippine dancers and musicians in the major ballet companies and orchestras of the world.

General Romulo had known Dame Margot's husband at the United Nations long before an assassination attempt, in his native Panama, had left him paralyzed and wheelchairbound. He had been shot by his own bodyguard, who had been paid to do it by a political opponent.

I asked the General if that could ever happen to Marcos. "No," he insisted. "The men close to the President are either his relatives or Ilocanos. They are totally loyal to him."

When Dame Margot and her husband visited Manila, they were always provided with a private residence, medical care, and physical therapists if she wished it. She actually performed much of her husband's care herself, with the help of a male attendant who traveled with them.

Dame Margot and her husband were frequent guests at Malacanang Palace, and whenever we saw them in the reception hall there the General and I would go over for a chat. Arias is a strikingly handsome man, with a beautiful head, steel-gray hair, and lively dark eyes. But he is totally paralyzed, even to his hands and larynx. He understands everything that it said to him however, and mouths his responses, which his wife then speaks. After sitting with them for awhile one evening, I realized I too could follow what he was saying if I sat close to him and watched his lips carefully.

Later Romy asked me, if he were in the same condition, would I be so devoted? And I answered in all honesty that I didn't know. In time I learned that one does whatever one must do. Dame Margot carried on with enormous grace and love.

The General was always disturbed by the fact that the Marcoses honored all manner of visiting dignitaries but ignored Filipinos who performed extraordinary service. After a United Nations Development Program conference in Manila when all the foreigners had been lavishly entertained at Malacanang, the General gave his own private party to honor Narciso Reyes, who was President of the UNDP Governing Council and the Philippines' permanent representative to the United Nations in New York.

Since the General was coming down with laryngitis, I went to his house to nurse him that day. I was fascinated as I watched the house and garden being transformed for a party. The staff of the Intercontinental Hotel, which was catering the affair, began arriving shortly after lunch. Tables were set up and laid. Spotlights were strung up in the tall palm trees. Excess furniture was banished upstairs. The piano was moved into the garden. The living room was cleared to accommodate the guests for cocktails in case it rained. In the patio a champagne fountain was set up, and the UN insignia was carved out in an ice sculpture that was lit from behind and backed the iced caviar.

By the time the first guests arrived—the African, European, and American delegates of the UNDP conference—everything was in order. The champagne flowed, the white-coated waiters stood at the ready with their silver trays. After cocktails in the garden, a sit-down dinner for 150 was held under the covered terrace.

Romy welcomed his visitors to his "humble home." Later, when we were alone, I told him the phrase might sound graceful in Spanish, but in English, he was lucky no one laughed.

He was so tired, and half-sick, that he was ready to drop from fatigue but, punctilious host that he was, he refused to take to his bed until he had bade farewell to his last guest.

The widowed General Romulo had been sitting home alone for six years when I entered his life. After I became his companion, he liked to go out nearly every night—to entertain me, show me Manila, and not incidentally to enjoy himself. One evening President Marcos called his house and was told by the maid that she didn't know where he was. The President dispatched his security chief, General Ver, to search out the General.

Ver went around the hotels asking if anyone had seen him, and at the Intercontinental he was told yes, indeed, General Romulo had come in and gone up to the supper club, El Castilliano, on the top floor. General Ver took the elevator, walked in, spotted us dancing, went to the phone, and called the President. "I've found him, sir."

"Where is he?"

"In El Castilliano, dancing."

There was a moment's pause. Then, "Does he dance well, General?" asked the President.

"Yes, sir, very well," reported Ver. "Do you wish to speak to him?"

"No, never mind," said the President. "Don't bother him."

The General dropped by my suite at the Hilton one December morning before joining the President for the annual Loyalty Day Parade. He read the news while I anchored a loose button on his shirt sleeve. Then, at the door, he kissed me good-bye, saying lightly, "I hope they don't shoot him. I stand next to him, you know!"

By the time Imelda's birthday arrived in July of 1974, she had gathered a collection of guests: Van Cliburn and his mother, Cristina Ford, the Italian actress Virna Lisi, and thirty other Italians whom Cristina had brought along for the partying. The entire diplomatic corps had also been invited, plus the Cabinet members and their wives and a goodly splash of generals. (Imelda, like her husband, believed in keeping in close touch with the military—they could make the difference as to whether you kept your throne or not.)

There must have been a thousand people at Imelda's little resort that year. One of the Italians—I think it was Princess Pignatelli (Luciana Avedon)—arrived at the solemn birthday Mass with her wet head impudently wrapped in a bathtowel.

During the festivities, Ambassador Sullivan and his wife, Marie, and the General and I went out for a swim in the sea. We were splashing around, amusing ourselves, when the Argentinian Ambassador came running down to the beach and called to the General.

"What is it?" Romy asked, wading in to shore.

"Perón is dead, General."

Later, when we were talking about it at the cabana, Ambassador Sullivan said he'd give Isabel Perón "three months" to survive her husband in power. Marie wondered about an attempted assassination. "No," Bill guessed.

"They'll think of a more gentlemanly way to get rid of her." And he was right.

I was fond of the Sullivans and I once commented to Romy how charming they were. But he gave me a quick lesson in diplomacy: "This is a man for whom personal feelings or relationships will mean nothing across a conference table."

I was brought up short.

"He's the highest caliber American ambassador they have sent us so far. Which is great for the US but dangerous for us. He understands the working of the Asian mind, so we can't put anything over on him."

In Manila he had managed to get in dutch with Imelda after he likened her, by inference, to Marie Antoinette. She never forgave him.

After his tour of duty in the Philippines, Bill Sullivan was sent to Iran—and diplomatic disaster. When the Shah fell, he had little choice but to resign from the foreign service.

I had much to learn about the diplomatic world. I recall once when I was reluctant to turn down an invitation to a reception, Romy, a veteran of fifty years of diplomatic socializing, said, "They don't care if you come or not. They just want to know how many glasses to order!"

A large part of diplomatic life involves travel—making official visits and attending conferences. When General Romulo traveled he took one personal aide (to pack, arrange appointments, make reservations), one political aide (who kept all the official documents and gave him the correct briefing papers before each meeting), and me. One hectic year I estimated we were in our house only nine days.

General Romulo seemed to believe that no Filipino would ever do him harm. Fortunately, his luck held. I think he was the only Cabinet minister without even one bodyguard; some had a whole platoon watching them.

Sometimes, when there had been a threat against the Marcos government, the State Department assigned security people to watch us in New York. In Manila we relied on the Foreign Ministry driver, Calixto Pascua, and, if I was not with the General myself, a protocol officer from the Ministry would go along to hold his arm if he needed support.

When Mrs. Marcos traveled the situation was vastly different: She took along anywhere from twenty to a hundred people depending on her mood and destination— her "Blue Ladies," her security, the media (not just reporters and still photographers, but the entire paraphernalia of a television studio so that her every move was faithfully filmed for the government-controlled TV stations back home).

Recently, when the new Philippine government's Vice President and Foreign Minister, Salvador Laurel, made his first official visit to the People's Republic of China, his small private plane containing the six members of his party was met at the airport in Beijing by no less than twenty cars sent by the Chinese government. They were so accustomed to Imelda's entourage—she had turned up once in Beijing with a retinue of two hundred—they couldn't believe that the Philippine vice president would arrive with such a small party.

No one was ever certain until the last moment whom she would choose among her Blue Ladies or peripheral friends to accompany her. When the word did come—usually with a telephone call from her palace secretary, Fe Jimenez, saying the First Lady was expecting you to leave—sometimes in a matter of hours—there was a grand flurry of checking or updating passports and hasty packing. Trips with her were considered a great honor.

In reality, as one friend told me, who was occasionally among the chosen, traveling with Mrs. Marcos was something of an ordeal. "If you got the call, you were supposed to drop everything and run for the plane. I remember once

Fe called and I said, 'But that's my twenty-fifth wedding anniversary! I want to be home with my husband,' and she said, reprovingly, 'But the First Lady is going to miss *her* birthday!' In short, I had no choice."

She always brought along her own doctor (a cousin) and hairdresser. And one man whose sole duty was to check on her luggage. Everyone else's was up for grabs and bags were often missing or left behind, with the result there was much wasteful replacement buying later in the trip. Also, there were daily arbitrary decrees: "Darling, you can't wear that. She wants us all in silk dresses." "Today it's wool suits. If you haven't got one, buy one." "Tonight we are all to be in long gowns." If her ladies didn't have enough showy jewelry she sometimes doled out some from her own collection. One cabinet minister's wife recalled attending a wedding in Houston, Texas, at which Imelda passed out diamond clip earrings to all her entourage: "I couldn't believe it. Every Filipina has pierced ears from birth, but Imelda had plain clips on her earrings. I was terrified one would drop off. They were worth thousands of dollars." Once, in Rome, she decided her party should all wear a certain sort of dress. When the wife of the resident ambassador, who of course knew how to dress appropriately for the city, showed up in something different, Mrs. Marcos wouldn't let her accompany her party, and sent her back home.

The Blue Ladies were not treated as guests, but more as ladies-in-waiting. One, for instance, always carried Mrs. Marcos's big alligator bag, a cross between a portfolio and a purse that I suppose contained bundles of cash. They ran errands, shopped, and sniped at one another. In New York, Imelda would suddenly decide on a side trip, and arbitrarily name someone to accompany her; the ones left behind would invariably cry or simply fret that they were out of favor.

On one such junket her supermaid, Glecy Tantoco, who

was said to be her silent partner and share large investment and business interests including Rustean's (the profitable department store in Makati), was left off the plane list till the last minute, and was in an absolute tizzy. Finally her name was included and the entourage all hurried for the Washington-bound plane. When Mrs. Marcos opened the door of her suite at the Madison Hotel, she let out a squeal of pleasure. The room was filled with "goodies"—fine jewels, the latest in watches (she had a passion for watches, especially as gifts), and the newest fashions. Apparently Glecy had set it all up so Madame could have a complete shopping spree without leaving her suite "That's Glecy's business," one of the Blue Ladies said acidly. "She gets a commission on everything Imelda buys."

Mrs. Marcos showed little or no interest in the comfort or pleasure of any of her entourage. Most of these women were deeply indebted to her: Through her benevolence they made vast fortunes running housing developments, construction businesses, department stores. She ordered them around and told them what she expected of them. For the privilege of being treated as her servants, they left their families, friends, the comforts of their well-staffed homes in Manila, and often ended up sharing tiny rooms ("When we got the baggage in we couldn't close the door"), carrying their own luggage. "I kept wondering why they put up with all this," said one of my friends, "then I remembered how much money they were making because of her."

One fall Imelda decided, as a treat for their loyalty, she would round up a pack of generals' wives and bring them to the Waldorf in New York for a week. I remember the night she took over Peacock Alley for a private dinner at which the guests included such New York friends as the Russian ballet dancer Natalia Makarova and her husband and Van Cliburn and his mother. I don't know whether most of the generals' wives had ever been out of Manila, but clearly they were not very comfortable with Mrs. Marcos's New York friends, and not adept at making space for themselves at the party. They simply stood in their long dresses in one line on one side of the room, like diamond-studded sparrows on a telephone wire. At one point my husband nudged me and said, "Why don't you go over and talk to them?" "There's no one there I know," I told him and added meanly, "or care to."

"You better be nice," he said with a wicked grin, "there might be a coup!"

In August of 1974, the General and I made a trip to three Eastern European countries—Yugoslavia, Czechoslovakia, and Rumania—to open diplomatic relations with the Philippines. This was the beginning of a foreign policy that would eventually include diplomatic relations with all the Balkan countries, the USSR, and the People's Republic of China. It was a major shift in Philippine foreign policy: to move unilaterally to normalize relations with Communist countries, instead of waiting to follow the American position.

General Romulo's official party, as usual, was small. With him were his political aide, Ambassador Felipe Mabilangan, his personal aide, Consul Julius Maloles, and myself. The list for the delegation of the Republic of the Philippines gave my name simply as Miss Beth Day, and I was assigned to car number four, with consul Maloles.

When we landed at the airport at Belgrade, someone thrust a big bouquet of red roses at me and I quickly learned why Imelda Marcos will not accept roses unless they have been de-thorned. This bunch ripped through my raincoat. A stranger grabbed my hand luggage and I was pretty frantic because it contained my good jewelry, travel documents, and even some of the Generals' secret papers. (At another airport, on that same trip, an overeager lackey lunged gallantly at what was in my hand and I pushed him off. "No, No," I yelled, "this is my *purse!*")

When we reached Budapest, I had as my companion the wife of our ambassador in Paris, Mrs. Moreno-Salcedo, whose husband would be concurrently assigned to Rumania. We were given a wildman for a driver. He insisted on tailgating the car ahead of him at about 65 mph. Mrs. Moreno-Salcedo was getting carsick. I yelled at the driver that we wanted to change cars. My interpreter kept trying to soothe us, but I had had enough and insisted that we change cars. We did.

In Belgrade we were assigned a government villa. A Filipino aide who was sent from the Paris office warned me, "They are so efficient here, you don't dare leave anything loose. They will fold it, pack it, or wash it." Too true! When we reached Prague, one of the General's pajama and robe sets was missing. The maid in Belgrade had taken it away to wash it.

I read in a newspaper one day while on this trip that Nancy Kissinger, on a trip with her Secretary of State husband, came into their room to find a porter grabbing from her bed the dress she intended to wear later that day. She had to chase him down the hall to get it back. He was going to take it to the cleaners.

Communism had not dulled the Yugoslavs' sense of humor. Our protocol officer told us that Marshal Tito was in the habit of asking an aide every few days, "What jokes are they making about me now?" It kept him in tune with the temper of his people.

We found when we reached Belgrade that the General's official appointments had been set up with Mr. Milos Minic, the Vice President of the Federal Executive Council. Tito himself was out on the island of Brioni, in the Adriatic Sea, where he spent much of his time. A site of ancient Roman ruins, and once the favorite resort of Mussolini's son-in-law, Count Ciano, Brioni had been ceded to Yugoslavia by Italy at the end of World War II. Tito made it his summer retreat.

General Romulo requested that we go to Brioni so that he could pay his respects to Tito, and he also asked to visit the beautiful resort of Dubrovnik, so that I could see it. At Dubrovnik, we were sitting at table one evening, looking out over the marvelous craggy shoreline, when I noticed an unfamiliar face at our table. I asked the protocol officer who he was. "The doctor," he told me. "Marshal Tito wanted General Romulo to have a doctor in his entourage."

At Brioni we were billeted in a government hotel. I waited there while the General was received by Tito. It was very private: only Romy and his ambassador and political aide; Tito had his aide and translator with him.

The General came back to the hotel, bubbling and elated over his meeting. He told me that despite his advanced age Marshal Tito appeared robust. (Tito himself was already eighty-years-old—seven years Romy's senior.) He was dressed in an impeccable all-white suit. As soon as they were seated, he offered his guest a cigar.

"I don't smoke, Your Excellency," Romy told him.

Then Tito offered him brandy from a decanter on his table.

"I don't drink, Your Excellency."

Tito stared at him a long moment. "What do you do, then?"

"I etcetera," Romy said with a sly smile.

"I drink, I smoke, and I etcetera, etcetera, etcetera!" roared Marshal Tito.

The fact that the General and I were not officially able to be married until 1979 created a protocol problem that got solved in different ways in different countries, and even at different embassies in Manila. The US Ambassador, for instance, always seated me to his right, either to take credit for my presence in Manila or to please the General—I wasn't sure. Often, traveling abroad, I was placed with the general's ambassador or his political aide.

When we landed in Belgrade, we were met with a fleet of Mercedeses and a red carpet. In Prague, it was a fleet of Czech-made cars and no red carpet. Czech Foreign Minister Bohuslav Chnoupek and his lively blonde wife proved to be enthusiastic hosts, however, and even took us up to a lodge in the mountains near Bratislava where the gypsies danced. (Chnoupek said to me, years later, "Don't forget—I gave you full honors in 1974!")

Our most elegant accommodation on that Eastern European trip was in Bucharest, where we were taken to a private villa with its own sauna and swimming pool and a lovely rose garden leading down to a river. But when Mrs. Moreno-Salcedo and I strolled down to the river one day, two armed soldiers suddenly appeared from around the hedge with their rifles at the ready. We gestured that we couldn't go farther and walked slowly back to our villa, praying they were not trigger-happy. Apparently the villa assigned us abutted the president's house, where President Assad of Syria was currently a heavily protected guest.

We intended to hit all the eastern bloc countries that season but protocol dictates that one is supposed to go home or to another country in between official visits, so from Bucharest we went to Paris and then flew to New York City. On September 19, publication day of my book *The Philippines: Shattered Showcase of Democracy in Asia*, General Romulo held a reception at the Waldorf. I put on a pretty *terno* for the affair. There was quite a crowd: Filipinos, Americans, the press, and even some gate-crashers. After it was over, I discovered that the books we had set out on a display table had all been taken. I guess people thought they were party favors!

Yassir Arafat decided to come to the United Nations that fall, and also stayed at the Waldorf, where most foreign diplomats usually stay when they are in New York. "The Towers," I complained to Romy, "look like the 50th Street Precinct!" I had never seen so much security. Riding the elevator down to the lobby one afternoon, I shivered at all the chants and screams I could hear coming off the street from demonstrators. "I wish the Palestinians weren't staying here. It makes me nervous," I said.

Romy said calmly, "You only die once."

Five days later I came in to our suite after shopping and Romy was sitting with Consul Abaya from the Philippine mission, who always served as his personal aide in New York. "Something serious has happened," he told me. "They've got Romualdez [a cousin of Mrs. Marcos who was the Philippine ambassador in Washington]. They have taken him hostage in the chancery."

I thought he might be kidding. He did sometimes tease people about the most serious things, and he knew I had been nervous about the Palestinians. But this was true: Mrs. Marcos, in New York at the time, had called and told him the story. A man who had an appointment with the ambassador had a gun and handcuffs in his briefcase and made the ambassador lie down on the floor after handcuffing him. The commercial attaché tried to grapple with the assailant, who shot and wounded him. Both men were being held hostage.

We started our vigil, turning on the radio and two TV sets. Supper was sent in. The phone rang every few minutes. The FBI. The consulate. The General sent his political aide Philip to Washington to see the crisis through.

We had no security. I double-locked the door and put on the chain. At about eleven o'clock there was a ring at the door. I opened it a bit, but left on the chain and peered through. A man flashed a badge. I looked closely, having seen enough TV serials to know about fake badges. Then I glanced down at his shoes. I saw flat feet and let the officer in. He was checking to see if we were all right, he said, and he gave me a police number to call in case of trouble. He said I was a good girl not to let him in right away.

We didn't know who Romualdez's assailant was or whether we might all be struck. Then about two A.M. we got a call that it was all over. The man was identified as a Filipino who wanted his son, who was detained in the Philippines, released. President Marcos agreed to these terms.

The General worried about the precedent. If that man got what he wanted, might not others be encouraged to do the same?

Three days later we went to the airport to see Mrs. Marcos off on a jaunt to Mexico. The General told her he was going to Washington to address the National Press Club. She told him to be careful, the ambassador's plight still fresh in her mind.

"I'm his security," I quipped.

She laughed. "You're his security blanket!"

On her return to New York, Mrs. Marcos gave a small dinner party in the apartment she was then using, next to Cristina Ford's, in the Carlyle Hotel. Among the guests we met Romy's old friends Mr. and Mrs. Richard Berlin. Romy was in great form that night, bubbly and funny, telling his Tito story and a lot of others he'd picked up or invented about our trip. Finally Honey Berlin leaned over to me and whispered, "Whatever you are giving the General, I'd like a bottle!"

The year after our official trip to Rumania, President Nicolae Ceausescu and his wife visited the Philippines. Part of the entertainment consisted of a yacht trip, to celebrate Bataan Day.

It was great fun to watch the ebullient Filipinos trying to warm up and entertain the somber "black suits." There was not only a language barrier but one of national character as well: The Rumanians all wore business suits and their manners were quite formal; the Filipinos were in their cruise clothes and displayed their usual high spirits. Imelda Marcos had put on a flowing hostess pajama outfit after she boarded the yacht. I was wearing a casual pantsuit and sweater. The Rumanian ladies were in day dresses with sturdy black shoes.

When we reached the peninsula of Bataan, six helicopters were waiting to whisk us off to Mt. Samat. There a brief ceremony was held at the World War II memorial, with the American Ambassador and President Marcos speaking. Then back in the helicopters again for a short ride to the tiny rocky island of Corregidor that guards the entrance to Manila Bay. General Romulo was never too keen about visiting Corregidor—he had been holed up there, under Japanese attack, with General MacArthur in the early days of the war and the memories of the bombings and the soldiers' deaths still haunted him.

We returned to the yacht for a buffet lunch, then the presidents and their foreign ministers retired to the closed cabin for consultation while Mrs. Marcos and the other Filipinos tried to entertain the rather taciturn Madame Ceausescu. She is a chemist by training and heads a government department. I heard she had been an underground fighter in the war and looking at her strong no-nonsense face, I could well believe it. I don't know whether it was her lack of English or simply her manner but no matter what was said to her, she answered only "Yes" or "No." Mrs. Marcos tried to engage her. We all tried. No response.

Finally Mrs. Marcos began to hum, then sing. Madame Ceausescu looked at her with some expression of interest. So Imelda continued to sing to her. By the time the gentlemen rejoined us, things had loosened up a bit.

Mrs. Marcos now called on other Filipinas present to sing. She kept at it, pulling people in, encouraging everyone. She finally got one or two of the Rumanians to sing— the foreign minister and President Ceausescu for one bar. I even saw Ceausescu slip his arm around his sturdy wife, while President Marcos and Imelda sang a love song together.

Back among our group, Mrs. Marcos whispered: "We'll stand on our heads if necessary!" But the ice had finally broken, through her tireless efforts, and at last the dour Rumanians were all smiling and singing with the Filipinos.

Imelda was an indefatigable hostess. She didn't deal in anything as simple as a small sitdown dinner party; she was into spectacle, celebration. Wherever she was there was music, professional and amateur. She pulled in everyone around her and made them part of the act. It was an irresistible performance. Recently a former member of her New York set sighed wistfully, "She really knew how to give a party!"

The constant directives from the office of the Social Secretary about what "Ma'am" felt was appropriate attire for her luncheons, dinners, and the like were all part of Imelda's sense of spectacle. Sometimes she wanted us all in national dress; other times "Western attire" was demanded. At luncheons she did not want to see casual clothes, but "afternoon dresses." She sent a rather tart message to one Cabinet wife that she should cease and desist from appearing in pigtails at the palace. The men were not spared: A luckless Cabinet member who came to the airport once in a brown suit to accompany her to New York was told to take a later plane. I asked someone what she had against the color brown. First I was told she thought it was unbecoming to Filipinos, who tend to have dark skin. But a braver soul confided that it was an aversion based on the fact that brown "is the color of human waste." The General had several brown suits he was fond of, but he never wore them when he was in Manila.

In addition to assuaging her sense of childhood deprivation, Imelda's own clothes served her needs as a world-class performer. Besides her enormous collection of *ternos*, in every color of the rainbow, Imelda owned spectacular designer gowns she had bought in Paris, London, and New York. There was one paneled chiffon with a sort of free-form hand painting of a peacock I would have killed for. And I only saw her wear it once.

On a European trip, when we were leaving Paris, a member of the embassy handed us a box to carry through for "Ma'am." It contained no less than three identically designed mink evening capes, in three different pastel shades.

Throughout the 1970s the parade of distinguished visitors to the Philippines continued unabated, and with it Imelda's gaudy spectacles. In December of 1975, President and Mrs. Ford came to Manila. The Ford party included their daughter, Susan, and Secretary of State Henry Kissinger. When we walked into Malacalang Palace the night of the state dinner, Ambassador Sullivan and Kissinger were standing together at the end of the long reception room. As soon as they spotted us, Bill Sullivan whispered to Kissinger and Kissinger stared at me, with a knowing smile. I felt like Madame du Barry making that long walk, on the arm of the General, while the Secretary of State sized me up, as his ambassador filled him in about me. It was like being caught in a scene in a movie, and I was half annoyed and half amused.

Then the Fords came in. Mrs. Ford seemed extremely frail, smiling gamely, but she looked really worn and exhausted. (During the dinner, she kept closing her eyes. Maybe it was the combination of pills and alcohol that she later conquered.) The Ford daughter was a strapping blonde girl with swimmer's shoulders. *"Muy guapa,"* declared the General. But Bill Sullivan noted naughtily that she had a "contact-lens stare" in front of the battery of TV cameras.

I was astonished at how utterly self-centered Dr. Kissinger was in the brief private conversation we had as we went from the reception hall to the dining room in Maharlika Hall. I said, "I understand you are leaving the presidential party here?" and he promptly regaled me with how uncomfortable it was to travel with the President and how he couldn't wait to get into his own bed on his own private plane. Apparently he was miffed that no bed had been provided him on the presidential plane.

He was also put out that he wasn't the "star" of this junket. When we walked into Maharlika, the two presidents and their wives stepped to the podium to form a receiving line and Kissinger asked me, "Where do I go?"

I asked Undersecretary Collantes and he didn't know, so I ran off and found General Romulo and asked him where Dr. Kissinger should be seated. "Not on the podium," he said. "That's for the presidents and their wives only. President Ford is the show tonight, not his Secretary of State."

I started greeting friends and never did deliver that message to Kissinger. But it struck me that my man knew how to be Number Two gracefully whenever President Marcos was present. It was apparently, a lesson Henry hadn't learned.

When King Faisal was assassinated in the spring of 1975, Mrs. Marcos and the President decided she should go to extend the official condolences of the Philippine government. But there was a problem about her reception, since women are not welcome in the Saudi court and there is no protocol to cover their treatment. It was Imelda herself who came up with a brilliant way to get around that.

"Isn't it true that the new King had heart surgery in the US?" she asked. It was true.

"Who performed the operation?" As she had hoped, it turned out to be one of the surgeons who had recently been her guest at the opening of the Philippine Heart Center in Manila. She cabled him, requesting that he and his wife accompany her. When she appeared with her party before the new King, Khalid, he broke protocol and rushed over to greet them, extending his hand to the surgeon who had saved his life.

Mrs. Marcos was then invited to occupy the palace with her party—the first woman guest to be so honored.

Later, she bragged to the head of the Asia Society about the splendor of her reception in Saudi Arabia:

"I admired the varieties of grapes and when I came back to my room, there was a sheet spread on my bed, heaped with every color and type of grapes. . . ."

"I admired the rubies and I came in and a piece of velvet was on my bed, covered with unset stones. . . ."

"I admired the white Rolls-Royce and when I landed at home in Manila there were five waiting for me!"

This was an exaggeration. The King apparently really had intended to give her only one, but she told him that she and President Marcos always traveled in two identical cars, to confuse their enemies, in case of a coup. So he sent her two.

Although President Marcos preferred to stay at home in Manila while his wife traveled, he always made a big production of seeing her off and welcoming her home at the airport. There was a lot of live television coverage, and if she was returning from a mission abroad she always made an "arrival statement," just as General Romulo did when he came back from the General Assembly each year and reported on the Philippine role in the United Nations.

Imelda always expected Cabinet members, Blue Ladies, friends, and family to be present for her arrivals and departures. One morning when her plane was due at five A.M. Romy let me sleep and went off alone. When she debarked, they all got in cars and went directly to the palace for breakfast. Suddenly she looked around, turned to Romy, and asked: "Where's Beth?"

It was the President who answered. "She doesn't have to

be as devoted as Minister Romulo and I do—and get up at three in the morning just to meet you!"

I remember one evening when I was in the VIP room at the airport with other "welcomers," including the President. The General had just arrived from Saudi Arabia, and was leaving for Singapore. Imelda was just returning from a trip to Iran.

While he waited for her, the President watched a basketball tournament on TV; the Philippines was playing Korea. As the arrival of her plane was announced, I heard him grumble, "Why did she pick tonight to come home?"

Television coverage of Imelda's arrival that night included one shot of the President glancing longingly at the TV screen as Imelda made her arrival statement.

"He was more interested in that game than in my report about Saudi Arabia and the oil crisis—or in meeting his wife," groused the General.

Portrait of a Marriage

During the Marcoses' official visit to Washington in 1982, columnist Jack Anderson quoted from an alleged CIA assessment of the Marcos marriage: " 'The Marcos marriage is essentially a business and political partnership, but no one is sure just how close this working relationship is. At times the two clearly compete with one another; at others, the President will give in to her unless he believes a vital interest is at stake.'

" 'Mrs. Marcos is ambitious and ruthless . . . She has a thirst for wealth, power and public acclaim and her boundless ego makes her an easy prey for flatterers. Although she has had little formal education, she is cunning.'

" 'In the event of President Marcos's death, his wife would doubtless make a bid to replace him . . .' "

Most Manilans believe that the balance of power between the couple shifted perceptibly after the Dovie Beams scandal. Dovie Beams was a minor motion-picture actress from Tennessee who was brought to Manila in 1966, ostensibly to make a film, but primarily to be introduced to the President by a golfing friend of his, Poten-

ciano Ilusorio, who had seen her in California and
contracted for her to come to Manila.

She arrived while Imelda Marcos was in Rome. Soon
after her arrival, the actress was brought to a safehouse in
Greenhills along with a few other of the President's friends,
and the President himself appeared, being introduced as
"Fred"—not too unlike his real name. An affair developed,
which Dovie later recorded in excruciating detail in a memoir. Apparently the President was quite smitten, even
singing to her and telling her he liked her better than Imelda—all of which she secretly documented by placing a
tape-recorder under the bed.

When Imelda returned from Rome, her spies told her
that the President had been having a little fling with the
American actress. Imelda went straight to the commissioner of immigration and told him to "arrest and deport"
the young lady immediately. Dovie appealed to the US
embassy for help and the ambassador asked that she be
released, since she was a US citizen and there were no
actual criminal charges against her.

As soon as she was sprung, the enterprising actress immediately called a press conference, at which she played
her famous tapes of her love scenes with the President.
Senator Aquino as well as other opposition leaders were
present, and the senator is said to have purchased one of
the tapes for $500. According to some palace insiders, this
incident was the beginning of Imelda's hatred for Ninoy
Aquino. She never forgave him for making fun of her by
playing the tapes.

That night Dovie Beams left Manila. Later she tried to
publish articles and a book about her love affair with the
President, but after the Philippine government put out
word that there would be enormous libel suits, the material
was temporarily withheld. Eventually the magazine *Oui*
published an excerpt and after several years the book itself
appeared.

Through the years, Imelda Marcos had endured the usual seedy little affairs of a philandering husband, but this was her first public humiliation. Probably her first thought was to leave him. General Romulo told me about a scene he had with her, just the two of them in her music room, where she wept over her humiliation. She told him she simply did not understand why her husband had so hurt her, "because I never refused him anything." (By contrast, Dovie Beams quoted Marcos as complaining to her that his wife was frigid, and that they had practically no sex life.)

During President Marcos's campaign for reelection in 1969, a member of the opposition, Senator Jose Diokno, played Dovie's tapes for friends and they became the favorite amusement of many anti-Marcos households. (Diokno was arrested when martial law was declared and jailed for three months.) It was infuriating to Imelda, and she threatened not to deliver the votes in Leyte. Then, since the power bug had obviously bitten her by this time, she decided to make a deal. She would stay married. She would work for her husband. She would deliver the votes he needed. But at great cost to him.

From that time on she was the aggrieved party. To atone for his marital sins, Imelda extracted from her husband a "hands-off" relationship in which she could indulge herself limitlessly—and he made no effort to stop her. Her whims and wishes, unchecked, became increasingly grandiose: for clothes, jewelry, eventually international real estate. People who respected the President were amazed at how soft he grew with her, never curbing even her most outrageous behavior.

In 1965, the first time Marcos ran for the presidency, a soothsayer of his acquaintance saw Imelda for the first time. "She will bring you up," the clairvoyant prophesied. "And she will bring you down." His marital gaffe with Dovie was the first step on the way down. He probably could have gotten away with his own secret graft, which was so well protected by layers and layers of clever legal manipulation and shell companies without his name on them. But once Imelda was turned loose she left large tracks. When she shopped, when she got into real estate deals, she liked to talk about it. Her spending was never secret. She told US Ambassador Michael Armacost, for instance, that she got her start in investment by taking money from the President's political war chest, to corner the market in garlic.

Imelda had always had her own power base politically, even before the Dovie Beams affair strengthened her hand. It was unquestionably she who delivered the southern province of Leyte to Marcos during the presidential election of 1965. At that time she was also a big vote-getter in other parts of the Philippines, including Manila itself. She was especially popular with the poor, who comprise the mass base of Philippine society. If she had enemies or political opposition, it was apt to be among the well-educated and well-to-do, who were suspicious of her sentimentality, grand gestures, and extravagance. Also, by now many of the wealthy had experienced the pinch of being told they must contribute heavily to Imelda's pet causes. It wasn't a particularly subtle appeal, implying as it did that you better cough up cash if you wanted to continue to prosper in the Philippines. Much of this dirty work was handled by her kid brother, Kokoy Romualdez, a shadowy figure who hovered at the sidelines in the palace. When I first began attending dinners there, a place was often set for "Governor" Romualdez at my table but he never appeared. When I asked about this missing guest, I was told, "Oh, that's Kokoy. He never sits at a dinner." He was finally pointed out to me, a tall, heavy-set, white-haired man skulking around the draperies, always within beckoning range of his sister, but never personally taking part in any of the festivities.

Kokoy is a street-smart, rough and tough type of man, wily, effective, and uneducated. Early on, he attached himself to the political members of the family, serving as special assistant to his cousin, Daniel, who was Speaker of the House. He became an assistant to Marcos after his sister's marriage.

Imelda had a driving desire to put the Philippines on the world map. Just as she had metamorphosed from a barelegged village girl to a "Queen" who hobnobbed with other heads of state and the world's wealthiest people, so too she wanted her little country to become a mecca for those seeking the most elaborate conference sites, medical facilities, or the finest of tourist accommodations. It was through her aggressive efforts that the striking Cultural Center theater and the giant Conference Center were built on Manila Bay, and Plenary Hall, meant to rival the United Nations.

Sometimes her priorities were highly questionable—but few dared question her, especially after the imposition of martial law that silenced her political opponents. In 1974 she angled for, and won, for Manila, the lucrative and publicity-laden honor of hosting the Miss Universe Pageant. To house the spectacle she ordered built, in a record seventy-seven days, a gigantic 10,000-seat Folk Arts Theatre at the tip of the reclaimed area of Manila Bay where the Cultural and Conference Centers were also located. She believed the Miss Universe Pageant was so important to Manila that she took the funds earmarked for a new National Museum of the Philippines, which was languishing on a couple of crowded floors of the old Senate building, solely for the purpose of staging this event.

Later, spurred by a similar attack of chauvinistic grandiosity, she had built an enormous Film Center and tried to establish an annual Manila Film Festival to rival that of Cannes. Much criticized by the local cinema industry, the festival was held twice and discontinued, to her chagrin.

If she ran short of funds she shook down local businessmen. "At least she flirted with you and invited you to the palace," recalled one nostalgically; "I volunteered money to the new government, and I didn't get a cup of tea!"

Her husband's infidelity continued to plague her. Not long after the Dovie Beams scandal had become a juicy gossip item for Marcos-watchers all over the world, Imelda came to New York on a trip arranged by Kokoy. As was his custom, he also acted as her protocol officer. Her purpose was to plead the cause of Philippine investment before the executive committee of the Philippine-American Chamber of Commerce. When the committee was assembled, and before Mrs. Marcos was brought in, Kokoy made a little advance statement, reminding them, among other things, that "if you have any problems in the Philippines, don't forget my sister sleeps with the President. She can help you."

After his sister entered, he repeated: "Don't forget, she sleeps with the President of the Philippines." At which point the irrepressible Jose Saggese, president of Borden International, whispered: "—among others."

Imelda overheard him. She turned and, looking straight at Saggese, snapped, "Joe, you are *right.*"

The President's affair with Dovie irrevocably damaged part of the Marcoses' potent political image: that of the loving couple. It would take years for Imelda to live it down, and meanwhile the President lost whatever control he had once had over her. In return for her staying with him and continuing to deliver votes, she assumed a regal autonomy, arrogating more duties to herself and taking a vocal part in political meetings.

In 1975 Imelda had her husband appoint her Governor of Metro Manila and Minister of Human Settlements—a Cabinet position of almost limitless power and authority. As she took on an increasingly active public life, her self-confidence spiraled. Her early demure three-line speeches evolved into half-hour harangues as she switched facilely from English to Tagalog. Not a reader—I can't recall ever seeing her with a book in her hand—she nevertheless was a quick study and absorbed information instantaneously. Her idea of preparation for a trip abroad or to greet a conference was to summon specialists who would give her an oral briefing. She would then use the information in her forthcoming interviews. She didn't bother with papers—except for prepared speeches.

Once when the President made light of some trip she was about to embark on, she cut him down in front of the entire Cabinet: "I am not going as your envoy. I represent the Philippine government!"

Watching Imelda and Ferdinand Marcos together, I never could make up my mind how much emotion they shared and how much was simply the result of a very successful political coupling. He seemed proud of her political prowess, referring to her as "my secret weapon." On her birthday, he would personally compose a sentimental love song, in dialect, and sing it to her, to the rapturous applause of all the palace cronies.

The only thing that could make the President lose his cool were attacks—verbal or physical—against his wife. When he first heard of the assassin's attack on Imelda, he confided to me: "I have met many disasters in my life, such as the killing of my father by the Japanese because I refused to surrender, the fall of Bataan, the death in battle of some of my closest comrades. But I have never felt at the same time such cold fury and deprivation as when I heard that my wife had been attacked and might have been killed."

Yet she often seemed indifferent to him. Once, in New York, when she was regaling her circle of ladies with a long story, an aide walked into the room and whispered that the President was on the line from Manila. She kept right on with her story, and finally got up languidly and went to her bedroom to take the call, after letting him cool his heels for a good ten minutes.

There was much talk and, so far as I know, no proof, of Imelda's extramarital love life. Once when she was suddenly, secretly hospitalized after a trip to Rome, the rumor went around that the President had beat her up because of affairs with some of Cristina Ford's Italian friends. At other times, when her invariably tall and handsome young male friends—such as Van Cliburn or George Hamilton—were seen with her, people assumed they were her lovers.

I doubt it. Imelda loved to dress up and dance all night. But as far as getting down to the nitty-gritty of a love affair, I was always reminded of the old New York joke: "She wouldn't break her hair." She was sensuous—but not especially sexual. Even her beauty had a frozen perfection. It was not the kind of face, hair, or body one would be tempted to reach for and ruffle up.

George Hamilton and his mother turned up as frequent guests at Malacanang. Mrs. Hamilton, enormously self-confident and aggressive, apparently was a favorite of Imelda and even came to Manila several times without her son. And of course Imelda saw George whenever she was in California or New York. One garrulous maid claimed she once walked in on Imelda and George lying on a bed smoking pot, in the off-limits top floor of the former Philippine Consulate on 66th Street. If indeed the sighting was accurate, I would guess the pot-smoking was as far as the orgy got.

I had the impression Imelda liked men for public display, not private pleasure. She always chose handsome security guards, tall escorts. Since the US ambassadors all tended to run tall, she usually flirted with them when they first arrived in Manila: Bill Sullivan, Richard Murphy, Mike Armacost. Later, when she didn't like the US media coverage of what she was doing, she dropped them, muttering threats about her friends in Russia.

Her most enduring extramarital relationship, with Van Cliburn, was practically maternal. At one point, she told me, giggling, he had said that she was the only woman he would ever marry. They carried on great long-distance talk fests, and he often turned up in Manila (though usually with his mother and his manager in tow).

Imelda liked giving him gifts. After her first trip to China, she told me she had bought Van a piano, since pianos were "so cheap" in China. Once, in New York, she showed me a little black miniature poodle she was fondling on her lap and said it came from Van. I was mesmerized by the dog's diamond collar—and wondered if it, or just the dog, came from him. I kept thinking: How many sacks of rice would all those little diamonds buy?

Once Imelda told me that New York gossip had it that she and Cristina Ford had gone through a secret "marriage ceremony." It struck her as hilarious. "I'm not a lesbian!" she laughed. And Cristina's history would certainly indicate a preference for men.

In one sense Cristina's friendship exerted a good influence on Imelda: The Italian beauty taught her the fashion lesson that "less is more." Before her Cristina days, Imelda was inclined to wear too much of her stupendous jewelry at one time. After Cristina advised her, she learned to wear a single large piece at a time, or just earrings, and so looked much more chic.

Unlike the svelte Cristina, however, she was always trying to keep her weight down, but she had a weakness for good food and enjoyed the full-scale Filipino lunch of rice, meat or fish, fruit, and a sweet. Whenever she wanted to diet, she sent word to the kitchen to serve her what the President was eating, usually boiled fish and a vegetable. The Romualdezes are from the south, and they are fairly heavy people, while the Marcoses—from the spartan stony shores of Ilocos to the north—are thin. Imelda told me once that at a buffet the big, hearty Romualdezes would ask "What's good?" while the thin, disciplined Marcoses would ask "What's good for you?"

I was with Imelda once at a luncheon at the Indonesian Embassy, where she sampled everything in the buffet: chicken in coconut, skewered pork, fried shrimp, roast lamb, vegetables—three plates full!

I think Imelda probably loved her husband at the beginning. Which made the publicizing of his infidelity such a heartbreak for her. Five years after Dovie Beams left Manila, Imelda, pointing to the President, said to a startled group of US bankers, "See that man? He prefers a slut to me!"

That betrayal hardened her. By 1977, she had directed her strongest emotions inward. In an interview at the time of her 25th wedding anniversary she spoke of love:

"You can love others, but you have to love yourself first. . . . I love the President, but it's a lot of hullabaloo to say that I love the President more than myself. You may listen to this kind of thing in poetry, but it is only some crazy fool who believes he loves someone beyond self."

Wild Beasts—Foreign and Domestic

TERRORISM is a modern fact of life, one that affects us all—but none more so than political leaders and diplomats. In early February of 1976 I dressed for a reception for one thousand delegates to the United Nations Conference on Trade and Development (UNCTAD) with the unsettling knowledge that a Japanese Red Army hit squad had arrived in Manila to launch an attack upon our delegates.

At the Hilton beauty shop I watched the other ladies having their hair done, as I was, and I kept thinking how ironic it was that we were all getting gussied up—in order to have our pretty heads shot off. I was scared. Not surprised. Just scared.

Out at the General's house later, I wandered restlessly around, checking the arrangements. Then I saw Olivia, the wife of the General's youngest son, come out of her apartment, leading her youngest, Tina, a gravely beautiful five-year-old with round Spanish eyes like her mother's, all dressed for the party.

I panicked. "Please, Olivia," I whispered frantically, "take her away! Send her to a neighbor, lock her in the house. Anything. But *don't* let her be out here in this party!"

I explained about the word we had received and Olivia took Tina inside.

As the crowd began surging in, I dutifully shook hands, smiled, went through the rituals of welcome, all the while glancing at the high garden walls to see if the attackers were scaling them.

They never appeared. But they were not arrested either. The next day we flew to Bangkok, then went by car to Pattaya, 90 miles away, for a meeting of the Association of Southeast Asian Nations (ASEAN). The following morning I read in the Bangkok papers that the terrorists had arrived in Bangkok the day before and were apprehended at the airport. Did they come on the same plane? I don't know. Just as I don't know what made them change their plans to attack us the night of our reception. There were six of them—with a full arsenal of handarms.

I was always amazed how "normal" the President and First Lady appeared to be when they were exposed in public. Once I was sitting at an outdoor ceremony, two seats away from Imelda, when a man came running across the little improvised stage, making straight for her, with something rolled up in his hand. We sat, frozen, while he reached her and muttered something; a security officer appeared and led him away. As it was, he was just a "crazy" trying to give her a hand-designed scroll. But how had he got there? Why hadn't anyone stopped him? Imelda shrugged and smiled good-naturedly and the ceremony went on, but I wondered if we were thinking the same thing.

The previous Christmas night, the Romulo family was enjoying a traditional dinner when a note appeared from the Thai ambassador that he was being threatened by the PLO. What on earth was the PLO doing in Manila on Christmas night? And why were they after the ambassador?

Calls were made. Security arranged. And then a reassuring call from the General to the ambassador, who was stammering with fright. The General was sympathetic. "They mean business," he said.

UN Secretary-General Kurt Waldheim and his wife and daughter, Crista, visited Manila in February of 1976. (Many of our guests came in February, since it is one of the best months in the Philippines, cool and dry.) The General and I saw a great deal of the Waldheims in New York each fall, and they had also been cordial to Imelda Marcos whenever she was in town. They came to Manila now as her guests.

Soon after they arrived, we flew to Leyte. Mrs. Marcos took the Waldheims and General Romulo on her plane and instructed me to ride with the President and UNDP director Donald Bergstrom and his wife, Mai-Britt, on his plane. The President was in an unusually relaxed mood and chatted about his guerrilla days during the trip.

Comparing notes with Romy later, I commented that I could surely use a cup of coffee.

"Didn't you eat on the plane?" he asked in surprise.

"Eat what?" I said grumpily. "We weren't offered even a juice."

"Oh, we had champagne, pâté, fresh fruits," he told me.

We changed and went down to the sea. Mai-Britt Bergstrom and Crista Waldheim water-skied with the President while the rest of us swam. Imelda, apparently aware of her husband's abstemious hospitality, sent a tray of fresh-cut fruit down to the swimmers.

It was a small group—Imelda had brought only three of her Blue Ladies along, plus a priest who helps her with her speeches and the usual assortment of aides. But it was more convivial than her usual beach parties. In the evening the President rounded us up for a game of pelota and insisted on teaching Mai-Britt, Kurt, and I how to play.

Since I had ducked his earlier invitation to water-ski, I decided I must join him on the court. They found me a pair of tennis shoes (Filipino men's shoes fit me) and I flapped around in my Ken Scott evening pajamas, even managing to hit a few balls. There were no shoes big enough for Waldheim, so he played in his leather shoes—and fell once. The audience, which included Imelda and Romy and Mrs. Waldheim, got some good laughs out of our antics.

In the evening Imelda invited a few of us to take the two-seater golf go-carts and tour her domain. She drove the Secretary-General around in the first one; a guest drove Mrs. Waldheim in the second; and I drove Romy in the third. With a police jeep escort, we went around the village of Tolosa and over to the monument Mrs. Marcos had erected to her father, then down to "the Governor's Mansion," which is actually Kokoy's little beach cottage.

Kokoy, of course, was in Olot since Imelda was there. He appeared once on horseback, leading some other horses for the Waldheims to ride. He reappeared as the driver of the bus that took us back to our planes. His costumes alternated from bush jackets to jumpsuits—but always there were the bare brown feet in Gucci loafers. (I never saw him wear socks, even in the coldest of New York winters.)

Since it was Valentine's Day, Mrs. Marcos gave the Blue Ladies and me golden hearts from Cartier with her name on them. She also gave me a Philippine freshwater pearl ring, identical to the ones she gave Mrs. Waldheim and Crista. Imelda gave gifts because she enjoyed doing it. (When she wanted to control people, she gave them money.) I thought of the actress Esther Williams, who, when she first became a star, said the thing she enjoyed most about her new status was being able "to buy really nice presents for everyone I love." Imelda loved to give beautiful gifts, and when she did, she sort of stood on one foot, tensely expectant, hoping for a delighted response.

On the trip back from Leyte, I was again riding with the President. I always enjoyed our conversations. The President, unlike his wife, is an extremely well-read man with a sharp sense of history. (Marcos enjoys talking, reminiscing. And he listens when you address him privately. But he makes little or no comment, so you don't really know what impression you have made.) He told me now, with a twinkle of pride, that he was writing a book—a history of pre-Spanish Philippines.

I was quite surprised. "But Mr. President," I said, "when on earth do you have time for that?"

"Between eight and twelve at night," he replied.

He spoke of his fascination for Genghis Khan, marveling that he might well have gobbled up all of Continental Europe, even reaching the British Isles, had he not got lonesome for his son and called a halt on the eastern perimeter of Europe.

During our talk he also mentioned that he is a Virgo. This surprised me. It accorded with his concealed emotions—but Marcos has so much strength and drive that I don't associate him with this rather timid sign.

Imelda opened her fabulous Philippine Heart Center for Asia in February of 1975. I personally would much rather have seen her put her phenomenal energies and funds into renovating the sadly neglected Philippine General Hospital, which was the only public hospital with adequate facilities for the poor in Manila. But someone had sold her on the idea of grand edifices for specialized medicine. And the Heart Center was grand. There was a huge ceremony to inaugurate the building and a flock of foreign guests including famed heart surgeons Dr. Denton Cooley and Dr. Christiaan Barnard. (Dr. Barnard's wife looked like a schoolgirl; a British doctor's wife told me she is younger than his daughter by his first marriage.) Cristina Ford and the jet-setters were also there, along with Mr. and Mrs. Winston Guest. Looking over the crowd, I decided I had never seen so much wealth concentrated under one patch of night sky: Besides the complete diplomatic corps, Imelda had invited all the wealthiest families of Manila. Imelda's foreign friends all pulled up before the grandstand in palace limousines, while the Cabinet members were forced to park their cars three blocks away and walk.

Her reception that night was a new type of spectacle. She had taken over historic Fort Santiago on the Pasig River (originally built by the Spaniards to protect the city and used by the Japanese during the occupation as a prison), and turned it into a beautiful garden, with lights strung in all the trees and along the fortress walls. Filipina hostesses welcomed the guests at the great stone gates. Food and drink were set out beneath five white tents, and there was a presidential box draped in red velvet from which Imelda's honored guests watched a program—part dance, part fashion show, with slides and a narrator and beautiful Filipina models.

That night Romy told me his Valentine gift to me this year was that I would receive an honorary Doctor of Letters degree from Philippine Women's University for my work in serving as a bridge of understanding between the Philippines and the United States. "You'll have to make a speech," he warned me as he started to coach me in the Spanish way of accepting such an honor ("I don't deserve . . ."). I stopped him.

"That's not my style. I'm not big on false modesty. I'll say I'm grateful. That's enough."

I did prepare a fairly long serious speech on the role of women in Asia and America. But I had it handed out instead of delivering it. There were several other speakers, and that, plus the passing out of the degrees to the graduating class, made it so late by the time they called on me, I just got up and said a few words of thanks. Later, Ambassador Sullivan told me I really deserved the degree in "Humane Letters" since I was so humane to my audience!

In March, a long profile that I wrote on Imelda appeared

in the *Reader's Digest*. The *Digest* managing editor, Ed Thompson, and his wife, flew out from Pleasantville, New York, the business and editorial directors came in from Tokyo and Hong Kong, and there was a "presentation" luncheon. Imelda seemed to enjoy all the festivity centered around her, but she never did say whether she liked my article. It was actually quite favorable, recounting her prodigious activities. But perhaps she wasn't keen on the fact that I mentioned her background was poor, and that she was often referred to as the Iron Butterfly.

The General gave a dinner for the *Digest* group. But it was almost ruined by the lateness of our guests of honor. Mrs. Marcos decided to take them all shopping at 5:30 and ordered formal *barongs* for the men, which they had to be fitted for, and wait for, to wear. The *Digest* people were also uncertain whether Imelda herself would attend our dinner or not, and were waiting for her at the Malacanang guest house. The General finally got everything squared away, and pulled them in, but it was already time to sit down to dinner and they missed the receiving line. This was not an unusual occurrence. Plans would be made, to the hour or minute, and then Imelda would decide to take over, throwing everything into chaos.

We just got the *Reader's Digest* group swept out Sunday morning and the guest beds hardly cool when King Hussein of Jordan arrived, with an entourage of forty people. There was the usual round of entertaining, with a special concert, dinner, and an all-day excursion on the presidential yacht. Since the King had his foreign minister and his wife in his party, General Romulo and I were asked to be on duty to stay with them and help entertain our opposite numbers.

King Hussein wanted to water-ski, so the yacht put in at Bataan and we all went to the Marcoses' seaside guest house there. The King's foreign minister, his wife, Romy, and I sat in the sun watching them. It was quite a sight— the two trim-bodied, muscular heads of state water-skiing in tandem, with frogmen, for security, on all sides. Hussein is as short as Marcos—they looked like a well-matched pair in a water ballet.

His queen, Sofia, seemed a bit reserved at first. She seldom smiled and was not friendly with the group of Blue Ladies and Cabinet wives. But then the inimitable Imelda started teaching us all a new fad dance, the Bus Stop. It had a catchy rhythm (I guess she had had her tapes brought aboard the yacht), and pretty soon we were all rocking and laughing. And the pretty Queen—who was a quick study, and graceful—began to smile. We then showed her how to do the Salsa, which was enjoying a vogue at that time. (We were shocked a year later to hear of the Queen's death in a helicopter crash in Jordan. She was out on one of her official duties representing her husband.)

In May of 1976, I made my first and only trip abroad with President and Mrs. Marcos. Usually if the President and First Lady were both going abroad, I was not included. But when General Romulo told me they were both going to Kenya, I said I would really like to go along if possible. I had never been to Africa, and this was not an official visit: It was simply a trip to attend the UN Conference on Trade and Development in Nairobi at which President Marcos had been invited to speak.

Romy told the First Lady I was keen to go, and she said, "Why not? Tell Beth she can come."

I'm not sure she told anyone else, though, because when I presented myself at the steps to her plane on the evening we were to leave, my name was not on the passenger list. The airport manager, who knew the General well, ran off and came back saying it was all settled and I boarded.

We traveled on his-and-her passenger jets. I was on the First Lady's plane, with a group that consisted of several of her Blue Ladies and two or three men, including a new tall and handsome favorite who had recently surfaced at the palace, the Italian socialite and business executive Mario d'Urso. Mario was a longtime friend of Cristina Ford and of every other celebrity, as far as I could judge. He was amusing and full of gossip and he could make Imelda laugh. He made it his business to know everyone, and one of the Blue Ladies said it was he who eventually wangled a much coveted introduction for Imelda to Princess Margaret. (Another story had it that it was Imelda's own ambassador to London, Mike Stilianopulos, and his very social Spanish wife, Petita, who saw to it that Imelda met the Princess, who later visited the Philippines as Imelda's guest.)

The first leg took us to Bangkok, then Rome, and on to London. At each stop, a welcoming commiteee, headed by the Philippine resident ambassador, came to greet our planes.

We had a two-day layover at Claridge's, then left for Cairo. Egyptian Vice President Hosni Mubarak met us, along with a fleet of cars. We saw the Sphinx and climbed the Great Pyramid (I was disappointed not to see out, after climbing all those steep steps inside to get to the top) and played tourist like everyone else. The President even got on a camel to have is picture taken. Filipinos are fun to travel with—playful, lively, and not too sophisticated to be caught enjoying themselves in public.

In Nairobi, there were the days at the UN conference, the President's speech, and then a side trip was planned to see the animals in their native habitat. Unfortunately, we didn't stay at the famous resort, Treetops, which was considered too much of a security risk for the President. Instead we were put up at Keekarock Lodge, which is at ground level in an open plain.

On the flight from Nairobi to Keekarock Lodge, we made a stopover to visit Kenya's aging president, Jomo Kenyatta, and his young wife at their country home outside Nairobi.

Apparently Kokoy, who was directing all the trip's arrangements, took a dislike to his sister's new favorite companion, Mario. I don't know whether it was jealousy or whether the rough-and-ready Kokoy had an instinctive negative reaction to the languid cosmopolite. But when the list of seventeen was drawn up for the coveted trip by small Cessna planes to Keekarock Lodge, where we would view the wild animals, Mario's name was missing. It was too late when Imelda found out—we were already boarding—for her to do anything but sulk.

At Keekarock Lodge Mrs. Marcos saw the sign: "Please Don't Feed Monkeys." In a playful mood, she called a few members of the Cabinet, and her photographer, and had a picture taken of her "feeding her monkeys." Then she looked around, saw me,—I had backed off, to watch the fun—and called, "Where is our White Monkey?" So I joined them, posing on a fallen log.

When you are living on intimate terms with people of another race and color you quite forget the "white" and "brown" designations—yet strangers notice. When I went in with the Philippine group to greet President Kenyatta— a marvelously fierce-looking old man—he gave me a piercing stare, sorting me out from the others. It didn't help any when President Marcos introduced all the Filipinos and then, nodding to me, introduced Miss Day. Perhaps Kenyatta thought I was their mascot.

At the Romulo family dinner table one night, the General suddenly gave me a sharp look and said in a concerned tone, "You are pale. Are you sick?" One of his granddaughters giggled and said, "No, Lolo [Grandfather], she's *white!*"

We all enjoyed ourselves at Keekarock. It was new to most of us and a thrill to watch an elephant family strolling on the plain, or a fleet of pretty little Thompson gazelles leaping like ballerinas through the air, or watch the wicked-looking water buffalo—so much fiercer than the Philippine carabao. I still have photos of a pride of lions feasting on a gnu, and a sleek pregnant leopard asleep on a rock.

We were all sitting around the dinner table at Keekarock Lodge after an exhilarating day spent viewing the wild game when Finance Minister Cesar Virata commented pointedly to the President: "For every King there are vultures." He went on to summarize what the guide had said: that the great lions killed only for food, not greed, and thus retained respect. President Marcos listened carefully and later was heard repeating the statement: "For every King there are vultures." Unfortunately he didn't heed it personally.

The Englishman (a hunter) who organized our tour said he would miss us when we left because "there isn't a sorehead in the lot. You're such a jolly bunch, it will seem very quiet here when you are gone."

President Marcos made arrangements for the hunter to assemble pairs of non-predatory animals and bring them to an uninhabited grass-laden island in the Philippines. I thought it was a lovely idea to have a Philippine wild game preserve—until I heard that the President's son, Bong Bong, went there regularly to shoot game.

On May 9 we left Nairobi and after a short three-hour stopover at the Seychelles Islands in the Indian Ocean— long enough for the President to water-ski and the rest of us to have lunch—we flew on to India. We were told that we would be on the ground for several hours when the plane landed in Delhi, and that all the ladies should be in long gowns, since we would be guests of the Indian government for a formal dinner.

On her plane Imelda had a special dressing room-bedroom-and-bath arrangement fixed up for her own use. Sometimes one of the bravest or brashest of her entourage would ask to use it to change. Normally it was not offered, and the other ladies shared one small plain toilet. I struggled into my dress in that tiny toilet—a memory that still makes me shudder. I recall walking off the plane and being introduced to Prime Minister Indira Gandhi wondering if the bottom of my skirt was wet, and if the back of my dress was zipped.

Mrs. Gandhi was a much smaller, more feminine woman than I had envisioned, soft-voiced and hospitable. She, the Marcoses, and General Romulo went off for a private dinner while the rest of our party were the guests of members of her Cabinet. They took us to a sort of supper club at the top of a hotel, for dinner and a floor show. Since Filipino food tends to be very bland, the Filipinos had a hard time with the dinner—every dish was made with curry. They couldn't understand how I could swallow it. Then I showed them the dishes of yogurt placed at strategic intervals down the long table. If you slathered the hot dishes with cool yogurt, it was easy going.

When we left Delhi that night, Imelda told me that Indira Gandhi had confided to her that she believed herself to be "an old soul" who had lived at another time in history, since she had answers for things she could not have learned in this lifetime.

After the late dinner at Delhi, and no more than two hours of sleep in the past twenty-four, Baby Araneta—the jolliest of the Blue Ladies—came to me and whispered that she could not stand it anymore, and she disappeared into the back of the plane and hid under a blanket. "Don't let her know where I am."

Mario told me my eyes looked very bad, and several of us held a conference. I suggested placing a placard, "Sorry, Ma'am, but we are tired," on her table and then all sneaking off to the back of the plane to rest. Finally, when everyone was looking glassy-eyed from exhaustion, I got up the courage to suggest the President would want his wife to look her best when we reached the next stop, so shouldn't she retire to her compartment and take a little rest? With some reluctance, she accepted the suggestion and disappeared in her room. Everyone kissed me and thanked me and we all finally went to sleep.

In my notes scribbled during that trip, I wrote: "She never wearies, never tires, never apparently, like us lesser mortals, seems to need rest. After each stop she is charged up, eager to discuss who and what we have seen, to chat, to reminisce, talk of her hopes and dreams and past experiences. We try to stay alert and attentive and make appropriate comments . . . but it's hard going even keeping one's eyelids open after so many hours flying . . ."

Later, Romy told me that the President asked him several times how I was holding up. He was familiar with the hours his wife kept. In the President's plane, life was easier since he liked to doze during a flight, or read, and his entourage was allowed to do the same.

On the last leg of our journey we had a five-hour layover in Rangoon. The Burmese were very well organized: A fleet of air-conditioned Mercedeses met us at the airport and we were taken to government guest houses with bathrooms supplied with talc, toothbrushes, and so on. But the country is extremely hot. And walking barefoot through the pagodas didn't help.

There was a well-appointed luncheon held in a government house. The menu consisted of a very good chicken soup with both soft and fried noodles in it, a Burmese version of shad, roast turkey, and mangoes. The one odd offering was a fluted pastry shell on each plate, filled with cold canned baked beans.

In the afternoon, the ladies of the party went shopping. A jewelry store was opened for us, and Mrs. Marcos headed upstairs to the second floor where the finest stones were kept. She beckoned me to a case filled with enormous, unset rubies. "Which do you like?"

I had no idea. It wouldn't occur to me either to like or dislike an item so out of my price range. She fingered a few, couldn't decide on any, lost interest, and walked away. She had plenty of rubies at home.

It was hard for her to make up her mind. On the plane

earlier, leaving London, I had mentioned how fashionable her elder daughter Imee always looked. "Yes," she said, her voice wistful. "Imee always knows exactly what she wants. She can see a roomful of things and pick just one. Not like me. I try on everything and can't decide."

During the summer of 1976, President Omar Bongo of Gabon and his wife paid an official visit to the Philippines. I didn't know anything about Gabon, but at the state dinner I was fascinated with the jewelry his wife and the ladies of her party were wearing: sapphires big as pigeon eggs. I asked their minister if Gabon is rich in precious stones and he said no, but they did have forests, oil, and uranium— more than enough to buy gems! Mrs. Bongo was such a great shopper and left her husband alone so much that during their visit he managed to fall in love with a Filipina, whom he later brought back to Libreville. (His wife eventually had her deported back to Manila.)

As usual, Imelda had arranged a special cultural performance to be followed by a lavish midnight supper. The General sat in the presidential box with the Marcoses and their guests. I was assigned to one of the adjoining boxes, which were subscribed by rich friends of the Marcoses.

On the way home, Romy told me that when he asked President Marcos if he could be excused, the President answered him, in Ilocano dialect: "Go ahead. I wish I could go, too!"

I noticed that night that the President had that pinched look he gets when he is exhausted. His features draw up and seem smaller, his face becomes more closed and Oriental-looking. The more tired he gets, the more he resembles his old mother.

Clare Boothe Luce came to Manila on holiday that summer. I had first met her the previous winter in New York. Already in her seventies, she made it clear she was still "a worker" commuting between her home in Honolulu and

Washington, D.C., where she served on the president's National Security Council. She still wrote occasional columns when the spirit moved her. Mrs. Luce and General Romulo served together in the US Congress when she was the Congresswoman from Connecticut and he was the Resident Commissioner from the Philippines. At a dinner we all atended, she paid tribute to him for his initial refusal to leave Corregidor.

Mrs. Luce's main problem was her eyes—she had had several operations for cataracts. Her vision was impaired, but she was self-assured and articulate, and age had not dimmed her famous wit.

In line with their new, independent foreign policy, President and Mrs. Marcos and General Romulo went to the People's Republic of China in 1975 and normalized relations with the Chinese. At that time both Mao Tse-tung and his foreign minister, Romy's old friend Chou En-lai, were both alive.

Romulo and Chou had become acquainted at the first Asian-African conference in Bandung, Indonesia, in 1955. When Chou saw Romy next, he said drily, "Well, it took you twenty years to accept my invitation!"

Romy's impression was that there was "no sex" in modern China—nothing to arouse ardor or even mild interest. The women wore no makeup and dressed in dark, drab unisex suits. There was nothing to tempt one, he lamented. He said as much to President Marcos, who agreed, laughing, that "this is the place for us"—nothing to do but work. Romy also reported that Chou told him in all seriousness that this was calculated, the way they kept down their population. Nowhere in China was there visual stimulation for sexual activity, and couples were fined if they had more than three children.

On May 30th of the following year, the Marcoses and General Romulo went to Russia to open diplomatic relations. In Russia, Romy saw his longtime colleague Andrei Gromyko. Nimbly surviving many changing regimes, Gromyko had the unique distinction of being a foreign minister longer than anyone in the world—twenty-two years. (Before he retired Romy was second in line, with fourteen years on the job.)

Romy was sobered and shaken by the new military strength he saw in Russia, and recalled to me that Vishinsky, the former articulate representative to the USSR at the UN, with whom he had many a sparring match, had warned him: "Someday Soviet Russia will rule the world."

Much of Romy's work at the UN in the last few years of his participation there was trying to keep down the Russian presence and threat in Asia, especially in Cambodia and Afghanistan. Yet he believed it was time for the Philippines to open diplomatic relations with Russia. Only through diplomatic efforts would the world survive. "There is no winnable war anymore," he said.

I was surprised to read James Reston, a usually very reliable writer for *The New York Times*, refer to the Marcoses' trip to Russia by saying they "turned up" there "suddenly," implying it was a spontaneous trip to try to lever the US into granting more aid to the Philippines. In fact, the Philippines had announced that it was opening relations with China and Russia over two years earlier. It was part of Romy's master plan of neutralizing the Philippines by opening relations with the Communist block, independent of American protection. To his way of thinking, the days of the Cold War were over. The Philippines must get along with all nations and survive through its own diplomatic skills.

As she traveled the world over and observed what was being done in other countries, Imelda Marcos began increasingly to "think big" about her own country. In Manila alone she built the Cultural Center, Convention Center,

Heart Center, Kidney Center, and Lung Center. When the Philippines won the bid to play host to the International Monetary Fund Conference in October of 1976, she used this to promote Manila as the convention center for all of Southeast Asia. Fourteen new hotels were built to serve the conference, four of them luxury class, including a restoration of the historic old Manila Hotel on the bay.

The Manila Hotel soon became her favorite place for late dining. I unknowingly angered Mrs. Marcos by mentioning her as not a participant in the restoration of the hotel, but only as a frequent guest, in a book I wrote about the hotel. She wanted credit for the restoration—which was actually planned before the government took it over. She liked to bring foreign guests there—to the beautiful formal Champagne Room, or later, to the small, plant-filled Roma restaurant. A call would come from the palace: The First Lady will come at 9:30 with eight guests. A red carpet was rolled into place at the main entrance, a bouquet of orchids was prepared to be presented her by the general manager, whose duty it was to personally greet her. The orchestra would prepare to serenade her. But 9:30 often became 11, while the manager and the musicians waited. Fortunately the orchids—the strongest of flowers despite their fragile beauty—never wilted. Then the security cars would whoop into the circular drive, lights flashing. The long black limo followed, the door opened, and out she stepped with her pet guests spilling out behind her.

The group of eight may have grown to twenty by this time. She liked to scoop up people to be with her for her nightly ventures. Since the President did not leave the palace, it was her custom to dine late—with friends, acquaintances, hangers-on, whoever was around at the moment. They might stay till two or three in the morning with the yawning musicians hanging in there, knowing the management would pay them overtime.

Once when she arrived with a party of twenty and

wanted to be seated in the Roma restaurant where she enjoyed the capelli d'angeli with crab, she was told it was full and that the seated guests could not be thrown out. A compromise was reached. Since only a table for eight had been originally requested, her party was seated in the Champagne Room and Italian food was brought in from the Roma.

I was there that night with Chloe Romulo. We had dined in the Cowrie Grill and I was waiting for the General to emerge from a stag dinner in the Champagne Room. As Mrs. Marcos swept down the corridor, there was no way to avoid her. "We can't duck," I whispered to Chloe, giving her a nudge. We dutifully rose and walked forward to greet her. She kissed me, introduced me to her guests. They swept on.

In June the ASEAN ministerial meeting was held in Manila and the General gave a dinner for the foreign ministers and their delegations at the Hyatt Hotel. The hotel had recently been refurbished in native motif and at the presidential table were tall gilt chairs, with backs upholstered in a soft, wooly material.

I was wearing a beautiful new *terno* that Moreno had fashioned for me from blue satin flowered damask that had been sent me from China. I had had a bit of trouble hooking myself into it—and apparently entirely missed one tiny last row of hooks that held the back flap flat to the tight midriff. We were sitting at the head table—I was between the foreign minister of Thailand and the foreign minister of Malaysia—when I realized as I turned from one partner to the other that I was caught on the back of my chair. I felt the back with my hand and managed to free the soft thread of the chair. Then I got caught again, just as Romy was making the toast. I tried to rise, and the chair came along with me! I sat back down and whispered to my guests that I was caught. One minister tried to extricate me—and failed. The other tried—and failed. They called for the waiter to bring a knife. Romy, seeing that something was wrong, kept the toast going until I was whacked free from my chair, and then I suddenly popped up like a champagne cork for the toast. Before I sat down again, though, I had the good sense to put my napkin between my dress and the chair so that I could rise for the return toast.

The next time I came to the Hyatt I noticed the hotel had replaced those soft woven chair backs. Maybe somebody reported my predicament.

Nancy Kissinger came to Manila with her sister-in-law, Diana MacGinnis, the first week of September in 1977. Imelda put her up at the Antique House, one of the palace guest houses furnished completely in European and Asian antiques. I went to call for her there. She was a bit late getting herself together and someone explained that she was suffering an attack of shingles, alas. But she was very game about it and we went on with our planned tour and luncheon. She's a good conversationalist, and even more important, a good listener, asking highly intelligent questions and then paying attention to the answers.

The General was hosting an ASEAN–US Dialogue reception and dinner at our home that night and Mrs. Kissinger was due to arrive. Just as all the guests began to arrive, the skies opened and the rains came down. Within two minutes all the table settings, flowers, placecards, and linen were drenched and the waiters and musicians ran scattering like quail looking for cover.

At that moment Imelda, who had been with Nancy, decided at the last minute to accompany her to our reception. It was a madhouse, with all the palace security added to our own rainy confusion.

Nancy was supposed to have been our guest at the dinner, but Imelda decreed this was the only time she could devote to her. We all had to crowd into the house to escape the rain, and I saw the little maids peeking through the kitchen door to catch a glimpse of the First Lady and Mrs.

Kissinger. (The next morning Basing told me she found the American lady "very high." She had always thought I was tall—until she saw Nancy!)

There was nothing to do but to move the dinner to a hotel, which we did after Imelda finally left. The General went into action, and commandeered cars as they appeared to transport the musicians and protocol officers—who had no cars—over to the hotel. The poor fellow with the bass viol sat a long time before we caught a station wagon for him.

We spent Thanksgiving in Mexico City for the inauguration of President Lopez-Portillo of Mexico. The Kissingers had gone ahead for a few days of sun in Acapulco, then came in for the festivities. Senator Mike Mansfield was also there—another old friend of General Romulo. By now the US election was over and Kissinger was a lame-duck Secretary of State, with a new administration coming in.

Rosalynn Carter, wife of the president-elect, represented her husband in Mexico. I was curious to meet her in the flesh. In a Barbara Walters interview she looked sort of small-town prim and pretty, with a rather tight little mouth. But when she greeted the new Mexican president on her husband's behalf, I was reassured: She was well-dressed and made a graceful speech in Spanish. Obviously a lady who would do her homework.

Dr. Kissinger apparently wanted to tuck in the bases negotiation with the Philippines before he left office. He and Romy conferred in Mexico City, and Romy sent a message through to President Marcos about the offer he had received from Kissinger. To Romy's surprise, when we landed in New York, an ambassador from the US mission to the UN met him with a joint paper to sign for a press release about the agreement. But Romy said no; he had only transmitted the terms to Marcos, and had no authority to conclude the deal himself. Next morning *The New York Times* came out with a front-page story saying the US and the Philippines had reached an agreement. Romy called the State Department and asked that the story be rescinded. The next day there was a *New York Times* story saying Marcos had rejected the US offer, which had been agreed on by Kissinger and Romulo.

Romy was furious. He got an Undersecretary in the State Department on the phone and accused them of pressure tactics. He was told that the State Department was not responsible for the leak, and to please relay that message to Manila.

"I won't relay that message because I don't believe you," Romy said flatly. "You are trying to pressure us."

"That's not very diplomatic," said the Undersecretary.

"It may not be," Romy agreed. "But it's the truth and I refuse to relay it."

In the end, the bases agreement was not concluded until 1979. One of the Manila papers carried a cartoon of Kissinger chasing Romulo with a butterfly net, and Romulo, small and fast, outrunning him.

In New York that fall, I included one of my *Reader's Digest* editor friends who was curious to meet Imelda in one of our dinners. It was already fashionable in the Western press to condemn the Marcoses, with no other side ever presented. Even my profile of Imelda had appeared only in Asian and European editions of the *Digest*. My friend Helen, who had a lengthy chat with Imelda, commented it was a pity she was only presented as an extravagant jet-setter, when in fact she was also warm, voluble, and full of humanitarian plans and ideas. In fact, both Marcoses are much more complex personalities than the Western media have ever credited them with being.

Imelda attended the World Federalists Association presentation of the World Peace Award to General Romulo that was held at the Waldorf in December of that year. Our hosts were Mrs. Oscar Hammerstein III and Norman Cousins. UN Secretary-General Waldheim spoke first and Romy responded—a nice balance of a serious plea for world peace with touches of humor.

We had missed the New Year's Eve celebration in 1974 because of the General's attack of flu, and in 1975 he went alone to Malacanang Palace because I was in the hospital. For New Year's Eve 1976, he decided to really celebrate. His son, Dick, and Dick's wife were going with friends for a "package deal" at the newly renovated Manila Hotel, which included dinner, a floor show, and New Year's Day brunch.

We checked in at the hotel, had drinks with Dick and their friends, then went on to the festivities at Malacanang. It was not a very large celebration: The guests were limited to Cabinet members, Blue Ladies, and the generals, with a smattering of overseas guests, including Lillian Berkman from New York who was arranging to bring over an art exhibit from the Brooklyn Museum for the International Monetary Fund meeting. (At one time she was part of Imelda's New York set, and I used to run into her fairly regularly. I heard later that Imelda had wanted to borrow some of Mrs. Berkman's considerable personal collection of art and Mrs. Berkman, knowing how carelessly kept Imelda's paintings were in Manila, had refused. She had warned Imelda that the paintings she had bought in New York and Europe should be restored. But the First Lady wasn't interested. The climate in Manila is moist and moldy and paintings should be kept in air-conditioned rooms. Imelda's art was displayed all over the palace and in her private homes, with no special provision for their care.)

The New Year's Eve party at the palace was set up on the verandah. Mrs. Marcos had her New York guests at her table; General Romulo and I were assigned to the President's table. I guess she wanted to be sure he had someone to talk to, knowing the others might be too shy to converse with him. The other guests at his table were generals' wives and some Cabinet members who remained totally silent throughout the entire dinner. I don't know whether they were in awe of the President or just felt ill-equipped to join in on the wide-ranging subjects of our talk.

Finally the President asked some lady to dance and the General and I joined him on the dance floor. In all the years I was around the palace, the President never asked me to dance with him. Perhaps he didn't want a tall partner, or he simply may have preferred younger women.

Although I am considered of only medium height by American standards—five feet four-and-a-half inches—I often tower over Asian men. Once the Foreign Minister of Indonesia, Dr. Mochtar Kusumaatmadja, asked General Romulo with great curiosity, "Why did you choose such a tall wife?"

"I always like to look up to a woman!" the General retorted.

The General Runs for Office

BOTH General Romulo and Imelda Marcos worked hard and batted zero in their diplomatic efforts in 1976 and 1977. After six months of negotiations with Henry Kissinger, the bases agreement was shelved when the Carter administration came in. And Carter's people were so preoccupied with human rights issues that they didn't seem much interested in what was happening in Southeast Asia.

What looked to be a major coup for Imelda in 1976 was when she set out bravely to court the outrageous Colonel Qaddafi of Libya. The Philippine Moslem insurgency in the southern island of Mindanao was being aided and abetted by foreign Moslem sympathizers, most notably Libya. Mrs. Marcos asked for an audience with Colonel Qaddafi.

Her brother Kokoy later told me any visitor in Libya is in effect "a hostage." Imelda sat around, but no audience was granted. Finally they decided to leave. "We packed our baggage and shipped it to the airport and loaded it on our planes. If we had just put our bags in the lobby of the hotel they might have thought we were bluffing," said Kokoy.

Then the word came through that Mrs. Marcos should "pass by the palace" before she and her party left.

She saw Qaddafi, pleaded the cause of national peace, got him to agree to visit the Philippines, and to quit supplying arms to Philippine Moslems. She also called upon him to assume a leadership role in the Third World.

Apparently Qaddafi countered that Ferdinand Marcos was a spokesman for the Third World.

"But he's old already!" Imelda cajoled him. "You are but half his age." (Marcos was turning sixty and Qaddafi was thirty-four.)

Kokoy also revealed that when the Philippine and Libyan ministers were drawing up an agreement, the Libyan actually spat on the Filipino—twice. I asked Romy if, in all his years of negotiating, anyone had ever spat on him. "Never," he said. "What would you have done if one had?" "I would have spat back," he replied. "They are uncivilized by our standards," he added.

As a result of Imelda's trip an Islamic conference was held four months later in Manila. Then it was Romy's turn to negotiate—day and night. The first Carter man had also arrived in Manila to make a report to his president. It was a tense and trying time. The General's doctor and I stood by, worrying, while he had to go directly from a dinner to the Marcos yacht and work all that night and through the next day on both the US report and the interminable negotiations with the Libyans. ("They don't think like we do; its very difficult.") For two nights he did not get home to dinner or to rest in his own bed. They're killing him, I thought bitterly. I waited for him in his house.

I was dozing on a couch in his room the second night when I heard a car at two a.m. "A crisis," he announced wearily. "Almost to blows." The foreign minister of Libya had threatened to go home and call off negotiations, despite an agreement that had been reached, president to president.

President Ferdinand Edralin Marcos in 1973 . . .

First Lady Imelda Romualdez Marcos's favorite portrait of herself . . .

and as a Philippine "Adam."
(Manila Bulletin Library)

and as a latter-day Venus.
(Manila Bulletin Library)

The author interviewing Ferdinand Marcos in 1973.

The presidential home, Malacanang Palace, on the Pasig River. Marcos was the ninth Filipino head of state to occupy the palace. *(Bureau of National and Foreign Information, Dept. of Public Information)*

The Marcos regime played host to a varied collection of world leaders, including President Richard Nixon . . .

Pope John Paul II . . .

and Colonel Muammar el-Qaddafi. *(Manila Bulletin Library)*

The author and her husband, Philippine Foreign Minister General Carlos P. Romulo.

The Romulos and their youngest grandchild, Tina, at their home in the Philippines.

The author with (left to right) columnist Max Soliven, Abe Rosenthal of *The New York Times,* and Ambassador Steven Bosworth . . .

A state dinner honoring the Apollo 17 astronauts. From left to right are the author, General Romulo, Cristina Ford, the Marcoses, and the astronauts and their wives.

and with President Marcos, Van Cliburn, and the First Lady on their way to the Maharlika dining hall at Malacanang.

Prime Minister Cesar Virata, President Marcos, Defense Secretary
Caspar Weinberger, Imelda Marcos, and General Romulo in Washington.

General Romulo
with President and
Nancy Reagan
(Ambassador Jeane
Kirkpatrick is in
the background).

General Romulo and the Marcoses with Leonid Brezhnev and Andrei
Gromyko during the 1976 official visit to the USSR.

Ferdinand and Imelda Marcos and their daughters with Deng Xiaoping on a visit to the People's Republic of China.

Ferdinand and Imelda Marcos at General Romulo's retirement ceremony at Malacanang Palace. The ceremony was held on the General's eighty-fifth birthday, January 14, 1984.

Defense Minister Juan Ponce Enrile and General Fidel Ramos during the 1986 people's revolution that unseated President Marcos. Enrile recently resigned from the Aquino cabinet. *(Manila Bulletin Library)*

As Romy undressed and prepared for bed, a tiny note fell from his pocket. He showed it to me. It was in President Marcos's own hand: "My doctor is sitting right behind you." Marcos was not oblivious to his aging minister's health after all.

Despite all efforts, the talks collapsed. The Filipino Moslems—the Moro National Liberation Front—would not settle for anything less than total autonomy, amounting to secession. (They take the same line today, although they represent a fraction of the population.)

"I suppose the MNLF will try to kill me now," Romy said resignedly.

When some newsmen asked him about retirement that year he said, "God will decide when I die. The President will decide when I retire."

Spurred perhaps by the Carter administration's preoccupation with civil rights issues, *The New York Times* began a series of attacks on the Marcos government, contending that the relatives and cronies of the President and the First Lady had amassed great wealth at the expense of the country. But in Manila, these charges caused hardly a ripple. The Philippines was accustomed to corruption both in the old Congress and in high political office, and the charges did not rouse them. There was talk among the elite, however, that Imelda was the sole cause of the bad press because of her visible extravagances abroad. When she was in New York, for instance, the State Department security people assigned to her were aware of every purchase she made in every store. It was not just gossip. A number of Manilans, still loyal to the President, felt that she was ruining his international reputation.

Responding to the mounting criticism against his one-man rule, President Marcos called for an election for seats in the newly created Batasan Pambansa, or interim Assembly, which was to replace the old Congress, as the government changed from a presidential to a parliamentary system. Some Cabinet members were required to run for a seat in the Assembly, including the Minister of Foreign Affairs.

It was the first Philippine election since 1969—and the first time in his fifty years of public service that General Romulo ran for public office. Polls had been taken that showed his enormous personal popularity and he was asked for the Assembly to run in Metro Manila on the President's ticket, the KBL, which was headed by Imelda Marcos.

The President also lifted the ban against detainees running for political office. Benigno Aquino, who had been imprisoned since the declaration of martial law, decided to run from his jail cell. His wife, Corazon ("Cory"), campaigned for him. It was no surprise to Aquino or anyone else that the Marcos machine saw to it that he did not win a seat. But at least Cory was able to carry some of her husband's views to the countryside without being charged with subversion.

The only thing that worried the General about being forced to run for election was that I might become a political "issue" to the opposition. He asked me to stay out of sight during the campaign, and I never appeared with him at any rallies or events at which there were photographers. In fact, he passed up a lot of the rallies himself, sending his nephew, Alberto Romulo, who served as his campaign manager. Bert reported to us that my name never even came up. Friend and foe alike were apparently willing to let the widower have his lady friend, even if she was an American, without attacking him for it.

I read the absence of attacks on me as an indication that I had been around so long—it was five years now—that my horns had fallen off. People realized I was no threat to anyone and had caused no harm to their beloved senior statesman. Filipinos are a romantic people, and the image of their favorite statesman as "lover" delighted them. Also, by now, I had acquired my own quiet constituency. Many people had heard me speak or had read my articles or my book on the Philippines, and they knew I was sympathetic to their country.

During the campaign, one of Defense Secretary Enrile's children married and at the wedding I ran into General Fidel Ramos, the trim, scholarly Chief of Constabulary. He asked me what I was doing lately and I said, straight-faced, "I've been busy meddling in your internal affairs." He giggled. As the humorist Joe Guevara put it, the only place I meddled was "in the General's kitchen."

I had been told that Philippine elections were dirty, but I had no real idea what they were like since there had been none since my arrival. Now that she was running for office, Imelda was subject to constant attack. One of the leaflets distributed by the opposition asked the question, "Who is Imee's father?" which struck me as laughable. With a husband as sexy as the President, it was hardly likely Imelda would have sought out a lover as a young bride. Personally, I was glad she was the one heading the ticket. Otherwise, it might have been the General who was under attack.

At seventy-nine, he was amazed and gratified at his political popularity. Wherever he appeared he was cheered. Passing along the streets in his car, he was always recognized. People called out to him, flashed victory signs with their hands. When the votes were actually counted, he was told privately that his votes outnumbered those of all the candidates but since Mrs. Marcos headed the ticket, it was manipulated so that she came out Number One. He was Number Two. As he put it naughtily, "for reasons of my health!"

The Assembly met regularly, and those who had won seats had to attend the sessions, including General Romulo and Imelda Marcos. All of the Cabinet, who had been secretaries under the presidential system, now became ministers under the new parliamentary rule. Eventually the President named his former Finance Minister, Cesar Virata, Prime Minister, and kept the presidency for himself. But the interim government was neither fish nor fowl. And there was no Vice President. An Executive Council was established, supposedly charged with the responsibility of naming the next president in the event of Marcos's death. At first Imelda was named to the Executive Council, but later the US State Department urged the President to force her to resign from it and to issue a statement renouncing any intention of succeeding her husband. The Marcoses relied heavily on American support and the President was inclined to listen to, and often follow, advice from Washington in the interests of staying in office.

Imelda's relation with the American government was much more ambiguous than her husband's. She tried to court and charm members of Congress and the American ambassadors, but with relatively small success. Then she would become frustrated and angry and treat them as enemies. The same was true with the American media. She gave endless interviews, then was usually upset when she read the results. Outside Manila, she could not control the press or get her own way. It became a visible frustration.

After the election, the Marcoses held a big political dinner at the Philippine Plaza Hotel with the assemblymen from Metro Manila as special guests. I was moving around through the crowd, greeting friends, when the President came in. As he greeted me, I happened to ask about the new "find"—a Stone Age tribe, the Tasaday, that had been discovered in a rainforest in Mindanao. He stopped, and talked about it for at least ten minutes. I tried not to notice the people who backed off from us, then circled, silent and watchful as wolves, while we chatted. It was always like that and it made me uneasy: If I got into a conversation with either the President or Mrs. Marcos, everyone backed off. I deliberately went over to Imelda after the President walked on and mentioned the subject of my conversation with him so she would know that it had not been too personal. I wanted my record, to use Nixon's favorite phrase, to be "perfectly clear."

Carter's Vice President, Walter Mondale, visited the Philippines in May of 1978, along with his wife and son. Mondale looked in on the political detainees. A friend of Bobby Romulo who had been picked up during the elections for "subversive activities" along with other young anti-Marcos demonstrators said that showers were quickly installed and the rooms painted before the Vice President's visit. The result was that he and his friends were released a few days later.

One Marcos trait that used to bother the General was that for his toast at state dinners the President would extemporize. The General would carefully prepare the President's "remarks" for him, touching on major issues in the relationship of the two countries, paying tribute to the guest country, etc. Sometimes Marcos remembered the points he was supposed to cover. Other times not. The night of the dinner for Vice President Mondale, which was one of the best attended I had ever seen at Malacanang, the President got up and made a rambling toast, without enthusiasm. The ambassador sitting beside me commented, "Their meetings must have gone badly." Mondale, on the other hand, read his toast very well; it was short, upbeat, and to the point.

I found him more attractive in the flesh than from a TV screen. That hooded, bird-of-prey face lights up with a very nice smile, and a pleasant, friendly manner. The General had Mrs. Mondale for a dinner partner, and quickly revised his earlier estimate that she was "plain." He found her charming and an excellent conversationalist.

By 1978, I was getting a bit testy about being the perennial girlfriend, but never the wife. (In New York, Cindy Adams unkindly referred to me as Miss Abigail—who enjoyed the longest running engagement in the world, in Damon Runyon's *Guys and Dolls*.)

It came to a head with the election. I resented becoming a "political liability." One of the Cabinet members made an analogy to Nelson Rockefeller's abortive presidential campaign when he shucked the wife of his youth, who was well-connected politically, to marry his mistress. I hardly saw the connection, since in my case we were a widower and widow—and it hardly seemed an election of equal political importance.

We were married, privately in the home of close friends, Admiral and Mrs. Charles Parsons, in Manila, in September of 1978. The General was getting increasingly embarrassed about coming into New York with me each fall and facing all his old friends, and my family, with no change in my status. He decided we could keep our marriage secret in Manila, but share it in New York. This was a rather naive assumption. The morning following the wedding, the wife of an undersecretary in the ministry called me up to congratulate me. She knew the details—I later found out it was because the Chief Justice who performed the ceremony had ordered his wedding present (two silver goblets) engraved with our names and the date at Rustan's department store.

We denied it, and I continued to live at my hotel. When the bases negotiations were finally concluded, the following February, we were married officially, by the papal nuncio, at the *nunciatura*. Only the Romulo family and the nuncio's staff were present. I wore the same short pink chiffon dress to both ceremonies.

We had celebrated the General's eightieth birthday the month before, on January 14th, at Manila's huge Convention Center. Friends who organized the party seemed to think that eighty deserved a gargantuan celebration. There must have been a thousand guests, and one of the largest birthday cakes I've ever seen. President and Mrs.

Marcos attended, along with members of the Cabinet, relatives, fellow Assemblymen, and friends. It was a real gala. "I think I better plan to be abroad next year," Romy commented. "They can't do this again."

We soon followed the Mondales back to Washington for the US-ASEAN dialogue to be held there. At the ASEAN ministers' dinner for their US dialogue partners, the General introduced Mondale and told us the story of two brothers: One went to sea, one became Vice President, and neither was heard from again. The Vice President took the ribbing well.

Mrs. Marcos also attended the meetings in Washington. It gave the Asian delegations a chance to mix and meet with the State Department people and the Congress. I spent a cocktail hour talking to Senator John Glenn, whom I had heard was being considered presidential material. He struck me as a very responsible, low-key type, although I kept thinking of what FDR once said: He might be a good president, but what kind of a candidate would he make?

In New York we dropped by our old favorite restaurant, La Côte Basque, and found its owner, Madame Henriette Spalter, distraught. It seems Imelda had considered buying the restaurant and Madame, who was aging and anxious to be relieved of the burden and return to Paris, was thrilled at the prospect, then disenchanted and bitter. "She had my hopes up and then just backed out with no explanation."

Weeping, she told us the restaurant represented her life's work. She had built it up by herself and now all the plans for the sale had gone up in smoke. She clearly felt betrayed; the deal must have been well under way before the Marcos people dumped it—a deal that probably served as a practice run for Imelda's later acquisitions in New York. As we left the restaurant I heard my husband say to her, quietly and with great dignity, "Forgive us, Madame."

I was touched. The greatest gift a person, especially one of rank, can bestow is to ask forgiveness. Moreover, the

General had not even had anything to do with the transaction, except for introducing Imelda to Madame and her restaurant in the first place. There was a touch of sadness in his voice that made me realize he had said this before, when, as representative of his country and its leaders, he had had to apologize for some bad behavior he himself would never have committed.

The Marcoses celebrated their 25th wedding anniversary on May 1st, 1979, with two Masses. Imelda appeared wearing a white wedding dress with a train and a huge diamond rosary that dangled below her waist. The three Marcos children and the President's mother were all present, as well as the priest who had officiated at the original ceremony. There were several hundred guests, a full symphony choir, and a champagne supper afterward. I kept thinking it must have been different the first go-round.

By now I was Mrs. Romulo, so I had graduated to the head table and sat next to the Chief Justice. During dinner Romy, who was seated beside the Justice's wife, noticed that she was being bothered by the smoker to her left, and he leaned across and asked the guest to refrain from smoking. The guest, one of Imelda's titled friends from Europe, said haughtily, "I am Prince So-and-So." To which Romy replied, so clearly I could hear it at my end of the table, "Princes went out with the nineteenth century!" Angry but silent, he snubbed out the cigarette.

The anniversary party was the inaugural event held at the remodeled Malacanang Palace. All open areas had been totally enclosed. The airy, high white ceilings were covered with narra wood (Philippine mahogany) in a carved overlapping pineapple or basketweave design, which now lent a dark, gloomy look to the public rooms. The lovely open terrace overlooking the Pasig River was walled in and added to a smaller function room to form a grand ceremonial hall with red and gilt chairs on a dais for the Marcoses. Guests were relegated to backless benches ranged on either side. The entire building had been bullet-proofed, even the ceilings.

There was still the smallish dining room upstairs, across from Imelda's music room. But the big dinners were now held down below in a large, unattractive, low-ceilinged room. Its one advantage was that guests simply walked down from the reception hall above to the dining room, instead of going outside to another building.

As their special contribution for the evening, the famous "old beauties" of Manila and their partners staged a *rigodón de honor*, a Spanish ceremonial dance that traditionally had opened all the balls in Manila. The *cabacera*, or first line, of dancers always tried to outshine one another with their gowns and jewels—and this night was no exception. It was a dazzling display of glittering *ternos* accented with diamonds, rubies, emeralds, and sapphires.

In the same month Dr. and Mrs. Kissinger came to Manila on an official visit. I was at the airport to meet them, with Mrs. Marcos. It was a very pleasant visit: Kissinger seemed so much more relaxed compared to his former tense self as Secretary of State.

The Kissinger visit coincided with the UNCTAD V conference in Manila, the largest international gathering ever hosted by the Philippines. Since the General chaired it and couldn't meet his guests at the airport I was on constant airport duty, often with Imelda. Besides the Kissingers, we met the foreign ministers and heads of state of 168 countries and the US ambassador to the United Nations, Andrew Young, and his wife.

A luncheon for the Youngs at Malacanang proved to be a gala occasion with musicians, singers, and dancers. Then I couldn't believe what I heard: The Filipinos started singing "Dixie." I whispered to our guest of honor, "I don't think your hosts realize what that song means in the United States!" And Young said, graciously, "Oh, its been okay again for the last couple years."

The month-long conference caused enormous pressures

and tensions for the General. All-day meetings plus evening socials. Two or three times he developed fever and
diarrhea and had to go bed for a few hours, just from sheer
exhaustion. Finally his personal physician, Dr. Paulo
Campos, said: "I have the solution. Let me take you to the
hospital and let Mrs. Marcos preside. Then she can have
the diarrhea!"

The closing session, with Romy presiding, lasted all
night. I sat in our bedroom, watching it on TV. We were
due to leave for the States the next day and it was obvious
Romy was tired and wanting to get through with it, and I
could pick up the asides he was making to the Secretariat
around him.

After one long resolution, he said: "Any more?"

"No, sir."

"Thank God!"

Then the microphone picked up his aside: "Don't encourage them!"

One delegate was reading his speech, very slowly. At one
long pause, Romy snapped: "Are you still there—or turning a page?"

And when the Indian delegate was slow to respond, after
being acknowledged from the podium, the General demanded: "Is India awake?"

I had already had my breakfast brought into the room,
and the light was coming in the window, when I heard him
mutter, in exasperation, "This conference will cut short my
life!"

In July of 1979 there was a Cabinet shake-up. I was glad
to see that the embattled minister Virata survived but sorry
about poor Teddy Quiazon, a nice, unpretentious fellow
who got the ax.

The story had it that the luckless Teddy was spotted by
Imelda Marcos dressed in a T-shirt and blue jeans, munch-
ing a hot dog on a street corner in New York. It was only a
matter of time until his number was up. They called the
palace massacre "Imelda's cabinet."

I attended a very social wedding one evening that summer, at which I ended up across from Mrs. Marcos at the reception. She was chatting about her latest enthusiasms—a new prison reform plan, a plan for expansion of the Heart Center. She added lightly, "I'll have them all in good shape, in case I end up there myself one day. I don't expect to die a natural death."

The man next to me said, "Do you think she really means that?"

And I said, "Anyone who has survived an assassination attempt always has that in the back of their minds, I would imagine."

In the fall of 1979, in New York, I wondered why I was socially busier than ever until it occurred to me it was the first time I was "legal." I had always been included in evening functions with the General, but now that I was officially "Mrs. Romulo" I was also included in all the daytime events for ladies.

I attended one of Mrs. Waldheim's luncheons for First Ladies. Imelda Marcos was there, as well as the First Ladies of Mexico, Colombia, the Dominican Republic, and Bulgaria. A special guest was Churchill's daughter, Lady Soames, who had just published a memoir of her mother.

Estee Lauder was also there. A few nights later at another party, the Beauty Queen called me to her side and asked, "What makeup are you wearing?"

I told her I usually wore Elizabeth Arden cosmetics.

"The Arden look is passé," she pronounced. "I'll send you some new products of mine."

And she did. But it amused me that at a very social black tie dinner she would be peddling her lipstick.

While we were still in New York that fall, the General got a call from Senator Ted Kennedy asking for a private meeting. (General Romulo had been close to the Kennedy family since he had served as ambassador in Washington during President Kennedy's administration.)

They met in New York, with Arthur Schlesinger also present. When the General later told me the gist of their meeting, I was appalled: Senator Kennedy had told Romy he should resign in order to maintain the Senator's good opinion of him. His attitude was colonial, not that of a liberal. I found that sort of superiority galling, especially at a time when the US was still suffering from very low prestige in Asia because of the Vietnam horror.

Nineteen seventy-nine was a rocky year. Iran had fallen and the Shah was fighting for his life in New York Hospital. In our part of the world, Vietnam forces were invading Cambodia, with the backing of the USSR. Refugees were flooding into Thailand and the Philippines. President Park of Korea was assassinated. Mrs. Marcos cut short her trip to New York and flew to Seoul for the funeral, but was fogbound and arrived late. Romy and I were talking about the world at this moment—the problems in the UN and the problems that lay ahead for the Philippines.

"I wish I were twenty years younger!" Romy said.

He was thinking in terms of his own experiences, background, and fund of diplomatic knowledge and how it could be put to good use, either nationally or internationally in such perilous times.

"What would you do?" I asked.

"I'd be President of the Philippines or Secretary-General of the United Nations." (He had in fact been proposed as Secretary-General by the United States but was vetoed by the Soviets in the 1950's.)

I told him not to give up the thought. After all, Adenauer served his country at the age of eighty-four!

The Hospital Circuit

GENERAL Romulo and I attended a memorable dinner at Manila's Mandarin Hotel in early February of 1980. The first course was fresh foie gras flown in that day from Paris. Romy ate it, then excused himself and came back to the table a few minutes later and whispered, "I have to leave." In the car, I helped him loosen his cummerbund. Sweat was pouring down his face. He was having a full-scale gallbladder attack—brought on by the fresh fois gras—and was in great pain.

We had him in the hospital by the next day. After his fever subsided, he underwent surgery. He asked me to be present in the operating room and I was—and appeared later on television in mask and gown to announce the operation was a success.

It was to be the first of six hospitalizations that year. Twice he was hospitalized for heart irregularities; twice for flu; and once for a second surgery, a follow-up to the gallbladder operation, since he was unfortunate enough to develop an infection that required a fistulectomy.

Yet somehow he managed to carry on his duties as foreign minister. His staff from the ministry manned the front room of his hospital suite, accepting the many flowers, fruits, and telegrams, and taking dictation from him when he felt like it.

By May we were back in the travel circuit again, attending the Disarmament Conference in New York, then a conference on Kampuchea in Geneva. In June the General had to check into Imelda's huge, beautiful Heart Center for tests, yet in July he was in New York. The second surgery was performed in August, but the following month we were in residence at the Waldorf Towers as usual, attending the United Nations General Assembly.

Before leaving for New York, Romy got a call from the President, who informed him that he had decided to cancel the visit of President Pinochet of Chile. There was no secretary around (it was a Saturday), so I turned into a long-distance runner, scrambling for the telephone numbers of the Chilean ambassador, the Deputy Minister, and the Director of Protocol. President Pinochet had already left Chile and was on his way to the Philippines.

I think they finally reached him and informed him of President Marcos's decision in Guam or maybe Fiji. But it was a close call, since he was due to arrive on Monday and all the plans had been made for the official visit. This was the first time I had seen such a reaction to an official visit. A UN resolution had been issued against him and Japan had already refused to receive him.

We finally located the unfortunate Chilean ambassador, who had been enjoying a family lunch in a restaurant in Makati. The news certainly ruined his lunch. It also ruined his diplomatic career. President Pinochet was so angry that he recalled him and he was retired from the diplomatic service.

The official excuse for cancellation of the visit was that there were "threats" against Pinochet and that the Philippines could not guarantee his safety. When all our frantic calls had been made, and the General was dressed and waiting for the unfortunate ambassador to call on him, I asked Romy what might have made the President change his mind at such a late hour.

"My memo," he said quietly. He never told me what was in his memo but I guessed it had to do with the UN position, which was always closest to his heart.

Imelda was in New York that fall while Romy and I were there. Secretary-General Waldheim invited Imelda and us, along with several other special guests, including Pierre Trudeau, the Prime Minister of Canada, to share his box at a United Nations concert. I was seated on Trudeau's left, Imelda on his right. A gracious, somewhat flirtatious man, he gave us "equal time."

Later, when his name came up, I said to Mrs. Marcos, "Remember the evening we shared him at the UN concert?"

She didn't like that. "Oh, I've seen him since then," she said coldly. "And he has accepted my invitation to visit Manila."

It was quite clear that I was out of line for implying we were "girls together."

This was one of my problems with Imelda. I was never free to speak spontaneously and say what crossed my mind, since a carefree statement might offend her. Once when she was singing under her breath, I commented that some American friends had asked me if Imelda sang a good deal, and I told them, "All you have to do is coax—and wait." She was clearly not amused and stopped singing. I had not meant it unkindly: She sings well and enjoys it, and I didn't see anything wrong with her wanting to perform whenever possible.

But at least with me she was not capable of exchanging ordinary banter. She only wanted to hear things that were "good" and "beautiful" and entirely favorable to her, the Marcos administration, or her family. Once when I was

working on an article that included an economic picture of
the Philippines and I mentioned something to her about
the high rate of "under-employment" (as well as unem-
ployment) that plagued the country—one person with a
part-time job who was sole support for an entire family—
she turned and gave me such a withering look that I never
spoke of such matters again in her presence.

Another time we had just come into the Waldorf from a
very confused time at a New Jersey airport (she was traveling by private plane, which could not land at Kennedy)
where they kept running us from one side of the arrivals
building to another, with all her well-wishers scattering like
a flock of confused hens, clutching their bouquets, I observed to her, "They sure didn't give you a very well organized greeting this time, did they?" She fixed me with a
cold stare, then called to one of her minions and, fishing a
typed sheet out of her voluminous handbag, said, "Why
don't you serve Mrs. Romulo champagne in the study
where she can read this uninterrupted."

I took the paper, and properly chastened, went to the
library.

There was no possibility for an honest exchange, as one
would have with a friend. Anyone around her was supposed
to support her all the way and agree to everything—which
they did. While some of her projects were actually quite
good, others were sheer disasters because no one had had
the nerve to point out what was wrong.

It was always easier to talk to President Marcos. He
could tolerate questions or, to a certain extent, criticism,
but then never answered the point. He talked around questions in astute legalistic circles until you'd quite lost track
of what it was you had asked. Anyone watching his TV
interviews can see the President's style in action: After the
interviewer asked a question, Marcos would repeat the first
phrase as though he were going to answer, but then
launched into a diatribe on something else. He was a real

master of the sidestep. Questions made Imelda angry, but her husband always remained composed and cool.

In the fall of 1979 Ronald Reagan defeated Jimmy Carter, and we had a new team in the US to deal with—which actually was a pleasure for both Romy and the Marcoses. The Marcoses had picked Reagan as a front-runner while he was still Governor of California. The Reagans had been persuaded to visit Manila, and the Marcoses stayed in close touch with them ever since. They were elated that they had a friend in the White House at last.

In early December, just before we were to return to Manila, Romy paid a call on his old friend Richard Nixon, whose views on China he shared. Nixon was suffering from the flu and set the meeting in his residence, where he was recuperating. That evening at a farewell party we hosted, Romy didn't seem well, and that night he became feverish and disoriented. I canceled our departure and went with him to New York Hospital. It was frightening to have strange doctors assume his disorientation was the "normal" condition of an eighty-one-year-old. I kept telling them it was the result of high fever. "This is *not* my husband!" I remember snapping in frustration at a resident.

We finally stumbled home two weeks later, when he could travel. When his birthday rolled around in January, Romy announced he had no interest in a big party, and instead received guests at the house. I was a little shaken by the fact that five hundred people appeared to call on him. Fortunately the protocol department, which understands these things better than I, had ordered plenty of catered refreshments sent in.

In February of 1981, Pope John Paul II made a long-awaited visit to the predominantly Catholic Philippines. The arrival ceremonies were set for eight in the morning and we all had to be dressed according to instructions from the palace, each person carrying his own special pass. (Years before there had been an attempted assassination against Pope Paul VI at the Manila airport, and so the security was very tight.)

All the Cabinet ladies wore their new white *ternos*, with matching white parasols. Imelda was also, of course, in white—the color she had been denied at the Vatican.

Some months before, she had ordered a special stretch limo for the Pope's visit. The maroon limo was out at the airport waiting for the Pope, but he would have none of it. He also turned down Imelda's offer to stay in the Coconut Palace, a fascinating structure, shingled with coconut husks, its pillars covered with coconut bark, and bathrooms tiled with coconut shell, which she had had built for his arrival. The Pope chose instead to stay at the *nunciatura*.

During his visit to the Philippines, Imelda positioned herself close to the Pope at all times. When he flew to the provinces, she flew in ahead, so she could always be seen greeting him when he landed. Every news picture of the Pope included Imelda.

But he accepted none of her lavish hospitality, except for one reception at Malacanang Palace at which all the Cabinet and diplomatic corps met him. The Filipinas couldn't understand why I didn't kneel; Presbyterian that I am, I really didn't know how, and simply bobbed my head and shook hands.

At the private audience arranged by the papal nuncio for the Romulo family, Pope John Paul singled me out from the Asian faces and said, with that piercing blue stare, "You're European." "No, American," I told him. This time, with all my daughters-in-law kissing his ring, I made a stab at performing this Catholic ritual. I missed and ended up kissing his hand.

Accustomed to more ascetic-looking popes, I marveled at his physique. A powerful looking man, with strong, sloping shoulders, he looks as if he could work in the field all day. A good shepherd indeed.

We were at home, asleep, in our house in Manila, when we were wakened early on the morning of March 31, by a call from Consul Abaya at the Philippine Mission in New York. "President Reagan has been shot. He is still alive." Then the phones all began ringing, asking the General for a statement about the shooting.

I thought of Eldridge Cleaver's comment: "Violence is as American as cherry pie."

Fortunately, Reagan survived. But it was just one more reminder of how utterly vulnerable presidents are.

I am surprised that Marcos has lasted so long. He did tell me once there had been seven assassination attempts against him, but I think they were abortive plots only; no one got in firing range.

Being with the General was a daily lesson in diplomacy. In March of that year, he was guest of honor at a dinner given by the Philippine Ambassadors Association and attended by all the diplomatic corps. In his speech, he called attention to the recent Russian invasion of Afghanistan, whereupon the Russian ambassador bounced up, crying, "I object!" The other guests hissed and booed him for the interruption, but General Romulo with perfect equanimity bowed to the ambassador and said when he was finished with his speech he would be glad to give him equal time. And, at the end, he did turn over the floor to the ambassador, who blustered for awhile in defense of Mother Russia. Everyone was angry except Romy: "He has to defend his country. That's his job."

President Marcos, in a gesture toward the restoration of democratic principles, lifted martial law that year and put himself up for presidential reelection. No one seemed surprised when he was proclaimed the people's choice (the Marcos political machine was known to be so limitlessly rich and powerful that no one bothered to put up much opposition). An inaugural was set for June and dignitaries invited from all over the world.

In May the Marcoses gave a luncheon for Prince Faisal of Saudi Arabia. As luck would have it, since the prince had no wife and the wife of the Saudi ambassador was ill, I ended up seated beside President Marcos. We had a pleasant, wide-ranging chat discussing everything from gun control (he said since the US has a tradition of private citizens owning guns, guns should be allowed in residences but outlawed elsewhere—something like the way he handled the Moros in Mindanao who felt emasculated if they gave up their arms) to jungle survival—which was the subject of my current article. I hadn't been so close to him in a number of months, and was surprised to note that his eyes didn't look normal. Formerly they had a diamond-sharp glitter and now their color was dulled and they watered. I wondered what his ailment was. Later I was to learn that renal disease dulls the eyes and also results in a peculiar breath.

The Philippines hosted an ASEAN ministerial meeting in June. At the opening ceremonies, held at the Philippine Conference Center, Romy and I waited for Mrs. Marcos at the door, then escorted her in to the conference hall. She was to make the welcoming address. As I handed her a bouquet of flowers and walked at her side through the giant lobby, I commented that I was glad the elections were over without incident. "Thank God!" she said.

President Reagan's first Secretary of State, Alexander Haig, caught up with our ASEAN conference in Manila, for the final days, when observers attended. By now the ASEAN had become sufficiently important internationally that the US, Japan, and the countries of the European Economic Community regularly sent observers for the open sessions.

I liked Mrs. Haig from the moment she walked off the

plane with her husband. Girlishly slender, pretty, and soft-spoken, she is the perfect foil for her husband's brusk, hearty vitality.

As the wife of the Foreign Minister, I ended up sitting beside Secretary Haig at a palace luncheon and at the General's luncheon for him. A vital and attractive man, Haig is also extremely volatile and bombastic. I said to my husband: "Haig is charming but he's so thunderous. So Type A. How can he be a Secretary of State? A general, yes, but not a diplomat. They have to be cool."

When it was his time to speak, Secretary Haig told the joke about a patient who wanted a brain transplant and was offered the medical supermarket: a diplomat's brain for $10,000; a banker's for $20,000; a foreign minister's for $30,000; and a general's for $40,000. Why so high for the general's brain? "Because it's brand new. Never been used."

That got a good laugh. I enjoyed Haig but after spending a few hours with him, I came away with my first impression unaltered. "He simply doesn't have the temperament for a Secretary of State. I can't imagine he will last on the job."

He didn't. When I saw him later in Washington, after he had been replaced, he was bitter and blamed his departure in part on Nancy Reagan.

I was telling him about a list that had been published in one of the news magazines, rating the First Ladies of America in popularity. I think Jacqueline Kennedy and Lady Bird Johnson were among the first three.

"What about Nancy?" he asked.

Mrs. Reagan had not yet achieved popularity in the early part of the Reagan administration. "She was 28th," I told him.

"Too high!" snapped Al Haig. "Too high!"

The Marcos inaugural was a splendid event, with its bevy of distinguished guests and all-day festivities culminating in a ball at Malacanang Palace. Japan sent its foreign minister; President Reagan sent Vice President and Mrs. Bush and a rather large delegation that included Clare Boothe Luce.

Imelda Marcos, General Romulo, and I were all at the airport to greet the US delegation. I had seen the Bushes several times in New York—they were close friends of General Romulo—but this was the first time I had seen them in action on a political mission. I'll never forget the way Barbara Bush came off that plane—like a great, warm, all-embracing wave of friendship and goodwill. I had found her white hair a bit matronly, especially in contrast to her husband's rather preppy good looks. But at that instant it was beautiful—a white halo in the sunlight, framing her marvelous wide smile. And I realized what a enormous political asset she is. I commented once to Mrs. Holdridge (wife of the Undersecretary of State for Asian Affairs) about Barbara Bush's political appeal, and she observed that sometimes events come along in one's life that call for maximizing latent talents and abilities. And that was true of Barbara. She was at her best in her current role, although she had been primarily a wife and mother until her husband became Vice President. Her friendliness is genuine. She really likes people. The emotional Manilans responded to her warmth and she was tremendously popular during that visit.

Barbara Bush appeared at the inaugural ball in a stunning purple evening gown with hand-sewn paillettes and sequins that Imelda had had made especially for her. It looked striking with her statuesque height and white hair.

In July we went to New York, and from there to Cancún, Mexico, where the foreign ministers met to prepare for the Cancún Economic Summit. Lord Carrington was there for Mrs. Thatcher; Hans Dietrich Genscher was there for Chancellor Schmidt; General Romulo for President Marcos. The Chinese attended, and the Russians sent their regrets.

The Cancún resort had just been opened and the best thing about it was its short distance by air from New York. The Filipinos in our delegation didn't think it looked like much: just a strip of sandy beach and some new hotels. It wasn't special by Philippine standards, but I assured them that to be able to fly less than two hours and reach sun and sand in winter is sheer heaven for New Yorkers.

There was a whirlpool tub on the terrace of our suite, which I coaxed the General to try. He was so delighted with it that I was forced to order one for our house in Manila.

That September, in New York, General Romulo was awarded the UN Medal for Peace. And at the end of the month, he served for the third time as President of the Security Council. An old hand at this type of diplomacy, he held private meetings constantly and tried to thrash out sticky problems between the representatives before the Council actually met in session.

While we were still in New York, we attended a dinner at the Jordanian embassy in honor of the Crown Prince of Jordan, the younger brother of King Hussein. A small, compactly built man with black hair and dark, alert eyes in a lively and pleasant face, he was more informal and friendlier than his brother and quite easy to talk to. The Crown Prince explained that he was a student in London when he lost his parents and that after the newspapers wrote about the lonely young prince, the Ambassador of Bangladesh invited him to his embassy. He and the ambassador's daughter practically "grew up together" after that and eventually married. The Princess was young, pretty, and as friendly as her husband.

I was surprised and delighted to find myself seated to the Prince's left. At one point I commented that he must have had a big lunch because he wasn't eating. He told me he had lunched with the editors of *Newsweek* who kept grilling him, and since he could not eat and answer at the same time, he came home hungry and sent out for a hamburger, which spoiled his appetite for dinner. He made an excellent extemporaneous speech acknowledging all the guests present. Secretary-General Kurt Waldheim responded and offered a toast to him. "Oh, I forgot the toast," the Prince said. Then, looking over at my glass, "And you've drunk your champagne. Here, I'll share with you," and he dumped half his glass in mine.

"But you don't have to toast anyone, do you?" I asked. And he didn't.

In early December, before returning to Manila, we made an official visit to Madrid: Romy had finally succeeded in getting an ambassador installed there, and he also knew that I wanted to see Spain.

While there I heard from one of the embassy staff what had gone wrong for Imelda in Madrid. She had come to Madrid without an official invitation, then expected to be received by the King and Queen. Not only did the King not receive her, she was not so much as invited to tea with the Queen. She had heard that Queen Sofia admired the beautiful old-fashioned type of Spanish mantilla that is still handmade in the Philippines, the *mantón de Manilla*, and she had brought four as her gift to the Queen. They were returned to her by the Queen's secretary, who explained that since this was not an official visit the Queen would not be able to receive her, nor accept her gifts.

We were given a surprisingly warm and hospitable reception in Madrid. Romy seemed in his element, chatting in the beautiful courtly Spanish he had learned from his father. I found the wives of the Cabinet members quite elegant and charming. And the manners and grace of the men—it was a very young Cabinet, it seemed to me— made me realize why so many women prefer Spaniards.

Before we returned to Manila that fall, we accompanied our old friend Jean MacArthur up to West Point for a memorial service for her late husband at which General Romulo was the principal speaker. We were guests of the commandant in the historic old house where MacArthur had lived when he headed the Academy, then we went to the nearby inn for luncheon.

It was a pretty, warm day, and I was strolling out on the lawn with some of the other guests. Inside the restaurant, one of the American generals was talking to Romy and looked out at the lawn.

"General," he said, "how did you happen to find such a pretty American girl?"

Without batting an eyelash, Romy answered: "Why don't you go ask her how she found such a distinguished Filipino?"

The Edifice Complex

IMELDA began buying New York real estate properties in the fall of 1981. With her friends the Reagans firmly in office, I suppose she felt free to spend as she wished without fear of criticism or reprisal from the US government.

The first I knew of it was one afternoon that fall when she summoned me to her apartment in the Waldorf Towers, patted the sofa invitingly for me to sit beside her, and began to chat about her latest activities. I think she liked telling me about what she was doing in New York—the people she saw socially and the investments she made—because, unlike her traveling companions from Manila, I was a New Yorker and could identify and appreciate the names and places she mentioned.

Her eyes were bright with excitement, her tone low and conspiratorial. "You know the Crown Building?" she asked me.

"You mean the building at the corner of Fifth and 57th?" I asked. "The one with I. Miller shoes on the ground floor?"

"Yes," she smiled, in triumph. "What do you think of it?"

Think of it? I swallowed. This was harder for me to envision than rubies. "We'll, it's one of the most prestigious office buildings in midtown Manhattan," I finally said.

"I think I'll buy it!" she told me.

I couldn't wait to get back to our suite and report to my husband. "Imelda says she's going to buy the Crown Building!"

He shook his head. "She's nuts."

It had never occurred to either of us that one person, rather than a consortium of investors, would buy an entire building. Actually, as we were to learn later, the Crown Building was her second New York City real estate investment.

The first was the Herald Center building on 34th Street. She met, at the Waldorf Towers, with Joseph and Ralph Bernstein on November 10 of that year to ask them to represent her for the acquisition of Herald Center. She told the Bernstein brothers that she wanted to make it into a showcase for the retailing of Philippine goods.

As for the Crown Building, she told the Bernsteins she liked its "old world charm" and thought that it would be a "nice counterpoint" to the modern Trump Tower. She also gave them two different reasons for launching her real estate projects. The first was "for her children." Later she said it was to make a profit on the buildings in advance of the 1987 presidential elections in the Philippines. At Christmas of the same year, the Bernsteins later testified, she waved a Swiss bank statement in front of the nose of one of them over dinner at the Sign of the Dove. It showed $120 million on deposit.

Imelda kept changing the story of why she needed so much money abroad, and such large investments. One version, which she told a close friend, was so that the Marcoses could always "buy back" the Philippine government in the event of a Communist takeover. Apparently she believed that the Marcos dynasty could go on indefinitely, provided they always had enough cash to spend.

When stories of her mammoth investments in New York began to filter back to Manila, Imelda was accused of gross extravagance—but the President still came up roses. No one seemed to believe he had anything to do with it. Yet the Bernsteins testified that they traveled to Manila in the spring of 1982 and met with President Marcos himself three times. As a lawyer, he wanted to learn how the tax structure was set up via the Netherlands Antilles companies through which the real estate money was washed. (Mrs. Marcos's name did not appear on any documents. There was a complicated web of offshore companies designed to conceal the actual ownership.)

Once she got in the swing of it, Imelda enjoyed being a Manhattan landlord. She purchased 200 Madison Avenue and 40 Wall Street. Then, she boasted, she bought across the city with buildings eastside and westside, uptown and downtown. "My husband," she once told Ambassador S. P. Lopez, when he was her seatmate on a flight, "likes gold bullion. But I prefer buildings."

The Marcoses also purchased a house in New Jersey for their daughter, Imee, to live in while she attended Princeton. And there was a large seaside estate, known as Lindemere, on Long Island, complete with boat dock and helipad, where Imelda sometimes entertained her New York and European friends.

She also continued to acquire or build real estate in the Philippines. She built family guest houses all over the islands, in Leyte, Bataan, Ilocos, and Canlubang. The Marcoses may have stayed one night or two at these fully furnished homes but they never lived in any of them.

Imelda ordered the creation of a palace guest house directly across the circular drive from Malacanang. (Today President Corazon Aquino uses it as her office.) Originally built to house palace staff, the building was opulently redone for VIP guests. The entry is stunning, a huge double-story room with capiz chandeliers and narra-vaulted ceilings. There is a downstairs meeting room and a library and his-and-her master suites on the upper level.

At the time she was anticipating a visit from Colonel Qaddafi, Imelda had a mosque built in the Quiapo section of Manila, as well as a "Mosque-ito"—as she called it—on the palace grounds, behind the guest house, so that the visiting Moslems would have a convenient place to pray. Imelda told me she had the beautiful gold dome brought from Rome.

When the Philippine Consulate in New York outgrew its quarters in the charming old brownstone off Fifth Avenue on 66th Street and moved into the former Schrafft's building at 46th and Fifth, the 66th Street property was supposed to be sold and the proceeds used to help pay for the new building. However, the brownstone caught Mrs. Marcos's eye, and after looking it over she decided to make it into a townhouse for her own use. She told me that then she wouldn't have to stay at the Waldorf Towers whenever she came to New York; she claimed it would "save the government a lot of money" in the long run. Since she already had the use of several beautifully furnished apartments joined together at the Olympic Towers, her reasoning struck me as a bit specious. But once she had her heart set on a project—especially if it involved a building—there was no stopping her.

I don't know what the final cost was, but Imelda brought in fleets of decorators and designers from Manila who worked round the clock (she believed in 24-hour labor) repairing the old brownstone. A disco was added on the top floor, to indulge her love of midnight partying. The famous Samuels Collection of art and antique furniture that she purchased in toto for $6 million found its way to the town-house also.

Imelda loved to give small dinners there. One was for Adnan Khashoggi, the Saudi multimillionaire. Another was for Armand Hammer, whom she hoped to lure into Philippine investment. Hammer's Occidental Petroleum did some oil exploration in the Philippines, but insiders said Hammer was more interested in selling Imelda art from the Hammer Galleries than in drilling for Philippine oil. Still another dinner was for the King of Morocco, whom she had visited and apparently had her eye on for personal reasons. "I don't know whether she had a crush on him, or was just excited about having such a rich and attractive friend," said one of her Blue Ladies. "He was a Humphrey Bogart type—one of those weary, sophisticated faces." Apparently he didn't want to be seen coming in the front door of the townhouse and used the fire escape instead.

Kokoy hounded the Philippine consul general in New York to transfer ownership in the building at 66th Street to Mrs. Marcos.

"But it's government property," he protested.

"Oh, come on," Kokoy wheedled. "She loves it. Sign it over to her for her birthday."

Fortunately for the government of the Philippines and its impoverished treasury, Ambassador Pineda held out and the townhouse still belongs to the Philippines.

Kokoy was not above strong-arm tactics when he felt his sister had been slighted. When the Beatles came to Manila for a concert in 1966, Imelda sent word that they should appear at Malacanang Palace for a command performance. Booked into the Rizal Memorial Stadium for a public performance, the Beatles sent back word to the palace that if anyone there wanted to see them, they should come to the stadium like everyone else. In short, they chose to turn down her invitation.

The day the Beatles left Manila, they were roughed up

physically by two rows of goons who kicked, spat, and punched at them as they ran from the airport building to their plane. George Harrison later recounted that not only were they abused at the airport, but that they were not allowed to leave Manila until their manager gave back the money they earned in the concert. Not surprisingly, it was the last time they ever played the Philippines.

After Imelda began to assert increasing authority in all phases of the government, her brother followed suit by interfering everywhere he could get a toehold. Businesses miraculously came under his ownership, although no papers were signed and no money was known to be exchanged. To my husband's great irritation, Kokoy gradually built up what amounted to a shadow foreign ministry in a house on Aguado Street, near the palace. Orders were issued from there, names came through for appointment, certain individuals in the ministry were clearly committed to Kokoy and his machinations rather than to their true minister. The only recourse the General had, when he found proof of this meddling, was to take matters personally to the President. He was thus able to head off some disastrous and inappropriate appointments in the foreign service, apparently doled out by Kokoy in exchange for political patronage for his sister. Once, when the General caught Kokoy red-handed in some meddling, he stopped him in the reception hall of the palace and in front of several members of the Cabinet snapped, "Who do you think you are? You are nothing but the brother-in-law of the President—and a nincompoop at that!"

When that scene was reported to me I grew frightened. The Marcoses and the Romualdezes can be vindictive; they do not tolerate criticism or disloyalty easily. They all live by the rule: "You are with us or you are our enemy." But I had forgotten about what stuff bullies are made of. The next time Kokoy saw my husband, he knelt, apologized, and kissed his hand (in the Philippines younger people still kiss the hands of the venerable as a gesture of respect).

Few people aside from his sister and perhaps his wife have much love for Kokoy. Yet the President always found him useful. He once told my husband that Imelda and Kokoy were better instinctive politicians than he was.

The front man for his sister, and also for both the President and Mrs. Marcos when they traveled together, Kokoy was briefly appointed Philippine ambassador to China and then to Saudi Arabia when the Marcoses were to make a state visit there. In 1982 he was appointed by the President as Philippine ambassador to Washington. When General Romulo protested that no person without diplomatic training or skills should be named ambassador to the country around which 80 percent of Philippine foreign policy revolved, the President reassured him: "It's only to prepare for our [official] visit. Kokoy knows how to do that. We will send him somewhere else as soon as we have made our trip."

Unfortunately, like many other glib Marcos promises, this was not kept. Kokoy remained ambassador to Washington while serving concurrently as the nominal Governor of Leyte and member of the Philippine legislature. What he actually did was work for his sister. In New York, whenever I went to the airport for one of Imelda's arrivals, he was always ahead of me—sitting and waiting.

I knew Kokoy's wife and his children and was, in fact, quite fond of them.

Slender, pretty in a shy, soft way, Juliette Romualdez is an educated, ladylike woman. Religious, cultured, she is the precise opposite of her conniving, often vulgar husband. It was one of those marriages that is difficult to understand. "One of the great mismatches of Manila," as one Filipina friend put it.

I saw Kokoy on numerous occasions at the palace or in hotel restaurants before I ever laid eyes on his wife—and

then only by chance, at a restaurant near the airport on a
Sunday noon, a place where no doubt he felt sure he would
not meet any of his friends. It is a Filipino restaurant,
created specially for tourists. I had suggested to Romy we
make the drive there, for a change of scenery, on this pretty
day.

Kokoy was obviously startled to see us among the tourists, but we were introduced. I was immediately drawn to
Juliette's sweet face and gentle manner and wondered, privately, where on earth he had found her. Their children
were with them—three sons, two of whom later proved to
be talented in photography and writing, and a daughter, as
angelic in appearance as her mother.

When I asked around as to why I had never seen Kokoy's
wife before, I was told she was kept under virtual house
arrest. While Kokoy floated around, doing his sister's bid-
ding in all manner of nefarious deals, Juliette remained at
home. She was not allowed to visit friends or receive them
in her house even for lunch. In lieu of normal social relations, she appears to have turned to God and become very
religious (she is a member of the extremely conservative
Catholic group known as Opus Dei). Her former classmates
refer to Juliette as Little Bo-Peep. The only time I ever
saw her when she seemed relaxed, natural, and enjoying
herself was when her husband was ambassador to Washington and was obliged to produce a visible, socially active
wife who was allowed to receive callers and to entertain.

People were always trying to please Imelda and ingrati-
ate themselves with her. When called upon to introduce
her, they would practically drool with allusions to her
beauty and accomplishments. I used to fantasize, when I
was listening to one of those long-winded embarrassing
introductions: it would be refreshing if one day, after hear-
ing all that slop, she would stand up, smile sweetly and say
"Bullshit." But she never did. She soaked up flattery like a
desert soaks up rain. There was never enough. It bothered

me, as I saw her develop over the years and become more mature, more self-assured, stronger in her self-image, that she never could see through the flattery. Her appetite for attention was bottomless.

One of the most shameless examples of this was when Deputy Minister of Foreign Affairs of the USSR, Mikhail Kapitsa, visited Manila.

Imelda had made a number of trips to Russia, mainly to do with cultural exchange, and she frequently entertained Russian guests. It was clear, from the start of the palace dinner, that the big, wily Russian had sized up his hostess and got her number. I never heard such blatant flattery from a guest: "The most beautiful woman in the world," etcetera, etcetera. She giggled like a schoolgirl.

It seemed to me that the First Lady's greatest weakness as a political figure was that she could not deal with people who would tell her the truth. The ones she was close to either promised her the throne (like General Ver) or shamelessly flattered and cajoled her (like her assistant Minister of Human Settlements, Conrado Benitez, and her favorite architect, George Ramos, who must have accumulated an enormous fortune building all those grandiose buildings).

She liked to believe that she was enormously loved by her people, and no one dared tell her when her popularity began to waver.

The Beginning of the Fall

B<small>Y</small> the early 1980s it was becoming clear to observers that President Marcos's health was deteriorating and that he was suffering from some chronic disorder. This was denied by a wall of lies from the palace. "He is writing a book." "He has a slight allergy." "He has a slight cold and is staying in." Medical experts suggested that he was suffering from lupus erythematosus, a chronic and progressive disease that can attack any organ of the body. This would account for his occasional bloated look, since the disease is often treated with cortisone. He was also suffering from kidney disease, which the palace stridently denied. That was one subject that even the General was not allowed to tease him about. Once, after the General himself was beginning to have kidney problems, he commented that he and the President and Russian premier Yuri Andropov were in distinguished company. The President angrily denied that he had kidney disease.

The more physical problems her husband had, the more actively Imelda meddled in affairs of state. She was already responsible for the forced resignation of several members of the Cabinet and the foreign service. It was becoming increasingly clear who were her enemies and who were her favorites.

Whenever she was out of the country, Imelda worried that there might be a coup back home and was alert to all the rumors. She was in New York in the fall of 1975 when she called the President one day. He was being briefed by his efficient executive secretary, Alejandro Melchor, in his office when the red phone rang—the one that only the President answers. Imelda told him, in great excitement, that she had just been informed that Secretary Melchor was about to stage a coup and that a force of several thousand men were poised to take over Malacanang Palace. Her voice was so loud and excited that Melchor, sitting there, could hear all she was saying. Embarrassed, he simply left the room.

The office of Executive Secretary was soon abolished and Melchor found himself out of a job. Later he served as the Philippine representative to the Asian Development Bank.

Melchor had been in a position of considerable power and a few in the Cabinet believed he might have been planning to try to oust the President. On the contrary, however, my husband thought losing him was a pity, since he had been an excellent aide and the President's schedule and appointments fell into disorder after he left.

When we returned to Manila after Melchor's ouster, I asked twelve people what the reason was for his dismissal and got twelve different answers ranging from his desire to be President to his fights with Imelda. I'm sure if I had asked twenty-seven people I would have received twenty-seven different answers. Filipinos are such inventive gossips that if they don't have facts, they simply make up a good story.

I imagine the real reason stemmed from his fights with

Imelda. A plainspoken naval engineer, Alex tended to be frank and that was something Imelda could not tolerate.

Imelda hated anyone who put any obstacle in the way of her own imperious desire. Perhaps her greatest bête noire in the Cabinet was Defense Minister Enrile (who has since also caused trouble for President Aquino). The source of their feud seems trivial on the face of it. Immediately after martial law was declared, Enrile was given the responsibility of handling the travel ban. The mother of a Mrs. Manglapus (daughter-in-law of the expatriate opposition leader Raul Manglapus) asked Imelda to intercede so that her daughter could come to Manila to give birth, and then rejoin her husband in Tokyo. Imelda promised to take care of it. But when the woman appeared at Enrile's office, the request was turned down since it didn't fall in their guidelines. Later that day Enrile was attending a meeting in the palace when a telephone call came in to him from the First Lady. She screamed so loud the others could hear her: "You are swell-headed! But I can tell you this this—I am going to destroy you!"

"She never forgave me," recalled Enrile. "In her view, I had embarrassed her. I was insisting on applying the rules. She wanted to violate them by giving preference as she chose. I became a pariah."

Following that incident Imelda pointedly ignored both Enrile and his wife, Cristina. Cristina stopped going to Malacanang.

Imelda's hatred for Enrile seems larger than the incident would justify. He had failed to obey her—a cardinal sin apparently. The job of supervising the travel ban was soon given to someone else. But she appears to have thought that he might also be an obstacle in the way of her own secret ambitions. People spoke of the Defense Minister as "presidential" material and that was probably the real source of her hatred. She had him put under surveillance by Ver's men. When he campaigned for the Assembly in his own province, she threw her support, and funding, behind the opposition candidate. But Enrile won anyway.

Enrile's falling out with the President was not so abrupt as with Imelda. "We drifted apart a few years after martial law." The President critized Enrile's handling of political detainees. "He thought I was too liberal with the people under detention. I was being scolded much of the time." Marcos was also somewhat suspicious of Enrile's political ambitions.

While it was hard to discredit General Fidel Ramos, who was known as "Mr. Clean," Imelda also considered him a possible obstacle to her political ambitions, and she used her influence to keep him out of power. In 1981, when Chief of Staff Romeo Espino was due to retire, Espino and Enrile recommended that Ramos become Chief of Staff. The President agreed, and called his Defense Minister on the phone. "I'm appointing Eddie Ramos and I'm going to announce it." Delighted, Enrile notified Ramos. But Imelda insisted that the job go to her cohort, General Ver. The President then lamely attempted to justify the change by claiming that Ver was more senior, when in fact Ramos was. He finally got an "opinion" from his Minister of Justice to justify naming Ver.

It appeared, from the outside, that it was the President who always clung to Ver. But in fact, it was Imelda. He was her hope of taking the presidency. All palace security arrangements were in the hands of either Ver himself or one of his sons. In the event of the President's death, they intended to withhold the news for at least two days—long enough to arrest members of the Cabinet and military who might oppose Imelda's ascendancy. Heading that list were, of course, Defense Minister Enrile and General Ramos.

When Ver was named Chief of Staff, one of the Blue Ladies overheard the President saying to Ver, "You better thank the First Lady. You owe this to her."

A Cabinet member Imelda was especially hard on was Cesar Virata, the Minister of Finance and Prime Minister, who took his role as the "conscience" of the Cabinet seriously, and opposed a number of her grandiose projects. In official gatherings, she gave him no importance, and it was my protocol-minded husband who kept insisting the Prime Minister be given his proper place. The President, however, recognized that Virata was respected abroad in the international banking community, and so protected him even when Virata dared to say no to Imelda.

In 1982 the First Lady asked for public funding for her international film festival. Minister Virata blocked the request. Miffed, Imelda raised the money she wanted by allowing movie houses in Manila to screen previously banned pornographic films.

In a Cabinet meeting, Mrs. Marcos accused Virata of treating her ministry as if it were "an enemy." Her friend, and her husband's crony, Bobby Benedicto, also chimed in to attack Virata for his austerity measures and stringent policies.

But Imelda plodded along with her grandiose schemes, despite the downhill trend of her country's economy. She also ignored some bad omens. When she first decided to launch her International Film Festival, she had built a huge building that was designed on the lines of the Parthenon.

As usual with her last-minute projects, the building was still under completion when it was nearing time for the festival, and construction was rushed, round the clock. The cement was not given time to dry properly. An entire floor collapsed and caved in on the floor below. According to the Marcos-controlled press, 28 workers were killed in the accident. Rumor had it that 168 had died. Betty Benitez (wife of Imelda's Assistant Minister, Conrado Benitez), who was in charge of the project for the First Lady, was called to the scene. The mothers and wives of the men who died had come to claim the bodies. But the building was due to open for the festival, and Betty ordered, "Pour the cement." The bodies of the dead workers were thus covered over so that the relatives could not claim them. The women put a curse on her.

A few months later Betty Benitez was herself killed in a bizarre accident. She was a passenger in a car driven by O. D. Corpus, a former president of the University of the Philippines. They were on their way to Tagaytay at night. (It was never made clear why they were out driving in the middle of the night away from their respective spouses and families.) Betty was killed instantly when the car ran off the road on a curve and smashed into a tree. Corpus survived.

Manilans soon said the film festival building was haunted, and many refused to work there or go inside to see films. Imee Marcos called in a medium, who was said to be able to communicate with the dead, and brought him to the film festival building. The medium went into a trance. Normally, he spoke only in his native dialect. But in the trance, he suddenly spoke out in English:

"Now there are 169," he intoned. "Betty is with us."

One of the international events Imelda wished most to attend was the wedding of Prince Charles. The guest list was actually limited to very few foreigners, and the Marcoses were not among them. Knowing that her ambassador in London, Mike Stilianopulos, was a close personal friend of Princess Margaret, Imelda flew to the Canary Islands and sent for Mike. She asked him if it was true, as she had heard, that he and his wife had been invited to the wedding. He explained that it was true, and that all the resident ambassadors had been included on the palace guest list. She told Mike she wanted an invitation and he replied, in some pain, that he really could not arrange it.

"Ask Princess Margaret," Imelda ordered.

Mike, saying he was very sorry, explained that he could not do that. And he added that Princess Margaret was not feeling too cordial to the Philippines and had not really enjoyed her visit there.

That was the end of Mike's diplomatic career. Imelda flew home in a huff, and demanded his resignation.

While Imelda was increasingly meddling in affairs of state and investing abroad, the American ambassador, Michael Armacost, discovered by chance that "the really big deals were the ones the President himself was making. One of the problems of the economy was that any company that succeeded, he moved in on. So there was no incentive for success. The only companies that were immune to this had a foreign connection. The Marcoses had their hooks in every sector, and they had a deal in each commodity: Benedicto had sugar, Cojuangco coconut. Tanchangco manipulated the rice market."

Just how crooked was the President? His cousin General Ramos says Marcos "isn't the man I used to know. We knew him as a young man during World War II when he was guerrilla leader. For about two and a half months during the latter half of 1944 he hid in Pangasinan with my father and stayed with our family. We knew him as a military leader and then as a young political leader. Up to the time he was elected president, and a little after that during his first term, we felt he really was the person who could make the Filipino great again."

Marcos created a powerful political image of a simple, brave, frugal man, a patriot who loved his country. I bought it. So did millions of others.

There were some, however, who believe he was a crook from the start: a clever politician whose only interest in the presidency was self-aggrandizement. The evidence that is coming in today, and becoming the basis for the numerous lawsuits, and all the sequestered companies indicate that Marcos was the same man all along—a sort of Filipino Godfather who got his hands into everything that produced money, and pocketed it.

His accumulation of great wealth didn't get into high gear until he became President. Before that, according to a cynical colleague, "he didn't have too much to steal," although he was said to be involved in the Japanese reparations scandal, when money earmarked to rebuild a battered Philippines found itself channeled into private pockets.

Once in the presidency, Marcos used his cronies, and some members of his Cabinet, to muscle in on businesses, to collect by overpricing, inflating commissions, and securing monopolies on commodities. Mrs. Marcos was doing the same thing, but on a much smaller scale.

As an example of how the President worked, in 1967, only two years after he assumed office, he decided to move in on the Philippine Long-Distance Telephone Company and wrest it from the General Telephone and Equipment Company, a large American firm. He sent Ramon Cojuangco as his representative. Since GTE did not know Cojuangco, the President personally called a Filipino member of the GTE board to escort Cojuangco to them. PLDT wanted to import equipment from GTE and a letter of credit was needed that was to be guaranteed by a subsidiary of the Philippine National Bank. Marcos instructed them not to issue the guarantee until he gave the go-ahead, which was not given until GTE agreed to sell all their shares to Cojuangco. In papers discovered since Marcos left the Philippines, it is clear that one of his companies owns 26 percent of PLDT.

Among business insiders, the President's greed was so well known that during the revolution, when someone commented that they wondered what the President was doing, a business colleague said, "He's probably sitting at his desk, counting the day's proceeds from the casinos."

When the Marcoses fled the palace, the day's report on casino take was found on the President's desk.

Under the Marcos system of patronage, the control of Philippine exports was doled out to the intimates of the

President. Robert "Bobby" Benedicto, a college classmate, got the entire sugar industry (the major export) plus a shot at being the Philippine ambassador to Japan. He was known to the Japanese as the "absentee ambassador" since he was much more interested in wheeling and dealing at home than tending his embassy in Tokyo. The General and I had dinner with him once in Tokyo—the meal was catered; the building looked as though it hadn't been lived in for years.

Bobby Benedicto cannot get a sentence out without laughing. This must be a nervous tic rather than good humor because the eyes behind his glasses are always cold. After the Aquino assassination, Benedicto was said to have made the largest cash deposit ever received by a bank in Honolulu—fifty million dollars. Whenever he visited the sugarlands of Negros, his car was always accompanied by a caravan of security guards. He had good reason to fear assassination.

Bananas, another leading Philippines export, went to the control of the white-haired Antonio "Tony" Floriendo, who also served as aide and escort to Mrs. Marcos on many of her journeys. Handsome and affable, Tony was often assigned to "look after" Cristina Ford or whoever else needed an escort. It is his name or that of one of his companies that appears as owner of some of the Honolulu and New York property that the Marcos family uses.

A cousin by marriage, Herminio Disini was responsible for the administration's most spectacular white elephant, the abortive nuclear power plant on the earthquake-prone fault of Bataan peninsula, a grossly overpriced bill of goods sold at astronomical prices by Westinghouse to the Philippines, with such rebates to Disini that he was able to buy a castle and a phoney title in Austria and emigrate forever.

In 1974 President Marcos issued a presidential decree that created the Coconut Industry Development Fund, known as the coconut levy. Imposed on every 100 kilos of copra, and adjusted at will, it was a source of income for the coconut hierarchy, but many felt it imposed undue hardship on the coconut farmers.

Coconut, the second most important export, went to the control of Eduardo "Danding" Cojuangco, who became variously known, in dialect, as "coconut king," "sugared coconut king" (when he added sugarland to his holdings), and finally "sugared coconut bread king" (when he cornered the market in wheat). Cojuangco, a somewhat taciturn, socially shy man, was actually the only one of all the President's cronies who was successful in his business ventures.

Cojuangco entered the palace fold in 1975, when the government launched a coconut replanting program. Defense Minister Enrile became acting chairman of the Philippine Coconut Authority, and worked with Cojuangco to build up the industry. They bought United Bank from the family of Cory Cojuangco Aquino, and created a United Coconut Planters Bank. (Cory and Eduardo Cojuangco are cousins.)

As soon as the Philippine Coconut Authority began to prosper, Imelda decided she better move in on it before it became any threat to her. She sent Kokoy to try to muscle in on behalf of the Romualdez family.

At this point, her old enemy Enrile decided it was time for him to get out. He suggested to Cojuangco that if he wanted his businesses to prosper he would need political support and he might as well deal with the Romualdez family.

In 1982, while the Marcoses were in the United States, Mrs. Marcos called a meeting at her suite in the Sheraton, in Washington, at which Cojuangco and Enrile were present. Enrile told her, "I have no interest in politics. I suggest Cojuangco support you." After that the Cojuangcos were visible at every palace function, and Danding was in full favor.

There was some talk of Cojuangco succeeding Marcos as president. It was assumed the President might have dangled the possibility before him. However, Enrile thinks it was probably Imelda who gave him the idea he could rule "after her," and then possibly turn the chair back to one of her children. At one time Imelda was pushing Cojuangco as successor to Enrile as Minister of Defense, but her idea did not gain sufficient support to go through.

Despite his mild manner, Cojuangco is perhaps the most ruthless of them all. When the respected former Vice President and foreign minister, Emmanuel Pelaez, took a public stand in the Assembly to fight the coconut levy, Mrs. Marcos, according to Pelaez, warned him, "Be careful, Manny. Don't fight it, Ramon Cojuangco is a killer."

Pelaez attended a stag dinner given by my husband for the foreign minister of Vietnam at the Hotel Intercontinental one evening, left early, and was ambushed on his way home. His driver was killed and he was left for dead. Fortuitously, although he was gravely wounded, he survived. Later, when my husband wanted to retire and sounded out Pelaez about taking over his job, Pelaez said emphatically: "I will never serve this government. There was no investigation of who tried to kill me." (Today Pelaez is President Aquino's ambassador to Washington.)

Apparently Marcos's clever daughter Imee also caught on to the uses of business manipulation and strong-arm tactics. For years Lucio Tan, a wealthy Chinese businessman who heads a conglomerate, was observed personally hauling the take for each business day to the President's office in the palace—the Marcos cut from all of Tan's businesses, including the country's largest cigarette manufacturing plant, which was said to be printing its own Bureau of Internal Revenue stamps for use on its packs. (If true, this would represent loss to the government in tax revenues of half a billion pesos annually.) In 1981 insiders say that Imee Marcos discovered that Tan was "cheating" the President by failing to cough up the full share of his agreed take. After that the Marcos family moved in on Tan's conglomerate and were thought to have taken the majority control of all his companies.

I never know what prompted Imelda—a good heart, her conscience, or a feminine instinct to avoid violence—but she did often warn potential victims. In New York, she conferred with opposition leader Benigno "Ninoy" Aquino, who had been allowed to leave incarceration in the Philippines to go abroad for heart bypass surgery, and warned him not to try to come back. "Some of our people will kill you."

Not averse to going public about her deepest fears, Mrs. Marcos also told Salvador "Doy" Laurel, an opposition assemblyman in Manila who supported Aquino, the same thing. "Don't let Ninoy come home. They'll kill him."

A ground swell of charges against the administration was beginning to surface: crony capitalism, misuse of loans and aid from abroad. It was during Ambassador Armacost's tenure that a recommendation went through that any aid to the Philippines should be handled in such a way that there was no chance of its getting into Mrs. Marcos's Ministry of Human Settlements. It had been charged that money that found its way there eventually went into personal investments or personal bank accounts in the United States or Europe. Funds contributed by UNICEF and USAID, for example, to her Nutrition Center to feed malnourished children were later traced to her "intelligence fund" and to her private bank account in London. Appropriations for housing and "human settlements" were used for real estate investments in California.

Common scapegoats for anything that went wrong in Manila were the American ambassador or the CIA. Imelda Marcos blamed Ambassador Armacost personally for much of the bad press she and her husband were receiving in the United States.

The Marcoses banked heavily on American support to help them maintain power. They considered President and Mrs. Reagan personal friends, and felt they could always count on their backing. When the American media attacked them, or their finances and investments became an object of scrutiny, they blamed it on their enemies in Congress. They apparently believed the mounting charges of corruption in no way influenced President and Mrs. Reagan's friendship with them.

There were many well-placed older families in Manila who had never supported Marcos. (General Romulo had, in fact, voted for his old friend, the former president, Diosdado Macapagal, in 1965.) For the most part, though, the opposition was quiet. They wanted to get on with their lives and their businesses as best they could without government interference. One of the first to speak out directly against President Marcos, was Jaime Ongpin, president of the Benguet Mining Company. In a letter to the *Asian Wall Street Journal*, he accused Marcos of "crony capitalism"— coining an apt phrase that was very hard for the President to shake off. "Mr. Marcos," he wrote, "must choose between his cronies and his country." Ongpin described the Philippine version of free enterprise as capital that has been "free only for a favored few. The direct cost of such a policy can be counted in billions of pesos mired in crumbling crony conglomerates." Through Marcos's largesse to friends who mismanaged the companies doled out to them, the Philippines, from being at the top of the ASEAN economic success story, sunk to the bottom. At one time Marcos secretly bailed out his golf partner Rudy Cuenca's debt-ridden Construction and Development Company to the tune of 20 percent—nearly one-fourth of the total money supply of the Philippines.

It was, once again, Jaime Ongpin who blew the whistle on what Marcos was doing to the country's economy. In turn, the President called upon his Minister of Trade and

Industry, Jaime's own brother Bobby, to speak for the government position. It became a "family feud" played out on the pages of the *Asian Wall Street Journal.*

"We had always been very private people," Maribel, Jimmy's wife told me. "Now, suddenly everyone was asking Jimmy for statements about the government. He became the voice of the opposition."

Privately, Jaime Ongpin was doing more than make knowledgeable statements about the perils of a Marcos-dominated economy. With his friends in the church, he was feeling out a means of creating an opposition powerful enough to topple Imelda and Ferdinand Marcos.

The Last Hurrah

THE General had made up his mind that he would retire on his eighty-fourth birthday (in January 1983), and so the family compound was sold and we moved to a single-family house only a few blocks away, in Dasmarinas Village. That same month we heard the news—not surprising—that Secretary of State Haig had resigned and had been replaced by George Shultz.

In September of 1982, President and Mrs. Marcos made a state visit to Washington, their first since Lyndon Johnson was president sixteen years earlier.

The General and I were already in New York, for the United Nations sessions, and we flew to Washington to meet the Marcoses when they arrived.

In contrast to Vice President Bush and his wife, and her own husband, the President, Nancy Reagan tends to be chilly on first meeting. I saw enough of her that I decided it is a certain wariness on her part. She is very concerned about her husband, very protective of him, and therefore cool and wary with strangers.

The morning I officially met her I was coming down the

reception line in the White House, after the arrival ceremonies in the Rose Garden. I first greeted President Reagan, who held my hand warmly for a long moment while he
reminisced about learning an oration written by General
Romulo while he was still a student. Then when I passed
to Nancy Reagan, despite her husband's affability, she
gave me a very cool "hello" and that was that. As I reached
the end of the line, big Barbara Bush swooped down on me
and pulled me back to the First Lady. "Nancy," she en-
thused, "I want you to know a friend of ours, Beth, who
married our good friend General Romulo."

"Oh?" said Mrs. Reagan.

There was nothing for me to do but to move on.

Yet that night, at the official White House dinner, I
caught a glimmer of another side of her.

Since the General avoided stairways where possible, the
White House protocol kindly arranged that we could come
up on the private elevator from the rotunda of the White
House to the pretty gold room where the Reagans were to
greet members of the official party.

I guess because of our special arrangements, we were a
bit ahead of everyone. Suddenly the elevator door opened,
and Romy and I saw President and Mrs. Reagan standing
directly in front of us, alone.

We greeted them, then chatted a bit before the Marcoses
and the rest of the party arrived. Grace Kelly's death was in
the news, and I asked Nancy Reagan about that, knowing
they had been friends.

Immediately her face changed. The guarded look disappeared and her face softened with concern. Even her voice
took on a different tone. She told me she had been on the
phone with the family in Monaco and planned to attend the
funeral. She had just heard it was actually a stroke that had
killed Princess Grace and that the car accident followed as a
result.

By then President and Mrs. Marcos and their children

had arrived. Mrs. Marcos was wearing an exquisite *terno* with a petalled skirt, all in rose color. Most colors suited her. But this rose had brought a special glow to her skin. She looked very beautiful indeed. Mrs. Reagan was dressed in silver and white, which was especially dramatic when we finally went outside to the Rose Garden for dinner: The entire scheme of flowers, silverware, and linen was in also silver and white. I was wearing a dress of mulberry satin and black velvet, and wearing Romy's first "important" gift—long ruby and diamond earrings.

There was a certain irony for me in visiting the White House as an official member of a foreign delegation. Clearly it was only as the wife of a foreign dignitary that I was seeing the inside of the White House and its functions in a way I never could as an ordinary citizen. I thought of the first time I had visited the White House, as a child of eight, on a family trip to Washington where we traveled through the White House on a tour, saw the Washington Monument, etc. Later, as a college-age girl during World War II, I trained for six weeks at the Pentagon on a summer job I had with the Signal Corps in New Jersey. And later still, as a young wife, I lived in Washington for a year while my husband did research at the Library of Congress.

But this visit was very different. When the group had assembled upstairs—the Marcoses, Prime Minister Virata, Kokoy Romualdez, Michael Armacost, and their wives—we were brought to the oval sitting room overlooking the Washington Monument and Jefferson Memorial for cocktails. Then we all went downstairs to the ballroom, where the other guests were assembled and the two presidents and their wives formed a receiving line. The guests were then shown outside to a "fairyland." The entire garden was trimmed with tiny white lights in all the shrubbery, and all the tables were set with "trees" of white flowers and small candles for centerpieces.

Romy and the Marcoses were seated at President and

Mrs. Reagan's table on one side of the garden; I was lucky and drew Secretary Shultz for my host, and sat between him and Senator Denton. I learned from the Senator that the attractive blonde across the table from me was Diane Sawyer. I guess that's one way for an ordinary citizen to get into the White House: become a media star.

Shultz looked a bit forbidding at first and I had visions of business-only conversation (thinking of his days as Secretary of Commerce and president of the Bechtel Corporation), but I couldn't have been more mistaken. His conversation is delightful, wide-ranging, erudite, splashed with occasional humor. When I seemed surprised at some of his more literary allusions (unfortunately my face gives me away), he laughed: "Don't forget, young lady, I was a dean at the University of Chicago before I was ever in Washington." He watched with interest as I deftly maneuvered my way through the first course. "I never have learned to use the fish knife," he commented companionably. I myself had, because I'm so fond of fish I wouldn't think of passing it up for lack of expertise.

The Secretary asked me if I missed my writing and I replied that even though I wasn't producing much these days I'd still identify myself as "a writer" if anybody asked who I was.

He commented perceptively that people "scrambling around for their identity" probably won't find it because "you have to believe it yourself, first."

Obviously—despite his modest, soft-spoken manner—he is quite sure about who he is. Romy was the first man I'd ever been close to who had that same firmly established, easy self-assurance. It is a trait I have learned to admire. It was, I believe, that shared characteristic that made it easy for the Secretary and the Foreign Minister to deal with one another. Their relations were based on mutual respect and cordiality.

Mrs. George Shultz—whom I got to know later—is the

kind of wife that every foreign minister or other public man under great pressure should have. She is her husband's number one fan. A warm, direct, thoughtful person, Obie (so nicknamed for O'Brien, her maiden name) projects the idea that her George is the greatest. She's convinced me. And a lot of other people. I wish more public men had that kind of a wife.

One of my sideline projects, which I engage in in speeches and private talks with wives of ambassadors, ministers, and the like is that public men need their women very badly as a kind of back-up team. Male aides, as my husband told me long ago just "tuck you in and run off to nightclubs." But the man who has negotiated under pressure all day needs someone to commiserate with, someone to be alert to his physical symptoms of fatigue, and someone, if he is low, to tell him he really is "the greatest." It's not easy to back out of the limelight, without someone behind you, someone "to come home to" even if "home" is an inhospitable hotel room. If the shoe is on the other foot, and it's the woman who's under pressure, I think the roles should be reversed and the husband support her.

I looked around the White House garden to see who, if any, of Imelda's personal friends were there. I spotted Van Cliburn and his mother, and Sir Y. K. Pao, the billionaire Chinese shipbuilder from Hong Kong who had always been a palace favorite. Two former US ambassadors to the Philippines were present: Hank Byroade and his handsome European wife, who had been in Manila when I first arrived, and Ambassador and Mrs. David Newsom, who had served during the Carter administration.

The General had a good time greeting a lot of his old friends from his days as Philippine ambassador to Washington. There were even some present who remembered when he had occupied a seat in the Congress as Resident Commissioner of the Philippines before the country's independence in 1946.

The Philippine delegation stayed at the Sheraton Hotel for the length of the official visit. We had a suite with a huge living room-cum-library, only one narrow Pullman-type bathroom, and no place for me to dress. I thought wistfully of the Madison Hotel, where we had always stayed when we were in Washington, but they had to get us all in one place, large enough to accommodate all the necessary protocol and security people that go with a state visit. There were luncheons laid on by the State Department and a session at the Department of Defense as guests of Secretary Weinberger.

One day Bonny Armacost, Joy Virata, and I shared a State Department limo back from the White House and we got to talking about "public" wives. Nancy Reagan had struck us all as pretty cool and stiff on first meeting and Joy said that some women don't start out like that but end up that way after so much public exposure. I recalled that after receptions for 500 to 1,000 people, I found my smile had "frozen" and my jaw ached when I tried to relax my face. Bonny commented that the three of us were probably quite fortunate in that we each had roles of our own—Bonny is a pianist, Joy is an actress, and I am a writer—and so don't take the public side of our lives so seriously. It isn't our total life, and we can afford to be friendly and act like ourselves. We all agreed we considered our public persona temporary at best. There would come a day when we got out of the limo and back on the bus, and it didn't bother any of us very much to think that would happen.

Lord Carrington, the Foreign Secretary of Great Britain, and his wife, Lady Fiona, visited Manila in 1982. Watching the two of them was a lesson in the ultimate art of diplomacy. A political conservative, Carrington was very quick, alert, with a nice dry humor and as clever at handling himself in an interview as any public figure I've observed. As a pair, he and his wife were as professional as any diplomats I had encountered. I had seen Lord Carrington in action at an ASEAN meeting in Kuala Lumpur, and in Cancún, but this was the first time I was close enough to get acquainted.

I was advised that Lady Carrington was interested in gardens, so the British ambassador's wife and I took her to a private garden full of orchids. We also went to the presidential suite of the restored Manila Hotel (where she decided she would like to spend a vacation), and I hosted a luncheon for her at the Nielson Tower.

The General and I were both distressed when Lord Carrington soon resigned over the Falklands issue. Apparently through some failure of intelligence in his department, the imbroglio caught him unawares and he felt he had no alternative except to resign. Later he become Director General of NATO.

The following month Marvin Traub of Bloomingdale's came to Manila. Imelda considered this one of her major coups. She had interested Traub in creating a Philippine month at his store, which would showcase and promote Philippine products in the United States. He came to our house and I discussed with him what we could contribute to make the store-wide show of interest. Besides Philippine wares, it was decided to have one historical section, like a small museum, on one floor of the store, with exhibits from the personal collections of General MacArthur, General Romulo, and President Marcos. I agreed to lend some personal items plus some of the things we had already presented to the Ayala Museum. Bloomingdale's took about forty items in all. I did not get to New York for this exhibit, but I talked to a number of people who did and they found it very successful, especially the historical section.

Later, unbeknownst to me and without our permission, the Philippine government tourism department took over all the exhibits at Bloomingdale's and carried them off to the World's Fair in Tennessee to promote the Philippines there. Eventually the Philippine items were all thrown together and shipped back to Manila. Six items from the

Romulo collection were missing. The curator from the Ayala Museum went to the palace and tried to find them but with no luck; they had gotten lost or broken in transit. The most valuable missing item was a painting by the leading Philippine artist of the period, Amorsolo, depicting the landing at Leyte with General MacArthur, General Romulo, and President Osmeña. Since this was central to the Romulo exhibit at the Ayala Museum, the collection was forced to remain closed for many months. Finally I told Ambassador Jaime Zobel of the Museum board to have the collection rearranged so that the "hole" wasn't noticeable and to reopen it to the public since people were complaining they could not see the General's memorabilia. My letters, and those of a Bloomingdale's executive to the department of tourism officials who had taken the exhibit from Bloomingdale's remained unanswered. I still don't know who has our painting.

Later that year Al Haig returned to Manila, and we gave a little dinner for him in the garden of our new house. No longer Secretary of State, he was selling Sikorsky helicopters to his friends in the government. Our guest, included Ambassador Armacost and his wife—Armacost had been Haig's appointment. We also had Bill Moyers, who was in town doing a special for CBS on the RP–US bases agreements. I noted our guest of honor, Haig, was somewhat wary of Moyers. He told me that once he had been interviewed on TV by Moyers, who had been President Johnson's press secretary. When Moyers commented on the evils of wiretapping one's own colleagues, Haig said, "Johnson started it," and Moyers, infuriated, cried, "That's a lie!" Haig said it was later proven true that Johnson did start tapping his own people. But Moyers never apologized, so they remained cool toward each other.

Haig made a very graceful toast to General Romulo, and commented to me privately how important it was for younger men to have Romy as their guide and mentor. "They can learn from him."

In the spring of 1983 the Marcoses' younger daughter, Irene, announced her engagement to Gregorio Araneta, scion of a famous old Spanish mestizo family and son of a well-known architect, cultural leader, and art collector, Don Luis Araneta, who was in fact our next-door neighbor when we were living in our old house. His home was a veritable museum of beautiful paintings, statuary, and ceramics. As a wedding gift, he gave it to his son Greggy and his bride, and moved to San Francisco. He had never been an admirer of the Marcoses and apparently took this opportunity to emigrate to avoid embarrassment.

In the Marcos/Romualdez political dynasty there are two outstanding innocents: Kokoy's saintly wife, Juliette, and the Marcoses daughter Irene. When Irene was subpoenaed to appear before a US federal grand jury in Washington in May of 1986, and finally ordered jailed for contempt because she kept saying "I don't know" when she was asked the details of a munitions deal, I thought: "Poor Irene. She probably *doesn't* know—even if someone did get her to sign her name to a document.

Sweet by nature, unassuming, dedicated to the study of music, Irene is one of those who sailed through the seas of corruption washing around her without understanding what was happening. Unlike her shrewd and ruthless older sister, Imee, she didn't get into the swing of making deals on her own. Irene's idea of action was to direct a youth orchestra.

Once, asked about his daughters, Marcos surprised everyone, aware of his intellectual closeness to Imee, by saying he really preferred Irene. "She's the one who fetches my slippers when I'm tired." It was a chore Imelda or Imee certainly would not have performed for him.

The date for Irene's wedding, June 11, was set with an

eye on the solar system. On this day all the planets, including the earth and the moon, would be in a straight line from the sun, which was supposed to auger well for a unique life. Thus far, it's probably been more unique than comfortable.

The wedding was to be held in an old church in Sarrat, the President's birthplace, in the province of Ilocos. A total of $1.3 million was spent on its restoration. There were 500 invited guests and 100,000 local spectators.

The government used twenty-four PAL planes and fifty buses to bring in the guests. We flew in a borrowed private plane, and escaped immediately after the service, not waiting for the wedding breakfast. Unfortunately the catered food had been brought in the night before and there was not enough refrigeration to handle it all; several members of the diplomatic corps ended up in the hospital.

There had been three wedding gowns for the bride's inspection: a Givenchy, a Valentino, and a Balestra. Irene chose the Balestra, with a 20-foot train. (Later it was discovered that the Valentino was paid for out of the Typhoon Relief Fund.) The Balestra gown was a variation of the Filipina Maria Clara costume—in sheer ecru, with a *pañuelo*, a nineteenth century pinned-on collar.

As we entered the church, we found the groom's father seated before the door looking pale and fanning himself. He had just discovered that his collection of antique altar candles had all been painted white for the wedding, destroying their natural patina. As I found out later, he was having a heart attack.

President Marcos and his daughter arrived at the church in a flower-decked horse-drawn carriage. Instead of the traditional wedding march on the church organ, the ninety-piece Philippine Philharmonic Orchestra played a Vivaldi hymn for two trumpets and orchestra.

The wedding gifts from the President's closest associates were said to include two Mercedes-Benz cars, one yacht, and a $2-million trust fund. The members of the Cabinet were simply assessed 1,000 pesos each and a single gift was given, a grandfather clock.

A few nights later a reception for 3,000 "close friends" was given at Malacanang Palace. For the first time the Aranetas were all present. None of the family had supported Marcos, so they had never previously appeared on the palace guest list. But now they were relatives—a position that is respected above all other ties in the Philippines.

In contrast to Irene, Imee had a much more troubled marriage. A smart, strong-minded girl, Imee was always closer to her father than her mother. Once she said of Imelda, "We can't spend time together. We terrorize one another."

On Imee's eighteenth birthday, it was the generous Cristina Ford who played fairy godmother and persuaded her husband, Henry, to throw a magnificent bash at the Regency in New York, to celebrate her debut. For once Imelda agreed to take second place to her daughter. She flew into New York, with her arrival timed for the morning *after* the party. She explained to friends, that there had always been a certain rivalry with Imee because Imelda, by her own admission, was "more beautiful."

It was a generous gesture on Imelda's part, through it did not further her marriage plans for her daughter. Henry Ford had invited all the richest and most eligible young men, but nothing came of it.

Then Imee enrolled at Princeton University. She supposedly graduated in law at the University of the Philippines later, but there is no record that she ever completed her course or passed the bar—although there was a mock graduation ceremony with highest honors (magna cum laude) that enraged much of the faculty and student body. (All the Marcos children were sent abroad for schooling, as were the children of most wealthy Filipinos, but none ever finished a degree to anyone's knowledge.)

Imee was far more interested in men than in her studies.

But always gravitated to inappropriate types. The rumor went round that Imelda would like to have married her off to Prince Charles—or some suitable royal of a slightly lower category.

When Imelda was invited to the wedding of Franco's granddaughter in Madrid, she attended with Imee, who was then about seventeen years old. Imee appeared in a full diamond tiara. Her mother was told by protocol that "no young girl in Europe wears a tiara." Both Imelda and her daughter were furious—but Imee took it off.

Imee kept falling in love with the wrong people. First it was Ricky Silvero—a romance her mother did much to break up (the Silverios' business was to all purposes ruined), and then it was a previously married basketball coach named Tommy Manotoc. She married Tommy. (He must have more than meets the eye since an American of my acquaintance left her husband and even threatened suicide over him.) No one will ever know Imee's motives. But many Manilans assumed it was to spite her mother, who had her sights set on some grand international "catch."

Because Mrs. Marcos found the match eminently unsuitable, Imee and Tommy were married secretly in the United States in December of 1981. Back home in Manila, the marriage was not recognized legally and the couple lived apart; they hung out where they could—although hardly invisible when you consider her small army of bodyguards. (Imee once said of palace life that the best perk was the security and running through red lights in traffic; the new president, Mrs. Aquino, stops at red lights.) One of their hangouts was the Ilang-Ilang restaurant (actually a coffee shop) in the Manila Hotel. Another was a modest but excellent fish restaurant in Makati, Las Conchas.

It was after leaving Las Conchas one evening in January of 1982—Imee in her palace car with bodyguards, her husband in a self-driven car—that Tommy was kidnapped. It seemed a rather melodramatic way to break up an unsuitable romance. That night at Malacanang, Mrs. Marcos was quite nervous, chattering with her Blue Ladies, twisting her handkerchief in her hand.

The facts were never made public. After six weeks Tommy reappeared, a bit bedraggled but unscathed, with some confused tale of being held by the New People's Army (Anything that happened in the Philippines was conveniently blamed on the NPA or the CIA.) Rumor, again, had it that Imee simply blackmailed her mother into bringing him back alive. She kept the books at the palace and threatened to expose some of her mother's more interesting investments, if her true love was not returned to her.

In December of 1982, Romy told President Marcos that he had decided to retire and would announce it at his birthday dinner the following month. Until then it would be a secret. His advanced age—he turned eighty-four on January 14—seemed good enough reason for him to step down. The President apparently accepted his decision graciously and kept the secret well—so well he did not even tell Imelda.

Each year it was General Romulo's custom to invite the entire diplomatic corps for a black-tie dinner on his birthday. On the night of January 14, Mrs. Marcos arrived first, alone. The President was detained but would catch up with us shortly. Our guests were already seated and we escorted the First Lady to the presidential table. She was seated beside the General; a vacant seat was left for the President, then came my place next to the prime minister. As soon as we sat down, she leaned across the vacant chair, started to whisper something, then motioned me to move over to the President's seat. I did, a bit reluctantly. As hostess, I would rather have faced my guests.

"Is it true?" she demanded in a low agitated voice. "Is he really going to announce his retirement?"

"Yes."

"He can't," she said sharply. "Not now. This is not the time. Don't you understand? There is no other one."

I was silent, wondering why she was so upset.

"Why would he want to do that?" she went on. "Did you ask him to do it?"

"No," I said. "It's his own decision."

"But why? Why would he want to retire? What will he do with himself? Sit in a rocking chair?"

"He's eighty-four years old, ma'am," I told her. "He's tired."

"But don't you understand," she repeated in that same agitated low voice, *"there is no other one!"*

Word came that the President had arrived. We went down to the lobby and escorted him into the ballroom. As soon as we sat down, Mrs. Marcos began whispering excitedly to him.

When it came time for him to speak, the General made a somewhat tearful fond farewell, to his diplomatic corps and to his president.

Then President Marcos rose to speak.

I don't know what he had originally planned to say. But what he did say, in effect, was that he refused to accept General Romulo's resignation. "I hereby extend his service for one year . . ."

There was a roar of applause. Romy's friends, the ambassadors, were delighted to keep their "dean of diplomats" in place for another twelve months. He was a father figure to them.

I looked at Mrs. Marcos. She was smiling broadly. She had won. It was the first time I had been exposed to the full impact of her personality when there was something she wanted. It left me shaken. Certainly if we had known what was coming we would never have allowed them to hold on to the General.

The Marcos family is a living example of the truism of Lord Acton that "Power tends to corrupt and absolute power corrupts absolutely." Twenty years of unquestioned power, with no accountability for one's actions in the long run, has demoralized every member of the family. There are advocates of Imee who remember her at ten or twelve as a warm and generous girl, yet, especially after great amounts of funds were in her control during elections, she became ruthless and people were imprisoned who dared heckle or contradict her. It was rumored that one student was murdered by the military because he challenged her at a public rally. And Irene, for all her gentle sweetness, developed a reputation for toughness with people who had to take orders from her. Even Greggy, who had a fortune and business interests of his own before he ever married her, couldn't resist the chance to squeeze out and control small businesses and act like a Mafia boss after their marriage. He became known as "Greedy Greggy"—an embarrassment to a distinguished family.

One of Imelda Marcos's problems, many of us agreed, was that she had been in the top job so long she acted as if she'd be First Lady forever. She couldn't seem to anticipate that it might end.

It reminded me of something the old bush pilots in Alaska used to tell me, when I was writing a book on their lives *(Glacier Pilot)*. They were spectacular pilots and they got a lot of publicity for their exploits. But they had a saying: "When you start believing your own press notices, you are going to crash." And when you hear nothing but praise and adulation, you lose your instinct for survival.

The Aquino Mystique

O N a quiet Sunday in August of 1983 the General and I were sitting in his study talking about our upcoming trip to New York in the fall when the phone rang. It was his son, Dick. "Aquino's been shot."

I turned on the TV and the radio. At first, only the Catholic radio station, Veritas, was carrying the news live. Announcers, shocked as ourselves, were stumbling over the known facts. Ninoy Aquino was returning to Manila on a China Airlines jet, with a planeful of reporters accompanying him. Cory, his wife, was still in Boston with their children.

It was so crudely done, and so ugly, that the initial impact on the Filipino people was more psychological than political. It was a national loss of face, a reaction of personal shame. A man returns home, is taken off the plane by military escorts, and shot dead before he sets foot on native ground. Then the body, pitched forward on the tarmac, is hauled and pushed into a military van, like a lump of meat. Rumor had it that a soothsayer had told Imelda that if

Benigno Aquino's feet touched Philippine soil, the Marcos days would be numbered.

The General said to me, his voice pitiful, "How can I ever defend this country again?" He worried about going to New York. "I don't want to see my American friends. I don't want to answer questions."

According to my diary, it was "black Sunday and black Monday." Nobody knew exactly what had happened. They just knew it had happened.

The President apparently was seriously ill. Some said he was recovering from a kidney transplant. It was not until the evening of the second day after the killing that he finally appeared on television to assure everyone he was alive (he was propped up like an Asian Pétain, his face bloated and full of pain, the screen carefully obscuring all but his upper torso) and that he wasn't going to declare martial law again (it had been lifted in 1981). Another rumor circulated: If the President did die, no one would know for five days; Imelda would put him in the deep freeze and not release the news until she had consolidated her own position.

Later President Marcos claimed Aquino had been shot by a civilian, Rolando Galman (who had in turn been shot dead by soldiers), and that Galman was the hired gun for the NPA. Nobody bought that. Aquino would never have been a target of the NPA. His hacienda was in NPA country and he had worked out a "live and let live" peace with them. Marcos claimed the murder was carried out to embarrass his government.

There was no doubt the Marcos government was embarrassed. Defense Minister Enrile, in whose charge Aquino would have been, carefully distanced himself from the entire event once he left the airport, implying that Aquino would have been safe if he had had the chance to be turned over to him.

I couldn't understand why the President didn't make a similar attempt to save his own skin. "If I were in his place," I told my husband, "I would come on the air and say 'It is with great regret that I accept the resignation of my chief of staff and chief of security, General Ver, until there has been an investigation of this murder.'"

In fact no one believed the President had given the orders to shoot Aquino. To begin with, he was known to be ill at the time. Second, no matter what anyone thought of him, he would never have done anything that senseless. "It was Ver," said outspoken Brigadier General Hans Menzi, a Swiss Filipino who owned the *Bulletin Today*. "It had to be Ver. Nobody else is that stupid."

The scenario most insiders finally accepted was that General Ver and another Marcos crony came to Mrs. Marcos to report the bad news: "Aquino's coming. He's landing in Manila."

"My God, what will I do?"

"Let me take care of it, Ma'am."

"*Sige, sige,* go ahead."

Recently it has been established that the President, far from being comatose on that fateful day, was alert and made several telephone calls, one to his Minister of Defense to proceed to the hospital and arrange for the disposition of the body. Perhaps the reopening of the Aquino assassination case will show that far from being a spontaneous outburst, the murder had been planned well in advance.

The day after the assassination all Manila was blacked out. Sabotage? The NPA? Maybe they were taking over the city. There were many tense hours until the electricity came back on.

The General told me he must go and view Aquino's remains. He had known the Aquinos all his life—they were all from the same province, Tarlac. I asked if he wanted me to accompany him. "No, stay out of this," he told me.

As usual he had no security, only his driver and a young protocol officer to hold his arm. When they reached the Aquino house, the streets were full of people. It was a hostile crowd. The car could not get near the entrance. "I'll walk in," said the General. The protocol officer told me afterward he was "really scared." When the Prime Minister had come to pay his respects, the crowd closed in on his car, rocked it back and forth, and wouldn't let him get out. The car of the Speaker of the Assembly was stoned, and he withdrew. But when the crowd saw Romulo—short, old, frail, and brave—they drew back and made a path. "It's the General, the General!" Obviously they knew he had nothing to do with the assassination.

Aquino was buried at the Manila Memorial Park. The hearse left Santo Domingo Church at about ten a.m. and it took eleven hours to cover approximately 25 kilometers to the cemetery, the largest attendance of a funeral on record.

In an effort to dampen the national fury and frustration that followed the assassination, President Marcos created a commission to investigate the murder, with Chief Justice Enrique Fernando as chairman. He also named some other justices from the Supreme Court, and Cardinal Sin—who promptly refused, citing "an assignment from the Vatican."

There was so much furor over Marcos's handpicked commission that Justice Fernando resigned, as did the other justices, because "credibility was essential" to an investigating body.

In October the President issued a decree, creating a new fact-finding commission headed by Appellate Court Justice Corazon Agrava and including a prosecuting panel composed of nongovernment lawyers known for their integrity. Over the next year the Agrava board heard 193 civilian and military witnesses and received 480 documentary and physical exhibits.

When the First Lady was subpoenaed to appear, she

showed up on her birthday and after a few polite questions, the board sang "Happy Birthday" to her. "That's the end!" My husband was disgusted. "They will only do what the President wants."

Surprisingly, the Agrava board did come out with a majority decision indicting the military, including General Ver.

As a gesture of apparent conciliation, the President told General Ver to step down and appointed General Fidel Ramos as acting chief of staff. But it was a farce. Ver kept his position in control of the National Intelligence and Security Authority, and he and his family continued to live at Malacanang Park.

After the Aquino assassination, the Marcos government was never stable again. There were spontaneous demonstrations every day. It was as though the entire country, shocked by that one ugly, pointless political assassination, had shaken off a twenty-year lethargy, to rise against their entrenched ruler.

First on the streets were the women. ("Our husbands followed a year later.") The controlled press grew bolder, photographing the demonstrators and front-paging the pictures. I was amazed at the faces I saw—prominent women one normally would find only in discreet club meetings or restaurants—out on the streets with the students, the workers, and clergy, their arms raised in the *Laban* ("Fight!") sign. There was one stunning photo of Bea Zobel, the Spanish-born wife of leading industrialist Jaime Zobel, her elegant face transfixed with anger—and strength. "She was just passing by and went over to see what it was all about," her husband said uneasily.

There was Bing Roxas, chairman of the Philippine dance company—a socialite known for her cultural, not political, interests. And sturdy little Maribel Ongpin, Jaime Ongpin's wife, pulled emotionally from the golf course and squash courts to stand up and be counted in the crowd. Some carried signs: IMPEACH MARCOS.

"The first rally you attend is the hardest," Maribel told me. "You don't know what you're getting into—truncheons, water-hose, maybe getting shot." Many of the women carried big handbags with wet towels that had been rubbed with calamansi juice—the native lime—in case they were tear-gassed. The lime relieves the burning of the skin.

My daughter-in-law, Tessie, wife of Attorney Ricardo Romulo, told her husband she wanted to go to a Mass and rally for Aquino. All the family were careful because the General was still Foreign Minister and no one wanted to embarrass him. "Go to the Mass," Dick told her, "but not the rally."

That evening when he came home, she ran to him. "Oh, Dick, I went to the rally." Instead of scolding her, he embraced her. "I'm proud of you," he said.

The rallies were started by concerned women's groups, conservative middle- and upper-class matrons, and previously uninvolved business executives—not by the radical left.

The welcoming committee at the airport to greet their returning leader, had picked "Tie a Yellow Ribbon" as their theme song. After Aquino's assassination, yellow became the symbol of the opposition. Nonviolent street demonstrations, complete with yellow confetti (mostly shredded yellow telephone pages), became a daily happening on Ayala Avenue, Makati's financial district.

Despite the constant denials from palace sources, the President was clearly undergoing a medical crisis that year. He would appear functional for a day or so, then simply disappear from sight. Other times he would sit, zombielike, through Cabinet meetings, while Imelda fielded questions and nudged him into an occasional answer. "Poor me," she said later. "I had to do everything—even run the Cabinet."

The President became increasingly out of touch with reality. Ambassador Armacost recalls that when he first came to Manila, Marcos would call around and try to get feedback and reports to find out how the public was feeling about his regime. But after he became ill, facts were hidden from him. "Kokoy was a sinister influence. And so was she. Kokoy, Ver, and the inner loyalist group kept telling him, 'You're great, Mr. President,' and that was all he heard. The burden of bringing bad news to him was left to me. No one else would tell him." But as he withdrew into his illness, the President didn't seem to care anymore.

One of the greatest worries in the business community was the problem of succession. In November of 1983, thirty business, professional, and labor leaders ran a full-page ad in the *Bulletin* appealing to President Marcos to help head off national financial disaster by resolving the question of succession if he should die or become incapacitated. Most people assumed Mrs. Marcos would make a play for the post—and that General Ver would support her.

General Romulo said, "If Marcos dies, they will find a paper naming her as his successor." Such a paper was indeed found among the President's possessions, which were frozen after he fled to Honolulu.

As their hold on the country weakened, the Marcoses turned increasingly to soothsayers, faith healers, and the occult for reassurance. Since college days, the President had been a student of Kabbalah, the ancient spiritual doctrine of the Jews. He regularly practiced rituals designed to raise one's consciousness to higher levels.

He believed that his lucky number was seven and his automobile and yacht bore that number. When he won over Vice President Emmanuel Pelaez in the Nacionalista Party Convention of 1964, it was by a margin of 777 votes. At the time he decided to hold a snap election in 1986, he first set the date for January 7, then when it was found there was not enough time to prepare the ballots, he chose February 7.

When he first was diagnosed as having kidney disease, Marcos used the best medical team in Manila as well as specialists from the United States to treat him, but he also called upon the services of a faith healer in Baguio named Jun Labo. Believing that Labo's ministrations made him feel stronger, the President brought the healer to Malacanang Palace, where he was in residence for several months. In exchange, Labo asked to run on Marcos's KBL ticket in the 1984 election for the Assembly in Baguio. The President assented. But Labo lost.

Another longtime psychic hanger-on at the palace was a curious young man known as the Bionic Boy, who took the name of Ronald (for the American president) Marcos. A foundling, he did not actually know where he was born or to whom, but early on exhibited psychic powers (he claimed his gift came "from the Holy Spirit") and was picked up by one family and then another, until a Marcos crony brought him to the palace. He stayed for several years. Plump, open-faced, he looked like a farm boy.

The length of his stay had to do with a fortuitous event. Friends of the Marcos family, including their children and their children's friends, had all gone to the President's home province to celebrate his birthday. On the way back, a planeload of younger Marcos cronies was about to take off, with Ferdinand Jr.—Bong Bong—aboard when the Bionic Boy sent word to the President that he must remove his son from the flight. Bong Bong was yanked off the plane—which crash-landed in Manila, killing several of the passengers and injuring others. After that the Bionic Boy was a favored guest at Malacanang.

The Bionic Boy was used and abused by the Marcoses and their cronies for everything from political prognostications to stock deals. He tried to get away several times.

When he came up with a prediction that President Marcos would not survive in power past November of 1983, he was allowed to leave the country.

We made our usual trip to New York in September that year, but the General was extremely uncomfortable about it. He didn't know how he could respond to questions. He was convinced the Philippine government was indefensible.

Actually his friends and colleagues in New York and at the United Nations were sympathetic. No one tried to put him on a spot about what had happened. I reminded him that he had his own reputation quite apart from the government. He had served every administration. People respected him for who he was—no matter what went on in his country.

While we were still in New York, in October, Information Minister Gregorio Cendana called General Romulo asking him to sign a full-page ad that the Philippine government was going to place in *The New York Times* and other papers, absolving President Marcos of any responsibility for the murder of Benigno Aquino. The General refused.

By the time we returned to Manila in December, there was no longer any reason for the President not to accept the resignation of his Minister of Foreign Affairs. General Romulo was ill and heartbroken. He couldn't get through his arrival press conference without tears. Part of it was the depression that accompanies renal failure. But even more was his feeling for his country. "All that I have worked for for forty years has gone down the drain," he told Abby Tan of the *Washington Post*.

In the last two years of his public service, saddened by the mounting exposure of corruption in the Marcos administration, the General described himself bitterly as "the deodorant of the administration."

Hospitalized for kidney failure, he went into regular dialysis, and officially retired on his eighty-fifth birthday, January 14, 1984.

There was a spectacular testimonial dinner given in honor of General Romulo by his friends and admirers on the day he retired. Individual business executives and companies subscribed tables, and there was a one-hour multimedia visual presentation of his life and accomplishments, toasts from his colleagues, and a special singing presentation by members of his own family. Ambassador Armacost had received permission from Washington to present the General the US Presidential Medal of Freedom, which is usually only conferred by the American president at the White House. Scholarships were awarded in his name; there was even a bottle of Bordeaux wine, from the General's birth year, 1899, which had been purchased by an admirer at auction.

The Manila society reporters called it the party of the year. But the Marcoses were not present. The guests for the most part were close friends and family. As though for a final grand salute to a grand gentleman, we were all dressed to the nines. The five Romulo granddaughters all had new gowns. I wore a red silk chiffon Stavropoulos and long pearl and diamond earrings.

The Marcoses hosted their own retirement ceremonies at the palace. The President's face was puffy, his eyes lusterless. His hands were so swollen he refused to shake hands. General Romulo pleaded, "Mr. President, it is time for *us* to step down." Those remarks were never allowed to be printed in the local controlled press and the President never so much as gave him a phone call again.

I saw Imelda once at a July Fourth celebration at the American embassy in Manila, then in New York in the fall of 1984 when I took the General there for medical care. When she found out he was in New York Hospital she appeared at his room with a camera crew from Manila. I never could decide whether it was a "photo opportunity" or whether she really cared that he was ill. By that time, of course, she had seen her own share of illness—despite all the denials. It was ironic that both her husband and mine suffered from kidney disease. Only mine admitted he did.

After the Aquino assassination, palace social life came to an abrupt halt. President Reagan canceled his prospective visit to the Philippines. Prince Philip's visit was canceled. Imelda stopped giving big parties and luncheons, and even her jet-set friends ceased coming to Manila. "It is easier for me," Ambassador Armacost told us. "There aren't all those invitations to turn down." By contrast, our own life continued to be full—with family, friends, and the constant stream of visitors who came to Manila and wanted to call upon the General.

Reporters from the foreign press all asked for appointments with the General when they were in Manila. He was always very proper and circumspect in his remarks. Since he had served President Marcos for fourteen years, he refused to criticize him publicly. But privately he was grief-stricken at what was being uncovered about the corruption, which by now was engulfing even the President himself— for so long only Imelda seemed the culprit. The General had always had excellent personal relations with Marcos and it was very hard for him to accept, or to understand, what the President had done to his country.

Despite the fact that he now had to go into the hospital three times a week, General Romulo was still keen to attend the thirtieth anniversary session of the Afro/Asian conference at Bandung, Indonesia, in April of 1985, and we made the trip with a nurse and doctor accompanying us. In June we set out for San Francisco to attend the fortieth anniversary of the signing of the UN Charter, as guests of the city of San Francisco. We saw many of his old friends there—many UN delegates had flown in from New York.

And Harold E. Stassen, the surviving signatory from the United States, was present with his wife.

But once back home, the General admitted that kind of extensive travel was more than he felt up to anymore. He canceled a trip to Bangkok, in which he was to have been a special guest of the government. On his good days, between hospital visits, he continued to receive guests at home, from the State Department, the news services, and the embassies. In October he insisted on hosting a dinner for the new American ambassador, Steve Bosworth, and his wife, at the formally elegant Romulo Salon, a private dining room in the Intercontinental Hotel that had been named in his honor. He received the opposition leader, Salvador Laurel (who is now Vice President and Foreign Affairs Secretary), with his nephew, Bert Romulo.

When President Marcos, in a sudden last-ditch effort to prove his popularity, called for a snap presidential election for the following February, the General was visibly depressed. "As it was, he might have been voted out in 1987," he told me, "but now he will claim he won, no matter what happens, and we're stuck with him for another six years. I don't think the country can stand it."

In November of 1985, Dick Holbrooke, the former Assistant Secretary of State for Southeast Asian Affairs in the Carter administration, asked, through the US embassy, for an appointment to call and pay his respects to the General.

I gave him a date. When he arrived, I took him out to the terrace where the General was sitting, then left them for a while. As Holbrooke was leaving he said to me, "I never saw the General so depressed. Is that the way he really feels?"

"Yes," I admitted. "He is depressed about what's going on. He doesn't see any way out."

Some weeks later he complained to me of abdominal pain. I called his surgeon, who couldn't tell what it was.

"We will watch it," he said. But the pain persisted. I called the kidney specialist, Dr. Ramos, who took a look at him and sent for an intestinal specialist. Dr. Pineda said to put him in the hospital at once. The next evening, after a consultation with about nine specialists, they decided they would have to operate. No one could tell what was wrong with him.

I was in the operating room with them from nine in the evening till two a.m. They found a massive infection and abscess of the lower bowel, cleaned it up, and performed a colostomy so the intestine could heal.

He survived the surgery, long though it was, but his condition never stabilized and it was virtually impossible to dialyze him and clean the blood. He lasted five days.

Before he went into surgery the General gave me instructions to carry on with a dinner he was giving for Abe Rosenthal, the Executive Editor of *The New York Times*, who was in Manila with some of his international staff to observe the upcoming elections and to interview Aquino's widow, who was running against Marcos.

Dick and Bobby Romulo helped me entertain the *Times* people and Abe sent a written message to his old friend.

I was never able to read it to Romy. By the time I returned to the hospital that night, his condition had worsened and he did not respond. A day later he died.

After his death, *The New York Times* ran an article by Dick Holbrooke on its editorial page quoting General Romulo as saying that Marcos "is stealing us blind." When it hit Manila, I got calls from UP, AP, Agence France Presse—and Malacanang Palace. The President wanted to know if I was going to retract it. I did not know what Romy had said. All I knew was that he had spoken privately to an old friend. Holbrooke had not asked for an interview, did not have a tape recorder, did not have a notebook—he did not indicate in any way that he was conducting an interview.

I issued a statement that I considered Mr. Holbrooke's

article "unfriendly and unfair." It was unfriendly to me personally, since it left me in such a dangerous and vulnerable position in Manila. And it was most certainly unfair to the General, who had a standing rule that he never spoke against President Marcos to the press. Later I crossed paths with Dick Holbrooke in New York and he claimed that it had done the General's image good in America to let people know he really was against Marcos. "But," I told him, "that was *not* for you to say."

I had calls from concerned colleagues of the General in neighboring Asian countries, fearing reprisals from Marcos. But nothing happened other than that one call from the palace. The Marcoses had their hands full by now, and I was the least of their worries.

The previously weak and fragmented opposition, sniffing blood, began mounting charges: The old cries of crony capitalism were followed by denunciations regarding "hidden wealth" and property abroad. There were a number of leads to go on, since Imelda could never resist bragging about her purchases. As the wily, amusing Cardinal Jaime Sin phrased it, "Imelda is into mining. This is mine, and this is mine, and this is mine." A disenchanted career officer in the foreign service put it another way: "They had been in power so long, the dividing line between public and private property had disappeared."

An "Imelda joke" that went the rounds in the fall of 1983 was that President Marcos is supposed to have said to Anatoly Karpov, the International Chess Grandmaster and World Champion, "Politics is like chess; could you give me some advice for winning?" Karpov is said to have replied, "Mr. President, sometimes to win, it is necessary to sacrifice your queen."

The Moral Revolution

I don't think Imelda Marcos, for all her political savvy, ever understood what hit her or what, in the long run, drove her and her husband from power.

In fact it was an unusual alliance that brought their downfall—a coalition of concerned women and the Church, which had joined together in 1984. Their shepherd was an unlikely hero by the name of Joe Concepcion, a businessman friend of Dick Romulo. If you look at Joe—plump, bespectacled, cherubic, his hair hanging limply over his glasses, you rather expect him to stumble over his own feet. Yet, owing to some personal impulse of his own, it was Joe who decided the Philippines deserved honest elections.

While other businessmen were afraid to antagonize the all-powerful Marcos regime, Joe resurrected NAMFREL, the Citizens for Free Elections, to protect the votes of the people in the 1984 election for the Assembly. He went looking for support for his project among the women who had been in the demonstrations—the kind of women who were willing to leave the comfort of their homes and their sports clubs and work around the clock to protect the electoral process.

He also called upon the Church, through his alma mater, the De La Salle College. The president of De La Salle, Brother Dizon, was also president of the Catholic Educational Association of the Philippines, which gave him automatic access to a national network of workers for NAMFREL. The college became the national headquarters for tallying votes. The Marcos government could have outlawed NAMFREL, but the President decided to allow it to function to give the image of "fair elections" abroad.

The Catholic bishops encouraged the people to support NAMFREL. Cory Aquino, who was close to the Church, believed it was possible, with their help, to work for change through the electoral process. Volunteers who manned the polls were drawn from all sectors of society. In Manila, my own daughters-in-law, Tessie and Olivia, and their children worked at the polls alongside secretaries, laborers, and laundrywomen. It was clear that the people wanted a change. And since the shock of the Aquino assassination they had lost their fear. They were willing to put themselves on the line even against the "goons, guns, and gold" of the Marcos machine.

The 1984 election in Metro Manila was a personal slap in the face to Imelda Marcos. The opposition candidates beat her ruling KBL party 14 to 7 in her own district. Her mayors and *barangay* (village) captains were not able to deliver for her as they had in the past.

Convinced that the answer to all political problems is money, she had scattered it about with a profligate hand in an effort to bribe voters. But local priests had told their parishioners it was no crime to accept the money and "vote your conscience." When the votes began going against the President's candidates, the General suggested it was time for Imelda to make a graceful concession. "She won't," I predicted. "She will blame someone else and she will be angry and vindictive."

First she called in her mayors and cussed them out for not delivering. "Now," I wrote in my diary at the time, "she is blaming the CIA." The CIA has always been a popular whipping boy with the Marcoses and a certain class of Filipinos. If the government is attacked, it's the Commies; if there is "meddling" or "intervention," it's the CIA (some of the Blue Ladies who distrusted me whispered that I was also with the CIA).

My diary continued: "Imelda's confidants, such as Glecy Tantoco and George Ramos (the architect who redid Malacanang Palace), fill her with lies which she snatches at to save face. They tell her the CIA poured in 'millions.' So now she thinks she is 'out-bought' instead of 'voted out.' She can understand that. It means she will have more money in her political war chest next time. She cannot accept that people are sick of her profligacy. The voters are sending a message but she won't listen.

"'The vote went against me because I'm the one who had to hold everything together [after the assassination],'" she complained.

The 1984 election was a direct repudiation of Mrs. Marcos and she took her defeat out on anyone near. One evening she turned on a group of her own Blue Ladies, and demanded jewelry back that she had given them. Two took off their necklaces, handed them over to her, and walked out.

After the election, the newly mobilized women of the opposition kept up the heat against the Marcos regime with daily demonstrations. They also appeared in the Batasan to encourage the minority opposition, who had won seats in the Assembly.

On August 21, 1984, I wrote in my diary: "A long march is planned to commemorate the first anniversary of Ninoy

Aquino's assassination. Bing Roxas is one of the wardens. Tessie and Olivia expect to join the march.

"I meant to stay home today—no errands, no cars on the street, because we don't know what will happen. Then Romy had a medical emergency last night and here we are on the 9th floor of Makati Medical Center.

"I can see Ayala Avenue and Buendia Boulevard (the main intersection of Makati) from our window. All the cars have yellow streamers. I see one float all decorated in yellow and many marchers. It is only 9:30. They are getting ready for a big rally. The marchers will go out to the airport to welcome the statue of Aquino which will arrive today in Manila.

"We came here suddenly last night. The General had an attack of low blood pressure, going into shock due to dehydration, hypoglycemia. Cristina Enrile, one of the most glamorous looking women I know—ethereally slim with acres of flowing red hair and a thin Spanish face—materialized at our door with uncurled hair and no makeup and I hardly recognized her. She heard the General was ill and rushed in, full of friendly concern. Apparently we were both midnight medical emergency cases. She was with her daughter across the hall, whose flu had suddenly turned into pneumonia.

"Tessie dropped in and plans to join the march after a Mass. She is carrying wet towels and calamansi in a plastic bag in case they are tear-gassed. She is wearing a yellow dress."

A group of women, headed by Bea Zobel and Bing Roxas, began to haunt the Assembly on a regular basis. Marcos's men, accustomed to having their way by sheer power of majority, didn't know how to deal with them. Sometimes the women gathered outside the Assembly with placards, denouncing the Marcos one-man rule by decree. Sometimes they sat, ladylike and decorous, in the visitors' gallery, then heckled the Speaker, or the President's hard-drinking apologist, Minister of Political Affairs Leonardo Perez, either vocally or with more placards.

Speaker of the Assembly Nicanor Yniguez, an old political workhorse, warned them not to continue to disrupt the Assembly. But they came back, again and again, either demonstrating outside or sitting in the gallery—a silent reminder of conscience to the Assemblymen below. As long as they were not vocal, Yniguez could not proceed with his threat to throw them out.

Marcos loyalists had the women watched. It was easy to recognize these henchmen, with their short-cropped hair and neat *barongs*. They were like the security officers who formed a cordon around Marcos wherever he appeared in public. One could also identify them by a bulging pocket or waistband, depending on where they carried their guns.

When the issue of hidden wealth was being discussed, the women appeared daily in the gallery. One day, at a signal, they all unrolled little flags reading IMPEACH MARCOS. They had carried them hidden inside their purses.

The Speaker, furious, banged for order. The opposition Assemblyman cheered. The guards got so excited they locked the doors to prevent the women from leaving, while the Speaker bawled at them to get out. Tessie found Assemblyman Bert Romulo, the General's nephew. "Let us out of here!" she pleaded. He ordered the doors unlocked.

"He was so angry," one of the women described Speaker Yniguez to me, "he was apoplectic. I think if he had a gun he would have shot the lot of us." Most of the group admitted they were glad to get out and return safely to their homes that night.

In addition to mistakenly believing the people would accept her unconditionally, Imelda miscalculated her personal military backing. She considered Ver's generals "her" generals and would not allow any of them to be retired. They were the force that would insure her access to the presidency. She relied on General Ver as the key to the presidency, if her husband died. Imelda's personal alliance with General Ver extended to his sons and her children. Colonel Irwin Ver accompanied Imee Marcos to London when she attended boarding school there and served as her personal security officer.

Mrs. Marcos was also incorrect in assuming General Ver controlled the entire military. In fact, Ver was cordially hated by much of the army. His power was concentrated in the Presidential Security Command, the men who guarded Malacanang Palace. Beyond that small circle, however, his authority was questionable. Too many young officers had been held back while he kept his corrupt old generals in place at the top. The majority of the military was far more loyal to the fair and honest General Ramos than they were to the corrupt General Ver and his family. In believing that Ver represented her military power base, and snubbing Enrile and Ramos, Imelda made what in the long run was to prove a fatal tactical error.

In late 1983 Defense Minister Enrile, in a conference with General Ramos and the President, warned Marcos: "You are concentrating all your powers in the hands of a group. Why don't you balance your forces? Your inner security is controlled by a Ver. Your armor unit is controlled by a Ver. The chief of staff of your Presidential Security Command is a Ver. Your Chief of Staff of your entire military organization is a Ver. You say anything against these people and they will manacle you. You will end up a prisoner in your own palace."

Enrile's personal belief was that if the President died, a group of generals close to Ver would withhold the information from the public. Then they would arrest him and Ramos and all other persons whom they considered obstacles to the accomplishment of their objectives. After the arrests, they would announce the demise of President Marcos and install Mrs. Marcos as the leader of the nation.

Then, after six months or a year, they would remove her from the seat of power and a military dictatorship would take over.

An exposé published serially in the *San Jose Mercury News* in 1985 dealt the Marcos regime a harsh blow. The series documented a devastating number of acquisitions of property by the President and his close friends on the West Coast. The clever Enrile promptly came forward and made a clear statement of what property he owned and how much it was worth (an apartment and a house in Cristina's name). Energy Minister Geronimo Velasco, apparently uncomfortable with the accusations, tried to resign from the Cabinet. But the President refused to let him go. Clearly it was a case of "let's all go down together."

In Washington, a Congressional committee headed by Republican Stephen Solarz documented the New York properties. These were the most damaging holdings because they represented the greatest visible wealth: the Crown Building, the Lindemere estate, 200 Madison Avenue, 40 Wall Street, and the Herald Center at Herald Square. The Marcoses tried to unload them before their representatives, the Bernsteins, could be subpoenaed and forced to identify the real owners. The Bernsteins were negotiating to buy the properties themselves when word came from Mr. Rolando Gapud, the President's representative, to hold everything until the hearings were over.

By August of 1985, the opposition members of the Philippine Assembly felt they had enough hard facts to present an impeachment proceeding against the President.

The corruption issue had become so potent, both at home and abroad, that it was seriously affecting the Philippines' relationship with the United States. Since President Marcos seemed certain that his relations with the American president were still good, the State Department decided to send an emissary to disabuse him of this idea. Senator Paul Laxalt was chosen. Because Laxalt was known to be a confidant of President Reagan, Marcos could not claim that he did not represent the American president's views.

Laxalt came to Manila in October of 1985, and he and Marcos had two days of consultations. They got along very well; the Senator recognized and respected Marcos's ability as a political tactician. But Laxalt was faithful to his instructions and he gave Marcos the message that the views of the State Department were the same as those of President Reagan.

This Marcos was not yet prepared to accept. He still believed, when the chips were down, that the American president would protect him. Yet he respected Laxalt and recognized that he would be his conduit to Reagan in the future.

Senator Laxalt later commented that Marcos reminded him of President Nixon in his love of "the craftsmanship of politics" and political strategy. But he found him unrealistically optimistic about conditions in the Philippines, especially the insurgency.

General Ramos told me that the President was provided regular reports on the military situation, but tended to hold to "preconceived ideas" about what it really was. He seldom left the palace to visit the provinces, and when he did what he saw was stage-managed to give him the best impression. It was in the interests of General Ver, Imelda Marcos, and her brother to keep the hard facts of the Philippine situation away from him.

Perhaps his illness had dulled his perceptions. But Ferdinand Marcos was living in a dreamworld so far as his country was concerned. He saw himself as the popular, strong leader he had once been. And despite the ravaged economy and the growing discontent among his people he considered his country stable.

Marcos had ignored other messages that came to him through the American ambassador or the State Department, and he blamed his estrangement from the United

States on his enemies in Congress and the Western media, especially *The New York Times* and *Newsweek*.

President Reagan and the State Department called for reforms in the Philippine military and in the economy, as well as the retirement of General Ver. They also called for free elections in 1987.

Marcos's answer to all that was his historic decision on November 3, 1985, not to wait for 1987 to prove his popularity and power, but to hold a snap election that would catch his opposition disorganized and off guard, and that would prove to the world he still had the mandate of the Filipino people.

On December 2, 1985, General Ver was acquitted of the Aquino murder and President Marcos promptly reinstated him as Chief of Staff.

The following day Benigno Aquino's widow announced she would run against Marcos.

Once Marcos called for an election, several of the opposition threw their hats in the ring, most notably Salvador Laurel, the younger son of the wartime occupation president. It was Jaime Cardinal Sin who brought Doy Laurel and Cory Aquino together and convinced Doy to take second place and let Cory lead the ticket against Marcos. Cardinal Sin believed she had the moral qualifications that would prove most effective against the entrenched regime.

I met Cory Aquino for the first time at my husband's wake. She was busy campaigning, and Bert Romulo told me she wanted to take time to come by the church and pay her respects. I think the first thing I noticed was her smallness—she is five feet two, a compact, slender woman. She was dressed simply, in one of her "campaign yellow" dresses. Besides Bert, she was surrounded by a few of her workers but no real crowd, and not much security. We talked a few minutes. I told her I had met her husband in Boston and had a brief visit with him when he attended one of the General's speeches at the Fletcher School of Diplomacy.

Mrs. Aquino speaks softly, but not hesitantly, and she is far more direct than most Filipinas, looking you straight in the eye while she talks. When she left the church, I told one of my daughters-in-law, "She has a cool center. I don't think anyone will push her around." She looks like one of those alert, calm, self-contained people who will listen to everyone—and then make up their own mind.

She was actually not as inexperienced politically as her early press coverage would have led one to believe. In 1978, President Marcos allowed Ninoy Aquino to campaign for an Assembly seat from his prison cell. Cory helped organize the opposition party, and actively campaigned for her husband. It was she who carried her husband's message to the country. Since Ninoy's death the opposition had gravitated to her as a rallying point, trying to convince her that she was the only one who could lead the opposition. An astounding 1.2 million Filipinos signed a petition urging her candidacy. The Church, in the person of Cardinal Sin, urged her to take up the challenge.

Still she insisted on making up her own mind. She went on a one-day retreat to pray alone with her God. Privately she joked with friends and family that she hoped God would let her off the hook. He did not. She came back and announced she would run.

They had a scant two months to campaign. President Marcos was so sure he had his opposition off guard that he invited observers to come from abroad and watch the proceedings. President Reagan appointed a group that included Senator Richard Lugar, head of the Senate Foreign Relations Committee, and retired Admiral Robert Long, the former Commander in Chief of the Pacific Command, among others. News and television crews flew in from all over the world. The President himself did a little campaigning, although he was obviously in poor health. There were pictures of him being carried to speaking platforms, and assisted on and off planes. His hands were either bandaged or swollen and pocked with scabs. Whatever medical treatment he was undergoing at that time, it appears there was a lot of intravenous work going on. Transfusions? Dialysis through hand veins? One doctor did tell me he was being given transfusions between appearances to keep up his strength. The palace certainly wasn't talking. (When the Marcoses finally fled, five dialysis machines were found in the palace, plus a completely equipped surgical room, as well as oxygen tanks in his bedroom.)

During the campaign the President, Mrs. Aquino, and Imelda traded insults. President Marcos (who never referred to Mrs. Aquino by name) suggested that women should confine their preachings to "inside the bedroom"— an odd statement for the husband of Imelda Marcos to make. He also chided Mrs. Aquino for her total lack of experience and "having the nerve to aspire to the presidency."

Cory answered: "I concede that I cannot match Mr. Marcos when it comes to experience. I admit that I have no experience in cheating, stealing, lying, or assassinating political opponents."

Imelda complained of Cory's lack of interest in "love" and "beauty," the two things that should claim a Filipino woman's sole attention. She insisted that "what our people want is a woman of beauty."

When the President campaigned, the indefatigable Imelda did the warm-up for him. She appeared on stage in vivid red or blue ("Marcos colors"), talked to the voters, sang love songs. She often had with her a group of professional entertainers as crowd-getters.

Then the President would appear. The thrust of most of his campaign speeches was to warn of a Communist takeover if Cory were elected. He played up her inexperience, portraying himself as the strong, experienced leader the country needed. He also doled out government funds recklessly, promising aid for every request, in every province.

Since the Marcos government controlled most of the media, Cory Aquino's appearances and speeches got scant mention. It was the foreign press that gave her exposure. But, coverage or not, the people knew what was happening. Marcos's appearances and rallies, choreographed and funded as they were, drew relatively small crowds. Wherever Cory appeared, masses of people clustered around her. She was their hope.

She always ended her speeches with the phrase blazoned on opposition banners and posters: *"Sobra na—Tama na— Palitan na!"* ("Too Much—Enough Already—Change Him!") It drew roars of approval.

At one point during the campaign I received a call asking if I would agree to be the moderator of a national televised debate between the two presidential candidates. I thanked them for the honor but refused, figuring the President would make mincemeat out of my efforts to keep order. But I couldn't resist asking, "Why me?" The answer came back: "Yours was the only name acceptable to both sides." Apparently my efforts at being discreet all those years—in the interests of my husband's position— had paid off.

It was said that Marcos's final decision not to accept Cory's challenge for a public debate was based on the fact that Filipinos traditionally hold women in high respect and it wouldn't look good for him to criticize a woman. When the President backed off, Cory taunted him that he should "stand up like a woman."

That the President had badly miscalculated was soon apparent. Despite his endless campaign funds (he had two war chests in the palace full of cash solely for political campaigns), he was no shoo-in. Millions of people "voted their conscience" and came out against him. But the more votes were tallied against him, the more fraud and violence was stepped up to reverse the flow.

By 1986, the government tactics were different and more sophisticated than in 1984. Instead of simple disenfranchisement or voter intimidation, there was massive juggling of voters' lists in order to discourage voters known to be sympathetic to the opposition. Voters' names were scrambled and moved to another precinct. By the time a persistent voter located his or her name, voting hours were over. One of our grandsons, Mike Romulo, found his name had disappeared from the list of eligible voters in Forbes Park.

During the campaign a popular opposition leader in Antique province, Governor Evelio Javier, was gunned down by KBL assemblyman Pacificador's goons. His funeral, in Manila, was like a replay of the Aquino assassination. Thousands of mourners gathered at the church. Once again Imelda missed the point of nationwide revulsion at the brutal tactics of the Marcos people. When she was told how many mourners showed up, she commented that his family must have spent a lot of money on them. (When her own sister died that year, Imelda bought a crowd of mourners for P100 apiece.)

Mrs. Marcos was rightly worried about the role of the Church in the election. Her method for dealing with the Church in the past was a combination of piety, cajolery, and contribution. She had managed to seduce a few lesser members of the Church to her side, but she had never succeeded in befriending the powerful Cardinal Sin. And she had far less influence than she believed with the reigning bishops.

Two weeks before the election, she sent for Brother Dizon, president of the De La Salle College, and talked to him for over four hours at Malacanang Palace, trying to get him to stop the NAMFREL Quick Count, which she knew would never agree with the padded figures released by the government agency, Comelec. Brother Dizon refused to stop the count.

No amount of cheating could disguise the public will. In Manila and throughout the provinces NAMFREL volunteers manned the polling places, covering 85 percent of the country. "It was no problem pulling in volunteers," Maribel Ongpin told me. "I was briefing volunteers morning, noon, and night. They poured in—young, old, male, female, rich, poor, jobless, employed—a cross section of Philippine society." Because of their brave efforts much of the vote that otherwise would have been lost was counted and reported to NAMFREL headquarters in Manila. It was to make all the difference. According to the NAMFREL figures, Cory had won. Yet President Marcos stubbornly claimed victory through the doctored figures provided by Comelec.

After election day NAMFREL asked all the provincial coordinators to come to La Salle in Manila and asked each one to give a personal account of the election. It was on the basis of these field reports that the Catholic bishops met in Manila on February 13 and made a decision to release a pastoral letter denouncing the election as a "fraud unparalleled in Philippine history."

When Imelda got wind of what the bishops were about to do, she turned up at the Catholic bishops' headquarters in Intramuros at two a.m. demanding to see Ricardo Cardinal Vidal, the Archbishop of Cebu, who had presided at the meeting. The cardinal was awakened and met with her. She pled with him, trying to convince him not to publish the bishops' letter, and, not incidentally, reminding him that she had personally recommended, in Rome, that he be made a cardinal.

Cardinal Vidal told her the letter could not be withdrawn, for that was the consensus of all the Catholic bishops in the archipelago, and that even if he acceded to her plea, he had only one vote in the conference. The bishops released their letter to the press.

On February 15, despite the evidence of massive cheating, Marcos had himself proclaimed winner at the polls, through the Assembly. Cheated out of the election, Cory Aquino responded with a nationwide call for civil disobedience. She called for a mass rally at the Luneta on Sunday, February 16, to follow the reading of the bishops' pastoral letter in all the churches that morning.

Cory's rally was attended by three million people, although the Marcos press reported only "a few thousand" in attendance.

Her seven-point program of nonviolent civil disobedience included work stoppage and cancellation of classes on the first working day following Marcos's inauguration. She asked for a boycott of the "crony banks;" customers were asked to withdraw their deposits and make no new deposits. A massive boycott of Marcos-controlled media was also called for. Citizens were asked to delay payment of electricity and water bills. They were told to boycott Rustan's department and grocery stores, and to stop buying products from the giant San Miguel Corporation, including beer, ice cream, milk, and cheese (of which SMC was the main supplier).

Beginning with Manila, Cory intended to carry her program of civil disobedience throughout the Philippines. It would seriously damage the national economy. Her call for boycott was immediately effective. People stopped buying the newspapers owned by the President's cronies: Kokoy's *Times Journal*, Benedicto's *Express*. Rustan's faced empty aisles normally crowded with customers. Cojuangco's Cocobank and Benedicto's Royal Traders faced a run on withdrawals. Coca-Cola and San Miguel Beer—favorite beverages of Filipinos—languished on the shelves. Stocks in San Miguel slipped on the stock market. Films starring pro-Marcos stars Nora Aunor and Ronnie Poe were boycotted.

A diplomatic boycott also took place. Of all the resident ambassadors, only the Russian congratulated President Marcos on his victory and that was, he explained sheepishly, only because he was already in the palace on another matter. Australia and Spain recalled their envoys. Canada, between ambassadors, detained its new appointee at home. The EEC countries came out with a joint statement condemning the Marcos election.

The Marcos inaugural, planned originally as a splendid event on the Luneta, was shifted to the palace itself. No diplomats were invited.

After President Reagan's unfortunate off-the-cuff comment that there was "probably cheating on both sides" provoked an avalanche of criticism, the State Department claimed the president "mis-spoke" and plans were made to send Special Envoy Philip Habib to Manila to correctly assess the situation for the American president.

Three days after Cory's rally, on February 19, the US Senate passed a resolution declaring the Philippine election "fraudulent." The election had turned into a morality play and, for the moment, the forces of evil were still in the saddle. Though President Marcos was now condemned by his own people, his own Church, and the outside world, he still hung on.

Imelda underrated the influence of Corazon Aquino. Cory, Imelda sniffed, "is a crude soul, a woman without facial makeup or a manicure." She simply could not understand how the plain, soft-spoken housewife could be a political opponent to reckon with.

She also lost her fight with the Church. She couldn't buy them and she was unsuccessful at wooing them to the Marcos side. No amount of soldiers, guns, or money could alter the course of things. The Marcos approach of buying off anyone and everyone simply did not work with the clergy. "For Church people," Brother Dizon told me, "money is not a primary consideration."

The most commonly heard comment from the poor people who today tour Malacanang Palace is: "She had all those saints—and they didn't help her!"

The People vs. the Marcoses

T HE government itself was divided over how to handle the threat of Cory's boycott. The technocrats, among them Prime Minister Virata and Trade Minister Bobby Ongpin, stood on one side trying to get what concessions for reform they could from the President in order to salvage the country's economy. On the other side, Imelda, Kokoy, Ver, and their cronies were not prepared to yield an inch to the opposition.

General Ver came up with a sinister scenario that he discussed with the Marcoses in private. It was similar to the scenario for the first declaration of martial law: His men would stage widespread bombing and arson throughout the city, which would be blamed on the Communists. A state of emergency would be declared and martial law imposed.

The master plan for putting down the nonviolent civil disobedience was code-named "Oplan (Operation) Everlasting." Following the declaration of martial law, 150 people would be arrested, including Mrs. Aquino, Doy Laurel, Defense Minister Enrile, and the entire executive council of NAMFREL. Ver, who had a private grudge against

Bobby Ongpin, also had his name on the list, along with Bobby's brother Jaime, a leader of the opposition.

Enrile knew full well he was on Ver's hit list. His own security had got wind of Ver's plans. And RAM, the reform group of the military of which he was a member, was considering a coup against Malacanang. There seemed no other way to unseat the recalcitrant President, who had been voted out of office but refused to leave.

The tip-off that Ver was ready to put his plan in motion came on February 21 when Bobby Ongpin's security force was mysteriously arrested. All were men supplied by Enrile. Bobby immediately reported to the Defense Minister.

Enrile, as was his custom, was having coffee with friends at the Atrium, a giant modern office building in the financial district of Makati.

"Johnny," Bobby blurted out, his voice shaky. "What have you done with my security? They've all been pulled off. I feel naked. I'm afraid to leave my house."

"What?" There was a moment's silence. "Okay, I'll call you back."

Johnny knew nothing about the fate of Ongpin's security. But the news catapulted him into instant action. If Ver pulled off Ongpin's security, that meant he was ready to start making arrests. Enrile decided to preempt Ver.

Johnny hurried to his home in Dasmarinas Village, across a vacant lot from my house, for lunch with his wife, Cristina. They had barely finished when his security and intelligence chiefs, Colonel Honasan and Lieutenant Colonel Kapunan, and his senior aide, Major Noe Wong, arrived. They confirmed Enrile's suspicions: There was an order for his arrest. General Ver's people had got wind of a plot by RAM to kidnap the President, and he put out an order for the arrest of the Defense Minister and all RAM members. They discussed their options. They could disperse—and then "we would be picked up one by one." They could go to the provinces. Or they could stay where they were. Enrile chose to take a stand in Manila. "We better take them on."

He went to his bedroom, came out dressed in sneakers, blue jeans, and fatigue jacket. He was carrying an Israeli Uzi machine pistol over his shoulder.

Cristina panicked. "What are you going to do?"

"A plot has been discovered," Enrile told his wife, "and we will be arrested. I'm going to headquarters. I don't know when I can come back. Contact Mrs. Apostol (a newspaperwoman who was a friend of theirs), call the media people, and tell them to meet me at my office. Then call Cardinal Sin."

He made one call himself, to General Fidel Ramos.

Lieutenant General Fidel Ramos—a tanned, trim, athletic man with horn-rimmed glasses, and a perpetual seven-inch cigar, had gone to his office in Camp Crame that Saturday morning, then went home for a late lunch with his wife, in the suburb of Alabang.

When he reached home, his wife, Ming, told him she had just received a call from Mrs. Betty Go Belmonte, a publisher of the newspaper *Inquirer*, warning them that there was a reliable rumor that Enrile had been arrested and the general might be picked up at any time.

"Eddie," said Enrile, "are you still with me?"

Without hesitation, General Ramos said, "Yes, all the way."

When Ramos left his house he was dressed in a civilian bush jacket and slacks. He had no arms.

From his office at Camp Aguinaldo, on the EDSA,* Enrile spoke by telephone to Stephen Bosworth, the American ambassador, to inform him that they were grouped at the camp in anticipation of their arrest. The diplomat answered only that he "would inform [his] government about it." Enrile also informed Ambassador Kiyoshi Sumiya of

*A large, four-lane highway; it was the site of the revolution.

Japan of the situation. He told the newsmen who were gathering at his office that he made these calls so that "the world will know what is happening in case we are annihilated." Then he ordered Colonel Honasan to prepare a defense of the area in the camp. He cautioned "Gringo" not to fire the first shot, and only to reply if attacked, because he wanted to maintain a possible dialogue with whoever might challenge their stand.

Enrile called Cardinal Sin. He explained they had broken with President Marcos and asked his help to call people into the streets to protect them. "Can you help us?" The Cardinal said, enigmatically, "We will pray."

The idea of a revolution against Marcos was not unacceptable to the Cardinal, despite Vatican admonitions to stay out of politics. For years he had been performing a remarkable balancing act: keeping close to the people by criticizing the government, yet keeping his channels open to Malacanang.

The defection caught President and Mrs. Marcos and General Ver by surprise. Confident of their own plans, it hadn't occurred to any of them that Enrile would move first.

The President tried to get his Defense Minister on the phone. But Enrile ducked him. Finally, after sending emissaries back and forth between Enrile's headquarters and the palace, Enrile spoke to Ver.

From there on it was a war of wits between the clever lawyer and the obtuse general. At the time Enrile made his stand, he had only about 150 men with him. What he needed was time. He played on Ver's main concern: protection of Malacanang Palace and its occupants, the Marcos family.

"If you approach us," Enrile warned Ver, "we will have to fight back."

Neither side really knew what cards the other held. En-

rile emphasized that his people were in a defensive rather
that an aggressive position.

"Will you commit yourself not to attack the palace
tonight?" asked the worried General Ver. He didn't know
what Enrile had in the way of helicopters or weapon capacity.

"We have no aggressive intention against the palace,"
Enrile assured him.

A little after six that evening Enrile and Ramos held their
first press conference announcing their defection. It was
not shown on the Marcos-controlled television stations.
The rumors about the defection were in the air and we
were all on the telephone to each other. We listened to it
live on the Catholic radio station, Veritas, after which it was
replayed at regular intervals, throughout the night, so that
all Manila and the surrounding provinces would know what
had happened.

The Defense Minister opened the press conference with
the announcement that he and General Ramos were no
longer part of the Marcos administration. He said that he
could not, in all conscience, support a government that
"does not represent the will of the Filipino people."

A reporter asked Enrile whether he would go to the palace if Imelda Marcos asked him to come to talk to her.

"That would be like going inside a prison camp," Enrile
answered drily.

He was then asked if he would support Mrs. Aquino.

"I am morally convinced it was Mrs. Aquino who was
elected by the Filipino people," Enrile replied.

This was astounding news to most of us. We had not
considered Enrile as an important player in the fight between Marcos and the opposition. And it hadn't occurred to
any of us that he would come out in support of Cory Aquino.

It hadn't occurred to her either. The news of the Defense Minister's defection reached Cory in Cebu, in the central Visayas, an hour's flight from Manila, where she was carrying her message of civil disobedience to the provinces. She called Cardinal Sin. The Cardinal had faith in Enrile and Ramos and in their intentions and reassured Cory. "I am sure they are staging this because they want you to be president," he told her. She then called Enrile herself, and made plans to return to Manila.

We all watched as the President came on all TV channels to hold his own press conference in response to his minister's defection. Before Marcos spoke, Imelda told the assembled newsmen that her husband had been far too lenient with Enrile. "I told him as far back as 1972 to watch out, it might be Johnny who will kill you!"

A personal blow awaited her. President Marcos paraded Imelda's very own chief security officer, Captain Morales, whom she had personally picked to serve her, before the TV audience—and denounced him as leader of the coup against them. The luckless captain read a "confession" that had been prepared by Ver. When he was being led away, he passed by Imelda. "We had no intention of killing you and the President," he said quietly. She burst into tears and left the room.

Enrile spoke once more to General Ver that night. "Our office is full of foreign correspondents," he warned Ver. "The highway outside is full of civilians. Don't fire on these people. It would look bad for the President if you fire on defenseless civilians."

"That's when he could have wiped us out," Johnny told me later, laughing. "But then he never was a good military man."

NAMFREL leaders Joe Concepcion and Christian Monsod appealed to Cardinal Sin to call out the people to protect Enrile and Ramos. "Our workers are just waiting for a word from you," they told him.

Cardinal Sin went on radio Veritas, calling on the people

to come into the streets and protect the defectors. The
NAMFREL volunteers poured out. Many of them had
been in street demonstrations three years before, after the
Aquino assassination. They were programmed for civil action. They came, whole families, with their plastic bags of
food and thermoses of water, their radio sets, and their
diaper bags. By Saturday night, all traffic on the EDSA was
at a standstill.

By now, the news of the Philippine revolution was being
carried round the world. I got a long-distance call from my
brother in New York. "Aren't you going to try to get out?"

It hadn't occurred to me. "No," I said. "This is my first
revolution. I wouldn't miss it for the world!"

The airport closed at Sunday noon. Dick and Tessie,
who had been in Hong Kong for the weekend, got the last
plane in.

None of us knew what would happen next. The defectors were holed up in Camp Aguinaldo. Ver and his security
were holed up in the palace. The people were out in the
streets. But what about all the military?

Unbeknownst to us, General Ramos was getting
through, one by one, to the commanders in the field. He
had gone to his office at Camp Crame after the press conference to make his calls. His message was simple: Join us
if you can. If you can't, stay neutral. It was a message most
were willing to accept. No one relished the idea of firing on
civilians.

The tennis and badminton courts at the Polo Club were
empty. So was the golf course at Manila Golf. Even the old
ladies' mah-jongg tables were unattended. Everyone was
either at EDSA or glued to the radio and TV. Maids asked
their mistresses' permission to join the protesters. One
maid, crippled with polio, walked four miles to join the
crowd at Camp Crame. Some maids and mistresses went
out together, carrying food and jugs of water to the people.

Food enjoys an almost mystical importance in the Philippines. It is offered as a token of hospitality at any hour of the day or night. It was true to the Filipino character that one of the first things Enrile did was warn the media people who crowded his office that he had "no food" to offer them.

The message was carried on Veritas: They need food at Camp Aguinaldo. Within a half hour, it began to arrive: simple rice and soft drinks from the poor people, great pots of hot meat and fish stews from the more well off.

Rumors spread like wildfire. Imelda had taken the grandchildren and left. Only the President is in the palace. The President left secretly by the river. The President is dead.

Calls came in from New York. "Are the Marcoses still there?" I didn't really know. I had heard they had been sighted in Guam. "Is there any shooting?" Not that I could hear or see from my house. I gave orders to my little staff to get what supplies we needed from the nearest grocery and then stay in. I had been advised to lie low, and didn't want my cars or staff on the streets.

Marcos suddenly appeared on TV, broadcasting in battle jacket from Malacanang. Our hearts sank. He was still here. Imelda, wordless for once, stood behind the President's chair, her face unhappy. Daughter Irene sat nearby, staring absentmindedly into space. Two of the grandchildren played at the President's feet. We were all shocked that the grandchildren were still there. Why hadn't they sent them abroad, out of harm's way? Was it to get sympathy for themselves? "That's obscene," said my youngest daughter-in-law, Olivia. "Keeping those poor children there. If he loved them he would have sent them out of danger."

He had nothing new to say—just rambled on about the "plot" against him.

"Marcos was relying too much on his generals," Enrile told me later. "And the generals thought by simply issuing commands they would be obeyed. That is the greatest error of a leader: to only deal with the top. Many of those generals were already washed out so far as their commands were concerned."

Since he couldn't contact him on the phone, Marcos sent two emissaries from his KBL party to see Enrile. At their insistence, Enrile finally spoke with the President briefly. When he put down the phone, he told the two men: "The bottom-line demand—which is nonnegotiable—is for him to step down!"

They were shocked. "And remind the President of what I told him in 1983. He will become a virtual prisoner of some people in the palace."

"I don't know whether he remembered," smiled Enrile. "But when he got my message he was furious."

To the surprise of everyone at Malacanang, Marcos promptly called a late-night press conference.

He accused Enrile of being "out to grab power and rule the country through a junta." His rage went beyond his defense minister. He called Cardinal Sin "an inciter to rebellion" and "a mouther of subversion statements!" He said Enrile, Ramos, and all the reformists would have to stand trial.

Some divisions remained loyal to the President and responded to General Ver's frantic commands to attack the defectors.

"Government tanks are approaching EDSA," announced Radio Veritas on Sunday. "It is necessary for a large crowd to meet the tanks and immobilize them."

Nuns formed the first line of defense, kneeling in the street before the line of armored vehicles that were approaching, saying their rosaries. Thousand of men, women, and children formed a solid phalanx behind them. "I was scared," admitted Butz Aquino, younger brother of the slain opposition leader. "And then you see those little nuns and you know you can't back off." The nuns became known as "Enrile's marines."

Three battalions of marines loaded on ten landing vehicle tanks armed with 104-mm howitzers and 50-calibre machine guns descended on the crowd. When the towering tanks reached the first line of praying nuns, the commander ordered them to stop. "Those 45-ton LVTs could have just rammed through the crowds," General Tadiar admitted later. "But I didn't want to be known as the Butcher of Ortigas Avenue."

"We have our orders," General Tadiar told the crowd. "Let us pass."

"No!" roared the crowd, as a single voice.

"I'll give you thirty minutes to make way," he said, "then we are coming through."

As the columns of tanks approached, Enrile made two telephone calls. The first was to Ambassador Bosworth, telling him of the imminent tank attack. He said that many people would die, including scores of media men from the United States. He hoped Bosworth would inform his government of the situation, and that officials there would caution the palace to take a more prudent course.

Then he called Ver. "General," he said, "I know your columns are coming toward us. I want you to know that this building is full of civilians, not only former officers who served under you and who have served the President, but more than that there are many foreign correspondents with us. And if you are going to kill us, you and the President will both go down in history as butchers of your own officers and men, of the Filipino people and foreign media men. Kindly tell your tank commander not to proceed, because you might end up killing a lot of civilians."

Ver replied: "Well, sir, I will tell them not to push the civilians."

The women, children, and nuns, all offering flowers from their gardens, food, and cigarettes to the tank crews, were a target that the soldiers could not, finally, fire upon. One sergeant thought he saw the face of his wife and child in the sea of humanity below him and threw away his gun.

Later at home he asked his wife angrily why she had gone there. "I didn't," she replied in bewilderment. "I was in the house all day."

Finally the marines turned their tanks away and withdrew to Fort Bonifacio.

As night closed in, fears rose of an attack under cover of darkness. Joe Concepcion and Dick Romulo left the crowd at Crame and went to the US Embassy to tell the ambassador of the gravity of the situation. "It's getting more dangerous by the moment. We don't know how long Enrile and his people can hold out."

Ambassador Bosworth was guarded. "I'm keeping Washington informed," he said obliquely. He understood the Filipinos' position only too well, but he knew from Mike Armacost in Washington that they were briefing President Reagan.

The American president's friendship with Marcos dated back a long way, and he was understandably reluctant to tell his old friend to step down.

President Marcos came on TV at midnight castigating the rebels for their stand. "If innocent blood is shed, it will be their fault!" He sounded angry and out of control.

Later he would say he averted bloodshed by giving orders not to attack. In fact, his orders to attack had not thus far been obeyed.

General Ver ordered a full-scale assault for Monday morning, before sunrise. General Ramos got the report through his intelligence: Ranger Units were advancing toward Camp Crame. Armored columns were moving on the camp from three directions. Artillery and mortar were being placed to hit the camp. Gunships were going to attack at dawn.

"Just before dawn I gathered all the civilians at Crame," General Ramos told me, "and I explained that the situation is very bad. "'All those who want to leave, feel free to do so. Do not be ashamed to leave.'" No one left.

The Ranger Units, dressed in black, were creeping through a side street under cover of darkness when a civilian spotted them. He honked a car horn, flashed car lights off and on. Other cars joined in. The Rangers were exposed. They were held back by the crowd that rushed to meet them. No shots were fired.

The civilian crowd protecting the perimeters of Camp Aguinaldo were not so lucky. Antiriot police and soldiers armed with truncheons, shields, and tear gas advanced on the civilians.

Soldiers in trucks in the front line tossed four canisters of tear gas into the crowd. The crowd broke and ran, gasping in the semidarkness, eyes burning, as the fumes engulfed them. Then they stopped running, covered their faces with wet towels, and regrouped.

The antiriot soldiers attacked again. More canisters of tear gas were tossed toward the civilians. At that moment, the wind suddenly shifted. The cloud of tear gas blew back into the faces of the soldiers, sending them, coughing and sputtering, into retreat. The soldiers did not regroup. When they withdrew the civilians were still in place. They began chanting "Our Father" as the sun rose.

At sunrise, the crowd in front of Camp Crame heard the distant drum of helicopter gunships. They watched them winging in—Sikorsky gunships—carrying enough mounted guns to wipe out all the civilians standing below.

Soon the gunships were directly overhead. The choppers swung in over the crowd, flying in low over the treetops. Families huddled together crying and praying. The choppers flew over their heads, past the gates of Camp Crame. The people stared in disbelief as they dropped down, neatly settling in the dust of the Camp Crame parade grounds.

Pilots and soldiers jumped out, waving white flags and tossing their guns on the ground.

The commandant, Colonel Sotelo, had made up his

mind to defect. His gift to Enrile and Ramos was five gunships, two rescue ships, one utility ship, and sixteen combat pilots from the 15th Strike wing.

The rotors of the craft were still turning when the people rushed to welcome them. Reporters shoved microphones at Sotelo's face, asking where they had come from. Minister Enrile and General Ramos embraced Sotelo and the pilots.

"I have not really done much in my life," explained the fifty-three-year-old commander, "and for once I wanted to make a decision for my country."

At nine o'clock word came through "a verified report" on Veritas that President Marcos had left the palace. Elated, General Ramos went outside to tell the people. The crowd was ecstatic.

At 9:30 Marcos suddenly appeared on Channel 4. It was a hoax. He had not left.

That is when General Ramos decided "to go after the TV and radio stations and utilize our forces to go out and get them by force." He sent word for the crowds to stay in place and gave the orders for squads of soldiers to secure Channels 4, 7, and 9, and several radio stations. It was Enrile and Ramos's first attack against the loyalists.

Next, the frustrated President ordered Camp Crame bombed by planes. Two jets flew over, but they did not drop their bombs. One of the pilots later told his priest that heavy clouds made the visibility poor. He went lower. There was still haze. He went even lower. When he did, he saw all his relatives below him. He flew back to his base.

Commander Sotelo told Enrile and Ramos that Ver still had control over several helicopters and jet planes in the Villamor air base. Reports came over the radio, from conversations overheard between the palace and the base, that an airborne commando team was being organized to wreck the Sikorsky gunships parked at Camp Crame.

"Destroy their craft," General Ramos ordered Colonel Sotelo.

Three Sikorsky helicopters were dispatched to bring them down if in the air or destroy them on the ground. Major Charles Hotchkiss, commander of the 20th Air Squadron, took off from Camp Crame leading the attack.

One pass was all that was needed to accomplish this mission. The six presidential air squads that would have ferried Ver's troops to attack Camp Crame and Aguinaldo were destroyed. Columns of black smoke rose to the sky.

I saw the dense plumes of smoke from my bedroom window. What was it? Loyalist or rebels? I didn't know.

Military defectors poured into Camp Crame all day. Someone put up a hand-lettered sign, DEFECTION CENTER, and strung it across the bleachers on the parade ground. The NAMFREL volunteers set up emergency kitchens inside the camp ground to feed the hungry soldiers.

At ten o'clock a gunship made a measured rocket attack on the palace.

"We instructed them not to hit the palace directly, but show that we could inflict damage to them," explained Enrile.

Six rockets were fired at Malacanang. Five hit the garden harmlessly. One shattered the windows of the bedroom of Imelda Marcos, but no one was hurt. The First Lady, in anticipation of an attack on Malacanang, had rearranged, with her helpers, the drapes, windows, book cabinets, glasses, and lamps in every room so that in case of such an attack they would not be showered by glass splinters. The entire Marcos family with the exception of the President were in the pantry, "cowering in fear," as the President himself said. He remained at his desk throughout the raid—apparently determined to die in the presidential chair, with the presidential seal behind him.

This vulnerability to death made President Marcos realize that he had lost the contest, for if his artillery and mortars could raze Camp Crame and Aguinaldo, so too could the rebel gunships destroy the palace and its occupants.

He got Enrile on the telephone. "You are attacking us!" he raged. "My family is cowering in fear!"

"No, sir," Enrile said. "We have not ordered a direct attack on the palace."

That same morning Ambassador Bosworth telephoned President Marcos to convey President Reagan's warning not to use heavy weapons on the rebels.

"The situation is still under full control," Marcos announced at a live TV news conference, in which he was expected to announce an ultimatum to the rebels. The TV interview, held shortly after Reagan's warning was received, was held at the reception hall, with local and foreign correspondents present. Marcos was positioned at the extreme left of the screen, while Imelda, their children, and grandchildren were arrayed on the other side.

"We are ready to attack, sir," interrupted General Ver agitatedly. "We have two fighter planes hovering above, awaiting my orders to stage an air strike." Apparently he did not know that the pilots of those jets were already taking orders from General Ramos.

Imelda didn't want a direct attack on the people for her own reason.

"If we wipe them out," she was overheard saying to the President, "what will happen to our assets in the United States?"

Marcos gave orders not to use any heavy weapons unless the rebels attacked government buildings and installations. "Use only small arms," Marcos ordered, when the picture on the screen abruptly disappeared. The news conference blinked off the air. Marcos, who had dominated the media for twenty years, had been cut off. The government TV channel had fallen into the hands of the rebels.

On Sunday noon in Washington (it was midnight in Manila), a meeting was held at the White House with Secretary Shultz and President Reagan present. It was decided to convey another message to President Marcos, that the time had come to prepare for a transition government, and to offer him safe haven and access to medical care in the United States. This message was cabled to Manila and Secretary Shultz and Armacost made an oral presentation to Blas Ople, Marcos's Minister of Labor, who had been sent to Washington to present the Marcos side of the election story only days before the revolution began.

When she arrived in Manila to take her place as the revolution leader, Corazon Aquino issued a statement that "she would be magnanimous in victory."

While the composition of her provisional government was being drawn up on Monday, February 24, the then Prime Minister of France, Laurent Fabius, in an interview on French television, said: "We must give our support to democracy and say we are on the side of Mrs. Aquino."

He was the first head of state to recognize Corazon Aquino as the lawful President of the Republic of the Philippines.

The Agence France Press, in a dispatch from Washington, stated: "The United States, for the first time, called Monday on Philippine President Ferdinand Marcos to step down, saying that any attempt to prolong his twenty-year-administration was 'futile.' White House spokesman Larry Speakes said that 'a solution to this crisis can only be achieved through a peaceful transition to a new government'"

President Reagan went on radio and TV to say: "Any attempt to resolve the military crisis by force would surely result in bloodshed and casualties, further polarizing Philippine society and [doing] untold damage to the relationship between our governments. We have heard disturbing reports of a possible attack by forces loyal to General Ver against elements of the forces who have given their support to General Ramos and Minister Enrile. We urge those contemplating such action to stop. President Marcos has pledged to refrain from initiating violence and we appeal to him, to those loyal to him, and all the Filipino people to continue to do so. Attempts to prolong the life of the present regime by violence are futile. A solution to this crisis can only be achieved through a peaceful transition to a new government."

On Monday afternoon, in Washington, Secretary Shultz, Michael Armacost, and Philip Habib went to brief the Senate. In the midst of the briefing, Senator Laxalt was called to the telephone. Marcos was calling him. (It was 4:30 Tuesday morning in Manila.) Marcos expressed deep disappointment at the message he had received from the US, and he flew several trial balloons such as possibly serving as head of a coalition government or "consultant" to a government. He indicated his determination to remain in the country.

Marcos asked Laxalt whether the message he had received from the State Department through Ambassador Bosworth saying that the Reagan administration wanted him to step down truly represented Reagan's views. Laxalt assured Marcos that it did.

"He was a desperate man, grasping at straws," said Laxalt later. Laxalt felt sorry for Marcos and said that the power-sharing scheme was "impractical." Marcos told Laxalt "the Philippines is my home, and I want to stay here and die here."

President Marcos then appeared on Channel 7 in Manila, the one TV channel that had not yet been secured by the rebels. He repeated that his family "were cowering in terror in Malacanang because of the bombing threat from helicopters." He vowed he would defend the palace "to the last breath of my life and to the last drop of my blood."

The final camera shot of him was from a distance, surrounded by empty chairs, a picture of loneliness and desertion.

Out at Last

I T was five a.m. in Manila when President Marcos took a call from Senator Laxalt in Washington. Laxalt was surprised at the subdued quality of the President's voice. "All the spunk had gone out of him. The options for him had come down to staying in the palace and dying, or taking a walk."

Marcos asked Laxalt what the Senator describes as the "gut question": "Senator, what do you think I should do? Do you think I should step down?"

"I think you should cut, and cut cleanly," Laxalt told him. "I think the time has come."

There was a long silence. So long that Laxalt asked if Marcos was still on the line.

Finally Marcos, in a low, sad voice, answered, "I am so very, very disappointed."

Imelda broke down and sobbed.

Still the President did not want to leave Malacanang Palace. "Take the children and get out," he told Imelda. "Let me die here."

"No," she said. "We will stay with you. We will all die here."

A few hours after Marcos's talk with Laxalt, Imelda called the US Embassy to discuss the specifics of the US offer to get the Marcos family safely out of the Philippines.

Mrs. Marcos was told that the Marcos family and their friends would be welcome in the United States, provided there was a peaceful transition. The President, however, insisted on going through with his inaugural. He wanted to leave as the duly elected and inaugurated President of the Philippines.

General Ramos decided to call President Marcos himself to encourage him to step down peacefully. "I talked to him as to a younger brother. I spoke to him in dialect, calling him *Manong* [brother]. I told him the real score as far as the military was concerned. I said we had 85 percent of the military with us. I appealed to him to respond to the clamor of the people for him to step down, to avoid bloody confrontation."

The President could not believe that his army had deserted him. It had always been his strength, the source of his power. Even later, from Honolulu, he insisted "the army is full of Ilocanos. They still acknowledge me as their commander-in-chief."

But this was no longer true.

There were two inaugurals that day. Cory's came first. Her inauguration was scheduled to be held at nine o'clock at Club Filipino, a rambling open-style country club in the residential area of San Juan not far from Camp Crame and across the city of Manila from Malacanang Palace. It is a building with many private function rooms, and conferences and meetings are often held there. People began arriving by eight o'clock. At nine, Vice President Doy Laurel and his wife, Celia, arrived. Crowds were already waiting outside. The participants were jammed inside. Justice Claudio Teehankee was present to administer the oath. But Cory was not there.

Finally, at 9:30, Laurel received a telephone call. It was Cory. "Come to me," she told him. She was at her own family house on Times Street in the suburb of Quezon City about a twenty-minute drive away. Laurel hurried there. "What's the matter? Everyone's waiting for you. Why are you here?"

She told him that Enrile had warned her not to go out to Club Filipino. "He thinks it's unsafe."

"But I've had my own people sleeping in the building all night! None of the President's people have come near the place. It's safe, I promise you."

She was undecided.

"How would it be if I asked Enrile and Ramos to join us there?" Doy suggested. "Would you come then?"

She agreed. He got on the phone to Enrile and asked him and Ramos to proceed directly from Camp Crame to Club Filipino and meet them there. Enrile agreed.

The inaugural finally got underway at 10:30 a.m.

"I was scared," admits Justice Teehankee. "I didn't know whether it was legal or not."

Cory wore a bright yellow linen dress with cut-work sleeves and her usual light makeup. Small diamond stud earrings and a blackstrap wrist watch were her only jewelry. Dona Aurora Aquino, mother of her slain husband, held a small red-bound Bible (owned by the Laurels) during the ceremony.

When they came to the line "as President of the Republic of the Philippines," everyone started crying: Jimmy Ongpin, Dick Romulo, Joe Concepcion, even the radio announcer who was covering the event.

We had waited twenty years—we never expected to hear those words.

The new Chief Executive stepped to the rostrum, and

before a battery of microphones announced in her soft, sure monotone:

"I am taking power in the name of the Filipino people. I pledge a government dedicated to upholding truth and justice, morality and decency, freedom and democracy."

The Marcos inaugural was scheduled for 11:30. No diplomats were present. Even Marcos's own Cabinet ministers seemed to have disappeared. I scanned the unfamiliar faces on my television screen. Marcos's vice presidential candidate, Arturo Tolentino, was also missing. The crowd of strangers looked like office workers who had been invited to come in off the street.

Imelda was wearing a white *terno*—the graceful butterfly-sleeved dress made her appear regal and beautiful again. But her face was flat, without animation, her huge dark eyes lusterless.

While the inaugural ceremonies were in progress at the ceremonial hall of the palace, some 2,500 Marcos adherents had gathered outside, waving flags, wearing Marcos buttons and white T-shirts printed with his name. They continuosly shouted, "Marcos pa rin" (Still for Marcos). He appeared with Imelda on the balcony to acknowledge the plaudits of his supporters. They sang a duet—her favorite, *"Dahil sa Iyo"* (Because of You)—for the last time in their conjugal reign. Marcos still appeared composed, but Imelda's eyes shone with tears.

Tanks and fully armed soldiers were seen behind barbed-wire barricades at all entrances to the palace.

The President's rubber-stamp Chief Justice, Ramon Aquino, read the oath of office.

The President was repeating the oath of office in a solemn voice when the television screen suddenly went blank. The reformists had seized the last of the loyalist TV stations.

By Tuesday afternoon, President Marcos had no means of communication with the outside world except the telephone, and no forces left under his command. Even his personal pilots had deserted him. He called Enrile again and asked him to request security for the Marcos family from US Ambassador Bosworth.

By 7:15 the Marcoses had made up their minds. Word came in to Washington from Ambassador Bosworth in Manila that the family was prepared to leave the palace. The Marcoses asked to be taken to Clark Air Base and from there they hoped to be allowed to proceed north to the President's home in Paoay, in Ilocos Norte.

Late that afternoon General Ver, wearing a civilian suit, appeared from his quarters at the park. He had called his home for his wife to join him at the palace, bringing her valuables and some clothes. And he had issued orders for his constant companion, Edna Camcam, and her children to be evacuated.

Until the last moment, the President resisted leaving the palace although he himself had made the decision. It was finally his two sons-in-law, Greggy Araneta and Tommy Manotoc, who convinced Marcos he must leave "for his children and grandchildren's sake."

At a little before nine o'clock a US Air Force H-3 helicopter from Clark landed in front of the palace.

When it was found the Marcos party had swollen to 89 people, two more helicopters were sent for. They landed in the open park across the Pasig River from the palace. The baggage, boxes, and personal effects belonging to this small army of people were sent down the river by boat to the Army and Navy Club dock and thence by trucks to the US Embassy grounds, where they were loaded on helicopters to follow the evacuees.

When the first helicopter waiting on the palace lawn was ready to load, Marcos still held back. A nurse gave him a tranquilizer and his family half-carried him onto the waiting chopper.

At 9:05 p.m., the first of the helicopters lifted off. Others followed, one at a time, as soon as they were loaded. Before leaving, Marcos, through his wife, asked permission once again to fly to his home in Ilocos "in a spirit of reconciliation." His plea was transmitted to Ambassador Bosworth, who, in turn, relayed it to General Ramos and President Aquino.

The answer was an unequivocal no. Marcos must leave the Philippines. It was Cory Aquino's first major decision as the new President.

The people at the State Department did not tell Marcos where to go. They were only offering the way out. First, he and his party were flown to Clark Air Force Base and allowed to go to sleep. But the Philippine commander at Clark requested that the presidential party be moved on quickly. He feared trouble from the local Filipinos and could not guarantee the Marcos family's safety.

The President was wakened after only a few hours of sleep. He was so exhausted, he was carried on a stretcher to a military transport C-9 and flown with two doctors, his family, and the Vers out to Guam. A C-14 Starlifter carried the rest of his party.

The plane was out over the Pacific when Imelda said, "Why are we flying over water? I thought we were going to Paoay." (Later Marcos would claim the Americans "kidnapped" him and took him to Guam when he thought he was going home to Ilocos.) Imelda sang for the rest of the flight, to keep up their spirits.

Upon arrival in Agana three and a half hours later, the President was taken directly to the US Navy Hospital for a medical checkup. He was able to walk down from the plane unaided, wearing a golf hat and jacket. An American sergeant held an umbrella over his head, for a slight drizzle had fallen that morning.

"The President looked sickly, old, and dog-tired," observed Guam's Governor Reyes. "All he wanted to do was to hit the sack."

After resting at Guam, the Marcos family asked to be taken to Honolulu.

Back home, Tony Floriendo, the "banana king," slipped out by private jet to Brunei. Dr. Pacifico Marcos, the President's brother, fled to Kota Kinabalu to wait out the revolution. Marcos's ninety-two-year-old mother hadn't heard about the revolution that unseated her son; she was left in the comfort of the presidential suite atop the Philippine Heart Center. The President's younger sister, Elizabeth Keon, a victim of Alzheimer's disease, stayed in a mental ward in the Veterans Hospital.

When news reached Washington concerning Marcos's departure for Clark and Guam, Secretary of State Shultz appeared before reporters at the White House. "Reason and compassion have prevailed in ways that best served the nation and the Filipino people," he stated. He called the Filipinos "the true heroes of today because they have resolved this issue in a way that does them honor." He also lauded the decision of Marcos to step down. "Obviously, Marcos was reluctant to leave his post. At any rate, he did leave."

Shultz paid tribute to Mrs. Aquino for her "commitment to nonviolence," which he said had earned her "the respect of all Americans. This is not something the US has done— this is something that the Philippine people have done."

The poor people living near Malacanang, who had been barred from the grandeur of the palace grounds and lived for years without a glimpse inside those hallowed walls, stormed the fences and raced through the grounds. They hit the office of media affairs first, tore out the typewriters, the TV monitors, smashed the huge photographs of the President and First Lady, which had been required decor in every government office. By the time they reached the palace itself, guards had assembled and the people didn't get past the ground floor. There, they toppled chairs, smashed more pictures in Heroes' Hall, the huge, ugly, low-ceilinged dining room. That was all. Reinforcements were sent, and the palace was saved from being ransacked. This was the only mob violence of the revolution.

Rumor had it that Imelda had begun secretly moving her finest paintings and antiques out of the palace, into storage and to trusted friends' homes, several weeks before the controversial election. Malacanang itself still had many paintings on the wall—mostly flattering images of young, healthy, beautiful Ferdinand and Imelda. One depicts Marcos, bare-chested, as a jungle creature—a Philippine Adam. Another shows Imelda rising from the sea like Botticelli's Venus. But several of the most valuable paintings by Philippine and European masters were missing. And she obviously hadn't left any jewels behind. A large jewelry display case was open and empty in her bedroom, and the floor of her dressing room and bedroom were strewn with empty jewel boxes. There was a half-eaten banana on her night table.

In the President's library was a blackboard with a detailed map of Camp Crame, showing entry and egress and possible routes of attack. Beside it was a list of the rebels' estimated strength in arms and men.

There were two pallets on the floor of the President's bedroom. For the grandchildren? For nurses? No one was sure. But they had been recently slept on, judging by the rumpled linens. There was only one clothes rack in the President's bedroom, filled with bright-colored red and blue campaign shirts. A pair of his elevator shoes was under a desk. As a grotesque note to playful consumption, the President's room also contained a five-foot child-size gas-burning automobile valued at $7,000.

The palace intercom designated the Marcoses' bedrooms as the "king's" bedroom and the "queen's" bedroom. Indeed, Mrs. Marcos's private quarters were queenly. An elaborate bathroom was equipped with a 15-foot sunken tub, mirrored ceilings, baskets of imported soaps, and magnum-sized bottles of a French perfume, "First Lady." The adjoining dressing room had a makeup area befitting a Broadway star, with bright rows of theatrical lights surrounding the mirror. There was also commercial beauty parlor equipment—a professional hair-washing sink with sloped board, and a standing dryer. Her bedroom contained a 12-foot-wide bed, two queen-size beds, side by side, piled with satin pillows, table and chairs, and a baby grand piano. Her only clothes at this level of the palace were a cabinet full of nightgowns, and a half dozen Italian dressing gowns in the bathroom.

Mrs. Marcos's great collection of clothes and accessories was kept in what has become known as the "mini department store" on the ground floor below her bedroom. Here were the rows and rows of shoes, many with matching handbags, the racks upon racks of evening gowns and *ternos*, the rack of furs (although the finest were kept in storage in New York and Paris), the dozens of girdles and bras, mostly black.

There was also a room for gifts she intended to give away: boxes of Yves Saint Laurent shirts, dozens of rosaries, bolts of cloth, stereos, fifty-nine boxes of watches and pens from Cartier in New York.

On this same ground level was a fully equipped hospital room such as would be used for post-op recovery patients.

The President's own quarters were a pathetic testimony to chronic illness. There was a king-size bed (complete with mosquito net—all the beds had mosquito netting because of his aversion to repellents and sprays), but alongside it was a regulation hospital bed, with standby oxygen tank, EKG machine, and IV equipment. His bathroom contained rows of medications—and boxes of Pampers. Apparently one of his illnesses resulted in temporary or permanent incontinence. (Later, when the Marcos valuables were impounded, much of the jewelry Mrs. Marcos had taken with her was found packed in empty Pampers boxes.)

Mrs. Aquino intended to make Malacanang Palace a people's park, a reminder of the florid extravagances of the Marcos dynasty. When she opened it to the poor, she said: "Perhaps your visit will help you understand what happened to our country because our former leaders did not care."

For years denied access to the home of their President, thousands of Manila's poor now line up patiently each day for a glimpse of that past grandeur. They file through, viewing the gilt throne chairs of the departed residents, Imelda's dresses, her much-reported shoe collection. They shake their heads. They mutter. Sometimes they show their anger. One ragged man leapt onto Imelda's satin- and silk-draped bed and urinated on it before guards could stop him.

Before the palace was opened to the people, the contents were officially inventoried by volunteers, working with the SGV accounting firm. Most of the volunteers were old friends, classmates, and campaign helpers of Cory Aquino.

The final inventory listed 3,000 shoes, 1,000 gowns. Later, hundreds more shoes and gowns were found in her house in Leyte. "No wonder the Philippines is so poor," said an early visitor. "She spent all the money we borrowed."

The job of listing the medical supplies was given to a classmate, Dr. Angelita Reyes, my neighbor and friend. Several of us were invited to dine at Lita's house one night and we were surprised when our hostess was not at home to receive us. Her husband, Peping, explained she would be with us later but had been delayed at the palace. Then he was called to the phone, and left the house mysteriously. Finally they both reappeared while those of us waiting at their house stretched out the cocktail hour with many speculations. When Lita joined us, she was visibly agitated and wouldn't give any clear answer as to what had delayed her. Later she told me that while inventorying the medical equipment, she stumbled across documents in the President's bedroom that listed many of his foreign assets, an incredible number, going back twenty years—money spirited abroad, gold bullion placed at strategic points around the world, secret bank accounts. Recognizing the value of the "proof of theft" to the new government, she called for help, stayed with the documents until the new finance minister arrived, and then with him saw them into safekeeping at a Central Bank vault.

These documents later furnished a part of the evidence against President Marcos and helped form the basis for the government's suit against him. "Perhaps it was because he was a lawyer himself," speculated the Commission on Good Government's Washington lawyer, Severina Rivera, "he couldn't resist keeping detailed records. It will be his downfall."

A fascinating case recently reported in a Sydney, Australia, newspaper involves the World War II Japanese gold—referred to in the Philippines as "Yamashita's gold." As the Japanese swept successfully through Singapore, Malaysia, and the Philippines in the early days of World War II, they stripped the countries of their visible wealth—in the form of gold bars. These were then buried in the Philippines, in a cave in the mountain recesses of Baguio. For years, Filipinos have tried unsuccessfully to locate the cache of gold. According to the Australian account, the Japanese were aided in hiding their gold by one Filipino guerrilla: Ferdinand Marcos. He tricked the Japanese, and, when their armies left, managed to take the gold for himself. He dipped into this fortune, selling off a few bars, for the presidential campaign. The whole story came to light last September, when President Marcos, through his son in Singapore, tried to unload 2,000 tons of gold bars in Australia. There were no buyers in Australia for such a large amount of gold, so a deal was in progress with a consortium of Arab buyers in London. The gold bars, which eventually were smuggled out of the Philippines, are said to be stored in Hong Kong, London, Singapore, the United States, Switzerland, Panama, and the Netherlands Antilles. The gold was estimated to be worth $22 billion. In this instance, the President was correct in claiming that he was rich before he became President.

Between the President's gold bars and Imelda's real estate, the Marcoses had control of funds that far exceeded the Philippine national debt of $30 billion. Enough evidence exists that the new government feels confident they can reclaim some part of the staggering amount of loot the Marcos family spirited out of the country. One government analyst suggested a deal might be cut whereby the government would allow the Marcoses to keep a tenth of their wealth—which would still leave them $2 billion—and return the rest to their ravaged country. Surely one family, even people who spend like Imelda, could live out their lives on $2 billion?

According to a US Customs Service inventory taken after their property was impounded at Hickam Air Force Base, the Marcoses and their associates took with them more than 400 items of jewelry, including a gold crown and three diamond-studded tiaras, more than sixty sets of pearl necklaces and chokers, and a 150-carat Burmese ruby valued at $290,000. In addition, they fled with twenty-two crates containing $1.2 million in pesos. (President Marcos said later he carried pesos because he still expected he was going to fly to Ilocos.) One case held bearer securities including two Philippine bank certificates of deposit with a face value of $1.8 million. The overall inventory showed stocks, jewelry, and currency worth $10 million.

Found among the impounded luggage was a suitcase

marked F. Marcos, full of old sex magazines. For father or son?

Someone in Manila figured out that the legitimate income for President Marcos for his twenty years of service—1966 to 1986—would have come to a grand total of $327,000. At Malacanang, the President's daily take from the businesses that remitted 15 to 20 percent directly to him was recorded, held temporarily in the palace "money room," and then sent out of the country. One of the means used, for several years in the 1980s, was for the money to be brought to the personal desk of the then president and chairman of the Security Bank and Trust Company, Rolando Gapud, who would issue a receipt in his own hand to the bearer (a file of these receipts was found among the President's papers at Malacanang). Then it was up to Gapud to move the money abroad. For one year alone, from January 1983 to January 1984, Gapud moved $278 million out of Malacanang and into foreign bank accounts.

Among the items that turned up at the palace after the Marcoses left were Imelda's own household accounts, blue-ledger notebooks of her activities and expenses filled in by her secretaries and sycophants. An astonishing mix of millions and cents, the ledgers include releases of millions of pesos to politicians next to a few hundred pesos for the repair of a household TV set, or fifty pesos for a couple of bottles of Tabasco sauce for the presidential table. A fairly recent notation in the ledgers indicated that the First Lady and her two daughters were taking private instruction in Japanese cooking. Their teacher came to the palace each Sunday morning. The ladies would cook all morning, then the President and his two sons-in-law would dine on the results at family lunch.

Imelda was always a good tipper. (I used to see her handing out bills to the maids, bellboys, and doorman at the Waldorf, according to their rank from twenty to a hundred. Once she thought she had missed an elevator girl and called me to the car window as she was leaving the hotel, handing me a twenty-dollar bill to give the girl.) Her ledgers showed items of cash put into her evening bags so she would always have tips for waiters, musicians, and chefs when she dined out. At one dinner she especially enjoyed at the Hyatt Hotel's Misono Room, her tips for the evening ran to P20,000. At the palace parties on New Year's Eve, part of each table's centerpiece were bright, freshly minted pesos, which guests were free to pick up as they left.

In her ledgers were listed gifts by the hundreds. A single order was for 963 Elgin watches. A thousand-dollar Cartier tank watch was purchased by the hundreds. Her standard gift for the endless weddings, birthdays, and anniversaries to which she was invited was P50,000.

When the Marcoses fled, a Commission on Good Government was formed, whose primary mission was—and continues to be—to see what, if any, of the Marcos assets could be returned to the Philippine government. It has been able to freeze properties and stocks identified as belonging to the Marcoses in the Philippines. Thus far, the government has recovered $150 million worth of Marcos assets in the Philippines. But the big money is abroad.

How much it can retrieve is anyone's guess. President Marcos's appeal for presidential immunity from suit was denied. On the Commission's list of known personal assets, backed up by documents in the Commission's possession, are real estate holdings in New York, California, Texas, London, Australia, and Canada that total $622,359,000. Three of Imelda's personal bank accounts in Manila and in the Bank of America in the US, which contain $37.9 million, have been frozen. Investments listed run to $500 million, and gold bullion comes to $300 million.

How the Marcoses were able to make so many investments abroad is now becoming clear. There was an elaborate system of codes and false names, shell companies, and offshore corporations. For Imelda's New York properties alone, for instance, there were two tiers of offshore corporations established in the Caribbean. The Swiss bank accounts, which were set up as early as 1968, a mere two years after Marcos took office, according to the Commission on Good Government, were in the names of "William Saunders" and "Jane Ryan." If either of the Marcoses wanted to make withdrawals from these accounts, they sent a "Happy Birthday" message to an agent in Zurich; this agent in turn contacted a Hong Kong agent, who then traveled to Manila.

The amount of thievery is so enormous as to scarcely be believed. While Imelda's flamboyant dealing in expensive real estate was shocking enough—and also so public as to incur much wrathful criticism—it doesn't compare in size and scope to the amounts of money the President personally drained out of the Philippines. It is a staggering array of wealth, perhaps unequaled in the world today, and deeply ironic—given his somewhat abstemious and ascetic personality. The Marcoses have been labeled the world's wealthiest couple, and when the evidence is all in, they may well prove to be so.

President Aquino made good her campaign promise: She would not live or work in Malacanang Palace. As her office she chose, instead, the modern palace guest house immediatley across the circular drive from Malacanang.

The new President made an unscheduled visit to the palace on March 5 and looked around curiously at the displays of ostentatious spending—the expensive rugs and chandeliers and crystal statuettes, the antique (some life-size) statues of saints, the rosewood tables and quarts of perfume, the rows of unused gowns, the stacks of shoes, the freezers full of US steaks, and cabinets piled high with caviar.

"It looks like a hotel," she murmured as she walked out. Surely it was no place to live in.

Cory Aquino preferred to stay in her own home on Times

Street in Quezon City. Later she was persuaded to move into a gracious old-fashioned house across the street from Malacanang Palace, for security reasons. Her round trip to the office today consists of a block and a half drive by car from her home to the palace guest house. The people who elected her and who line up each day to tour the palace are near her, milling around in the public grounds of the palace, now known as "People's Park."

Her closeness to crowds makes President Aquino's security people nervous. "I'm not afraid of the people," Cory says serenely. "They protect me."

The revolution that ousted Ferdinand and Imelda Marcos was a moral revolution—a moral revulsion against an incredibly corrupt regime. It was not simply their corruption that alienated the people—a certain level is tolerated as inevitable in the Philippines—but the enormity of it. A few million spirited away to sustain political power is perhaps understandable. But billions? Why so much? For the honest who labored in the Marcos government, the President's theft from the Filipino people was a bitter betrayal. Billions syphoned off from an impoverished country—that is difficult to comprehend.

Corruption is endemic in Philippine society. The very low wages paid civil servants, for example, almost insures routine bribes as a way of making ends meet, for everything from "fixing" a parking ticket to trying to get a judge to drop a case. The equally low-paid military are often involved in such illegal activities as log smuggling, dynamite fishing, and gambling operations.

Bribery exists in most countries. (Try to get a license to alter your house or change the plumbing in New York, or Milan, without paying off some inspector.) But in the Philippines it is perhaps more openly accepted. And whether it can ever be changed, without a dramatic upward shift in the economy that provides better wages and employment for all, is a real question. Skilled labor is the Philippines' major export. Because of low wages at home, everyone who can qualify goes abroad. Their remittances, in dollars, to relatives back home help keep the country afloat.

Corruption in the Philippines starts at the top—the higher the position the larger the payoffs. This became institutionalized during Marcos's twenty-year rule. The biggest payoffs of all went to the President himself.

The Marcoses boasted, in the beginning, of breaking up the old oligarchies, which left the wealth and power of the country in the hands of the few. They portrayed themselves as modern-day Robin Hoods returning ill-gotten wealth to the poor. The trouble was it never got to the poor. For every oligarchy or monopoly they disassembled, a new one was created in its place—with the wealth going either to a member of their own families or to their friends. When they drove the economically and politically powerful Lopez family out of the Philippines, for example, it was Imelda's brother, Kokoy, who inherited the Lopezes' lucrative Manila Electric Company.

The Marcoses' reliance on nepotism was, like bribery, a characteristic Filipino trait—but one that got carried to an extreme. The greatest loyalty in Philippine society is to the family. There are no old people's homes. Families take care of their own, often at great personal sacrifice. It is a matter of intense personal pride. No one who has a relative is left to suffer or die alone.

There is no instinctive loyalty to the government. During Spanish rule, the only way the average Filipino could acquire anything was to find a Spanish patron or bribe some minor authority for a favor. Forty years of American rule did little to dispel these centuries-old habits. When the Philippines finally achieved its independence, it was assumed that those in power, in the Congress and the palace, would benefit personally from their position. The Marcoses were merely more audacious and greedy than most power-hungry officials.

Money allocated to social projects had a way of evaporating on its way from initial disbursement to the recipient. A study carried out at the University of the Philippines established the loss at a standard 30 percent. This was true of money appropriated by government departments, or money dispensed through the former Congress. A new Congress has been created, according to the requirement of the Constitution, which has just been written. What will happen then? The same old thing? Or can there be a new moral order?

The free press, too, can now perform a real service to the country as a watchdog of the democratic process. Thus far, however, it has done little more than gleefully report personal gossip about the members of the new government and the constitutional committee, and describe fights in the Cabinet meetings. Perhaps, in time, a more responsible and informed press can develop in the Philippines, and fulfill the important role of calling attention to corruption in government before it reaches the astounding proportions of the Marcos years.

Can Cory Aquino change all this?

No one doubts that the President herself is "clean," as are many of the people around her. But can her ethical example alter an entrenched system? Can one administration achieve a moral and sociological revolution that will overturn years of ingrained habit? When Cory's new Commissioner of Internal Revenue, Bienvenido Tan, launched a program of "no bribes" throughout his department his employees complained. Without bribes their families will suffer, they asserted. The government has made an effort to counter that fear by permitting government employees to moonlight, holding other jobs in order to raise their standard of living by legitimate means.

Despite the backing of the Catholic Church in the Philippines, and the United States government, Mrs. Aquino faces severe problems. From the beginning she has reigned over a quarrelsome and, to a great extent, amateur cabinet. Her defense minister, Mr. Enrile, denied what he felt was his just role in power sharing with the President following the revolution, took his complaints to the public and has become a maverick critic of government policy. He also seems to be campaigning for the presidency, a job that is not open at the moment. President Aquino has been forced to take a stand, and demand the resignation of her entire cabinet. She named General Rafael Ileto, the assistant minister of defense, to take over Enrile's position. Other controversial cabinet ministers are also being replaced.

The Constitution provides for Mrs. Aquino to remain in office for six years before a presidential election can be called. There was considerable agitation, by Enrile and his colonels and some other political hopefuls, calling for an earlier presidential election. Mr. Enrile is sixty-three-years-old and he does not want to wait six years. Fortunately, his power base is limited and does not add up in numbers to the strength of the army under General Ramos, who continues to be loyal to the President.

The Communist insurgency continues to be a major problem for Cory Aquino. She campaigned for the presidency on a platform of amnesty and reconciliation, which is the position of the Church. Some of the Communist ideologues, however, seemed to show little interest in accepting her offer of amnesty. National peace negotiations have broken down and amnesty is now being offered on a regional level.

Mrs. Aquino's conciliatory approach to her country's problems is sometimes misperceived, both at home and abroad, as a sign of weakness. It is not. It is patience, and a commitment to hear all sides before she makes her decisions. "I'm going to get the blame anyway," she remarked realistically. "So I might as well do what I believe is the right thing."

Her months in office have sharpened her political skills.

Now she has the self-assurance and authority to go against her advisors when she thinks she knows better. In her memorable visit to the United States, for instance, she arrived in Washington from the West Coast, to be handed three different speeches prepared for her to deliver in her maiden appearance before the American Congress. She studied all three, and threw them out, then stayed up all night writing her own. Her appearance was a vivid, emotional success. She had hit precisely the right note to get through to her audience.

She still holds the popular support of the Filipino people. And she is making helpful friends for the Philippines abroad as she embarks on her official trips: to the neighboring ASEAN countries, to the United States, to Japan. If anyone can lead the Philippines out of the morass of twenty years of entrenched corruption, she will be the one.

Ferdinand Marcos, meanwhile, can be counted on to make mischief for the fledgling Aquino administration. Marcos money is still available in Manila to fund loyalist rallies. Marcos was proved to have been on the telephone to his vice presidential running mate, Arturo Tolentino, when Tolentino led what turned out to be a farcical mini-coup by taking over the Manila Hotel for a few hours in July of 1986 and proclaiming himself "Acting President."

Despite being reprimanded by the US State Department for his efforts to destabilize the government in Manila, Marcos master-minded another more serious coup attempt in January of 1987. Soldiers loyal to the former president attempted to take over Villamor Air Base and Sangley Point Air Base in Manila, as well as Channel 7 TV. It was a three-day standoff until General Ramos prevailed on the mutineers to give up without bloodshed.

The Marcoses had a chartered plane standing by in Honolulu when the plot was discovered and his US hosts warned him not to attempt to leave. As usual, Imelda had tipped off the plan by being observed buying $2,000 worth of army fatigues and boots at an army surplus store in Honolulu.

Again, Marcos had miscalculated his popularity. He thought when "his" soldiers (who were paid P500 apiece) made a move, others would join them, thus preparing his re-entry. His old mother had been spirited out of the Heart Center and taken to his home province in preparation for their reunion. (His sister had died in December.) Some of his cronies were standing by in Hong Kong and Singapore, waiting to join him on his triumphal return to Manila. There is no doubt he will keep trying to come back until he dies.

"What about Imelda? She still considers her husband "the strong man" the Philippines needs, and prophesies that without him the country will fall to the Communists. "The US will lose the Philippines," she predicts. "And without the Philippines, the US will no longer be a world power."

Epilogue

W HEN I first heard that the Marcoses were living in a military bungalow with two bedrooms and a single bathroom, at Hickam Air Force Base, I thought they must be going crazy. It's the closest they have had to be in twenty years. But eventually they moved to a rented beach house, and then, at long last, to one of the two beautiful homes they own in Honolulu, which they claim is being leased for them by friends.

What can Imelda of the prodigious twenty-four-hour energy do with herself, locked in with an aged and ailing husband in a house in Honolulu?

The President can study his law books and try to find a way out of their legal dilemma. He always was a reader.

The only thing I ever saw Imelda read was a prepared speech. She gets all her information by ear, and needs people around her always.

At first the family was all together, but constant bickering about who was at fault for their downfall apparently soured things. Imelda was said to have been especially hard on Imee's husband, Tommy Manotoc, implying that all their problems started when he joined the clan. In retaliation, Imee and her husband left Hawaii. When last sighted, the Manotocs were in Morocco on false passports.

Irene and her husband, Greggy Araneta, have been in and out of Hawaii, sometimes staying in the Araneta property on the west coast. Bong Bong apparently has his own household near his parents in Honolulu. The Ver family are thought to be in California, as are the Cojuangcos. Kokoy, distraught at the loss of his enormous powers, floats in and out of hotels in a variety of cities, incognito. His white hair is now dyed black.

Bright spots in the monotony of their days for both the Marcoses are reports of loyalist demonstrations in Manila (now outlawed) or pro-Marcos rallies in Honolulu. The Marcoses' wedding anniversary, formerly a splendid all-day event at Malacanang, is now celebrated more quietly. They appeared before a loyalist group in Honolulu, made speeches, and sang Filipino love songs for their thirty-second anniversary on May 1, 1986.

They both blame the US for their hasty exit and insist the US forced Marcos out of power. They are also bitter about Cardinal Sin and the role of the Catholic Church in their expulsion. When roused, Marcos has referred to the Cardinal as "an Ayatollah Khomeini," while Imelda called him simply "a son of a bitch." The former President also contends that the Catholic Church contributed $30 million to Cory's campaign, a charge that makes the bishops of Manila laugh. "We don't have that kind of money, let alone give it away," said Bishop Ted Bacani, spokesman for the Catholic Bishops Conference of the Philippines.

When her journalist friend Cindy Adams, who had often been a visitor in Manila, interviewed Imelda for the *New York Post*, she noted that the former First Lady punctuated much of her rambling remarks with fits of tears. "All those that I've been good to and I've helped over the years have disappeared," she complained.

Imelda's lifeline is the telephone. Her calls to Nancy Reagan were finally discouraged by the State Department after it was discovered the Marcoses taped their conversations with President and Mrs. Reagan. But her friends have not entirely deserted her. "Loyalists" who come through Honolulu still call on her. She gets long-distance calls from old friends who don't want her to feel deserted and unloved. She has talked to Dame Margot, to Mario d'Urso.

She has her friend Mrs. Ayoshi, wife of the governor, to go out with once in a while. She has her children, who float in and out of Honolulu. Irene and Greggy Araneta will have to testify, after all, on the munitions case. Their petition to take the fifth amendment was denied. Bong Bong's name has surfaced in the reopening of the Aquino murder trial in Manila. He is suspected of attempting to bribe a witness, the famous "Crying Lady" who is said to have seen Aquino shot—however, not enough evidence was found to bring him to trial. The legal snarls, involving the entire family will go on for years.

Imelda Marcos shows no remorse. "God will grant us justice," she told Mario tearfully. "Only God will judge me."

Ferdinand Marcos, the "quintessential Filipino," as my husband called him, will never give up trying to return to the Philippines. I remember being with him in London, Washington, Nairobi. He was never comfortable away from home. I commented to Romy, even then, "Marcos will never leave the Philippines." He did not leave by choice. And he will never rest in peace until he returns, even if it is only to fulfill his stated wish "to die in Ilocos."

Imelda, by contrast, could be happy anywhere—if only she were free. Confined to a house in Honolulu is, as she described it to a visitor, "like being in a tomb." What about her phenomenal energy? Her disdain for sleep or rest? What can she do with herself now to fill the hours? If she were free to flit around the world, to London, New York,

Rome, she could survive with some measure of happiness. But not in one city and one house. On her fifty-seventh birthday, July 2, 1986, she commented wearily, "If my next birthday is going to be like this one, I'd rather be dead."

I had thought perhaps she would have a nervous breakdown by now. She obviously is depressed. It shows in her weight gain. In her constant crying on the telephone. But she is stronger than I realized.

Maybe she, like her husband, still dreams of going home.

Index